Why You Buy

Some Books by Lorne Tepperman
for General Readers

Habits of Inequality (2013)
(with Nina Gheihman)

Problem Gambling in Canada (2012)
(with Kristy Wanner)

*The Sense of Sociability:
How People Overcome the Forces Pulling Them Apart* (2011)

Why You Buy

Lorne Tepperman and Megan Markus

Rock's Mills Press
Rock's Mills, Ontario • Oakville, Ontario
2024

Published by
Rock's Mills Press
www.rocksmillspress.com

Copyright © 2024 by Lorne Tepperman and Megan Markus.
All rights reserved. No portion of this book may be reproduced by any means without the written permission of the publisher.

For information, including permissions information and information about trade, library, and bulk orders, please contact the publisher at customer.service@rocksmillspress.com

Contents

	Preface	7
	Introduction: Which Buyer Are You?	11
1.	Why You Buy Tickets	19
2.	All the Lonely People	29
3.	The Pursuit of Novelty	39
4.	The Search for Experiences	51
5.	Specialization and Niche Buying	63
6.	Trophies	77
7.	Luxuries and Luxury Buyers	91
8.	Luxurious and Trophy-Worthy Brands	107
9.	The Trophy Treadmill	119
10.	What is Materialism?	131
11.	The Search for Enchantment	143
12.	Possession Love	161
13.	The Need for Treats	175
14.	Compensatory Buying, Compulsion, and Debt	189
15.	Comfort Food and Other Treats	199
16.	Nostalgia Marketing	209
17.	Embarrassment, Shame, and Guilt	219
18.	The Expansion of Basics	229
19.	Planned Obsolescence	239
20.	Final Words	249
	Sources and Selected References	255
	Index	269

Preface

We wrote this short book after one of us had co-authored a much longer one entitled *Consumer Society*.* That book was a textbook intended for undergraduate students and included a lot of references, concepts, and debates. Our goal in this book is to cover some of the same ground but more briefly, and in a less academic way. We also wanted to present a more focused argument about the pros and cons of consumerism.

In the larger book, it becomes clear that there is a huge difference—even a conflict—between two perspectives on consumerism. On one side is the social criticism literature, rooted in early work by European sociologists such as Adorno and Horkheimer of the Frankfurt School in Germany and Baudrillard in France. They put forward four important views that we build on in this shorter book. First, consumerism, when taken to its current extremes, is dangerous and destructive. Second, consumer goods are culturally significant objects that people use to achieve social and psychological goals. Third, consumerism is a cultural ideology or mindset that occupies most people's minds most of their waking hours. Fourth, this cultural ideology has the effect of tranquilizing people and helping capitalism to survive.

Another, opposite take on consumer society is found in marketing literature, a field largely dominated by marketing specialists, psychologists, communication researchers, economists, and other applied social scientists. It asks: How do you get people to buy stuff? It ignores the question of whether buying this stuff is good or bad, because it assumes that people are going to buy stuff anyway, and marketers want to sell it.

As you can imagine, there is an uneasy fit between these two approaches to studying the topic of consumerism. This gap or conflict is

* Lorne Tepperman and Nicole Meredith, *Consumer Society* (Rock's Mills Press, 2021).

clear in *Consumer Society*, which waffled back and forth between the two approaches. Here, we take a firmer position on the side of social criticism. However, there is also an applied focus to this book that is missing in the larger book: notably, a set of questionnaires that allow you, the reader, to situate yourself as a consumer: to figure out what kind of consumer you really are.

We think this addition is fun and may help you make up your own mind about the pros and cons of consumerism. We do not intend this book to be a "self-help" book, but it may help you nonetheless, especially if you are wrestling with shopping addiction, hoarding, or other consumer-related excesses.

In preparing this book, we benefited from the help of several people who deserve mention. One was Khulan Enkhbold, then an undergraduate student in geography and planning at the University of Toronto and currently a graduate student at the University of Pennsylvania. Khulan helped us clarify our thinking about materialism and other issues related to the consumerist mentality.

Another helper was Soli Dubash, a doctoral student in sociology at the University of Toronto. Soli helped us to design and administer a survey of student attitudes towards buying, and to analyze these data once they had been collected. This analysis required a great deal of skill and we are grateful to Soli for his insight and effort.

We also want to thank Nicole Meredith who, with Lorne Tepperman, co-authored a textbook on consumer behaviour that served as the jumping off point for this present volume. And finally, we want to thank David Stover, our editor and publisher, who (among other things) provided valuable advice about how to improve and tighten the arguments in this book.

We hope you like what we've written.

LORNE TEPPERMAN
MEGAN MARKUS
Toronto, 2024

Why You Buy

Introduction

Which Buyer Are You?

You probably think you buy things because you need them and there's nothing more to buying than that. And you may even deny that anyone else's opinion influences what you buy, or why you buy it. But you would be wrong. We will show you that other people's opinions influence almost everything you buy. And so does your unconscious need for control.

The COVID pandemic reminded everyone of one key fact: we don't control our lives. We couldn't control the onset of the pandemic, nor the course it took. Many of us suffered from a COVID infection despite our best efforts to avoid this. We also suffered from the lockdown, supply-chain shortages, a rising cost of living, and later, the rising interest rates meant to control inflation. We couldn't control any of this, could we?

Meanwhile, Russia invaded Ukraine, and we couldn't control that either. Nor could we control the effects of this invasion on the cost of oil, gasoline, and travel. We couldn't control Donald Trump's disastrous presidency in the United States and the legacy of bad government it bestowed on the American people, and secondarily on Canada. We couldn't control the Trump-like invasion of Ottawa to protest COVID vaccinations (in which Donald Trump, Jr., played a part.) Nor could we control climate change and the continuing destruction of our natural environment.

Putting all this aside, we haven't been able to control the growth of income and wealth inequality in Canada. Nor have we been able to control the effect of this inequality on homelessness, depression, anxiety, and a general loss of confidence in public institutions. This has also fed a growth in conspiracy theories, political disengagement, and social disengagement.

You haven't been able to control any of this, and plainly, neither has anyone else.

The world is out of your control—indeed, out of everyone's control—and you may feel anxious and depressed as a result. Maybe you even agree with the following statements:

- I cannot influence most of today's problems.
- Things have become so complicated that I don't understand what is going on in the world today.
- Life has become so difficult that I often don't have any idea what I should do.

If you do agree, you're clearly not optimistic about the future. Yet, amid all this tragic confusion, one thing remains certain: if you go online to Amazon, you can still buy a new pair of socks that are the right size and colour. What's more, the socks will be affordable and may even arrive at your home tomorrow. You still have control and free choice as a consumer, if you have the money to spend. And that means you can turn your attention away from all the things you can't control and just think about the things you can.

And besides the socks, you can choose whether to buy a new colour TV set, and whether to order out for pizza or chicken wings.

But isn't there something pathetic and even dangerous about our reliance on consumer goods to make us feel better? And what are the effects of living this way? What are the social, psychological, and environmental costs of our obsession with material goods? Besides, who will pay the bill for our consumer obsession, and when will it come due?

You should read this book if you want to know the answers.

We will start by showing you four types of buyers and help you figure out which type of buyer you are. After reading this book, you may want to change your buying habits—or at least, change the reasons you buy things. Understanding why you buy the things you do will help you make better buying decisions. Then, you will be a hero in your own life, not just a bit player who orders socks when you don't really need them. And you will be more aware of your behavior if nothing else.

So, which type of buyer are you? To begin, here's a quick quiz to find out what you buy, and why. Don't overthink your responses. Just give the first answer that comes to mind. Write a number from 1 to 5 next to each statement, to show how strongly you agree or disagree with it. Depending on how strongly you agree with each of these statements, use the following numbers: 5 = strongly agree; 4 = agree; 3 = no opinion; 2 = disagree; 1 = strongly disagree.

I try to buy things that...

1. Look beautiful or attractive.
2. Are in line with the things I value in life.
3. Are unique and one of a kind.
4. Are handy to have around.
5. Are worth every penny I spend on them.
6. Cheer me up and make me feel happy.
7. Connect me with other people in my community.
8. Every household needs to have.
9. Fit into my budget and are necessary.
10. Have social prestige value.
11. Help me fit in with my friends and neighbours.
12. Show that I fit into the group to which I belong.
13. I have usually considered carefully.
14. Improve my appearance or the way I look.
15. Let me blend in with everyone else, so I don't stick out.
16. Make me feel cheerful and excited.
17. Make me feel like I am part of things in my community.
18. Make me feel lucky and comfortable.
19. Make me stand out as someone with unusual taste.
20. Make people envy and admire me.
21. Provide comfort or emotional security.
22. Set new standards for taste and elegance.
23. Show me off to my best advantage.
24. Show off how successful I have been in my line of work.

Now, use the same scoring scheme to agree or disagree with the following statements:

25. I buy the best quality stuff I can afford.
26. Treats and luxuries are basic needs for people who can afford them.
27. Most people I know buy stuff of the same quality as I buy.
28. I admire people who treat themselves to gifts now and then.
29. The things I buy are important to have and use.
30. It matters a lot to me what other people think.
31. I would buy myself treats every day if I had the money.
32. I'm going to buy myself something special even if other people don't like it.

Now, complete the following three steps to find out what type of buyer you are:

STEP 1: Calculate scores A, B, C, and D in the following way:

Calculate Score A by adding up your results from Questions 2, 4, 5, 8, 9, 13, 25, and 29, and then subtracting from that figure the total score you received for Questions 3, 10, 19, 20, 22, 24, 28, and 32.

Calculate Score B by adding up your results from Questions 1, 6, 14, 16, 18, 21, 26, and 31, and then subtracting from that figure the total score you received for Questions 7, 11, 12, 15, 17, 23, 27, and 30.

Calculate Score C by adding up your results from Questions 7, 11, 12, 15, 17, 23, 27, and 30, and then subtracting from that figure the total score you received for Questions 1, 6, 14, 16, 18, 21, 26, and 31.

Calculate Score D by adding up your results from Questions 3, 10, 19, 20, 22, 24, 28, and 32, and then subtracting from that figure the total score you received for Questions 2, 4, 5, 8, 9, 13, 25, and 29.

YOUR SCORE A: ☐

YOUR SCORE B: ☐

YOUR SCORE C: ☐

YOUR SCORE D: ☐

STEP 2: Identify the highest total: whether A, B, C, or D.

STEP 3: Identify which person you are like.
If Score A is the largest, you are like Angelyn.
If Score B is the largest, you are like Anton.
If Score C is the largest, you are like Tamara.
If Score D is the largest, you are like Timothy.

Having done all this, you may wonder who these people are. You may think they are strangers or oddballs, but they're not. To prove it, here's a quick sketch of all four. In this book, we'll say more about each of them and their reasons for buying the way they do. But be assured, Tamara, Anton, Timothy and Angelyn are all like people you know. They are all typical consumers in our society.

Our first consumer, Tamara, obsesses about social acceptance. She is confident and purposeful, yet longs for social approval. As a consumer, she usually buys "tickets": items her friends and neighbours own and enjoy. By watching the people she looks up to, she learns what is in fashion. Then, by buying what they have, Tamara makes herself feel confident and secure. Yet, despite her need to fit in, Tamara does not spend more than her family can afford. She has a budget and sticks to it. Tamara's biggest fear, if she has one, is being rejected by her neighbours, friends, and co-workers. She is terrified of rejection and unpopularity. Above all else, Tamara wants to fit in and be popular, within her budget.

Our second buyer is Timothy, who wants to inspire envy and admiration in the minds of others. Timothy enjoys buying "trophies": items that no one else owns. To achieve this distinction, Timothy watches to see what is fashionable, then goes one step beyond the norm. By doing this, Timothy often spends more than he can afford, making it impossible for him to save money. Yet despite his high standard of living, Timothy often feels insecure and unhappy, and he is rarely comfortable. Before he's had time to enjoy the purchase he's just made, he's already planning the next purchase.

Timothy wants to appear distinguished, but apart from that, he has no clear values or ambitions. So, he often suffers from anxiety and depression. His greatest fear is that he will be mocked or ignored by the people he is trying to impress. When he feels bad, he locks himself in his "trophy room" and admires all his possessions.

Anton is a third consumer in our story. Often depressed, he obsesses about finding happiness through buying. Anton buys what we'll call "treats": items that help him cope with his depression and anxiety. Anton can never use (or use up) all the things he has bought, so he has a surplus of things at home that he hides in the basement. Many of them are in packages he never opened.

Preoccupied with trying to compensate for his lack of positive feelings, Anton doesn't spend much time researching what will make him popular or cool. Instead, he buys flashy items that make him momentarily feel better. Spending impulsively as he does, Anton often spends more than he can afford. He rarely saves money, and his reckless spending occasionally gets him into trouble with family, friends, and coworkers.

Aside from his craving for consumer goods, Anton has uncertain values, goals, and ambitions; and he feels lost in a dangerous world. Although he buys treats to make himself feel better, the things he buys never satisfy him, at least not for long.

Like Tamara, Timothy, and Anton, most of us try to feel satisfied about the things we buy. But you may not spend much time thinking about this, so maybe you are more like Angelyn. Like the other three, Angelyn wants to be happy, accepted, and successful too.

However, Angelyn feels less compelled to buy stuff than Anton, Tamara, and Timothy do. Perhaps she has less money to spend. Or maybe she's putting money aside to (eventually) afford a house, a vacation, or a comfortable retirement. Whatever the reason, Angelyn buys significantly less stuff than the other three shoppers mentioned earlier. And she is also less preoccupied with shopping than they are.

But it's not easy to be like Angelyn. Marketers encourage us to be more like Tamara, Timothy, and Anton. They want us to feel that we can gain control of our lives—even achieve happiness—through buying. They want us to display ourselves through the things we buy. But in living like that, we risk turning into mere curators of our belongings.

So why do some people live like Tamara, Timothy, and Anton? And what are the results? That's what this book will explore.

Chapter One

Why You Buy Tickets

In a world that seems out of control, many of us look for friends and allies to help us. We want to find refuge in a community we can belong to. This ideal community will give us a better chance to survive in this randomly cruel world.

So we look for other people to join, and seek their approval. We want them to know we belong in their world and want them to show us the same consideration (and protection) they give their family and friends. But how to gain this acceptance and approval—this belonging? The answer is, by leading lives like theirs, with the help of lifestyles and consumer goods just like theirs.

Joining their community means conforming to their rules and adopting their ways of dressing, eating, talking, and shopping. That is the price of gaining their approval and acceptance. It is a high price to pay, but not too high a price in a chaotic world we cannot control. Ideally, with their cooperation, we will find a haven in a heartless world—a safe harbor—even if it means hiding our individuality. We may even have to change ourselves to gain their acceptance, but at least doing that will help us to survive.

All around us, we sense chaos, and no wonder. Some people have a strong desire to incite chaos, especially when they sense themselves to be marginalized by society. These people see chaos as a way to invert the power structure and gain social status in the process. Some produce chaos because they want to rebuild society, while others enjoy destruction for its own sake. Chaos-seekers are not a unified political group but a divergent set of malcontents (Arceneaux et al., 2021). But they have a dramatic effect on our lives, nonetheless.

Not only do the groups we join help us survive the chaotic danger of our uncontrolled world: they also make us feel less lonely. They distract us from the anxiety and depression that many of us feel, faced with a chaotic, uncontrolled world. With our new friends beside us, we may be able to cobble together a shared social life. Together we can share backyard barbecues, Halloween parties, Christmas parties, and summer vacations. Together, we will celebrate the good times—the birthday parties, promotions, and other successes—and weather the bad times—the failures, bankruptcies, divorces, and deaths.

But the price of their support and belonging is conformity. We need to be like our neighbours for them to accept us. And, as mentioned earlier, that means buying what they buy and living the way they live. And that, in turn, means buying "tickets." *Tickets* are goods or services that people buy to become members of a community: the price of belonging to that community. Every ticket we buy sends a signal that we are like our neighbours and deserve their acceptance.

The specific things we buy as tickets are not important in themselves, so long as they have what sociologist Émile Durkheim called a "totemic" or ritual value. They are merely objects that bring people together. So, for example, we may buy an expensive vacation in the Galapagos Islands so we can invite neighbours over to see our snapshots of huge turtles.

Tickets are a pretext for sociability. Throwing a party, going out to dinner with another couple, or buying a season's subscription to the opera are some ways that people create occasions for sociability and conversation. They all signal conformity and provide an opportunity for sociability and belonging.

In an "other-directed" society like ours, we value our membership in the community, even if the psychic cost is high. In their classic work *The Lonely Crowd* (1950), Harvard sociologist David Riesman and his colleagues Nathan Glazer and Reuel Denney noted the other-directed person "looks to the mass media for guidance in his design for living and hierarchy of values" (198).

David Riesman was smart enough to realize modern societies were facing a problem. Trained as a lawyer, Riesman initially clerked for Supreme Court Justice Louis Brandeis, and then worked as a professor of law before shifting his focus to sociology. *The Lonely Crowd* had a profound impact on sociology and remains one of the best-selling sociology books ever published.

Other-directed people, as Riesman describes them, mainly worry about how the rest of the world sees them. But this preoccupation with appearances leads them to "lose their social freedom and individual autonomy in seeking to become like each other," as Riesman says.

Even seventy years ago, people saw a need to conform if they were to survive. And their preoccupation with buying stuff was as strong then as it is today, though today our buying is also propelled by the Internet. Gideon Lewis-Kraus (2013) writes in *The New Yorker* that the Internet has given other-directed people even more reference points to consider today than in Riesman's time. He writes, "Gone are the days when calling someone a 'conformist' was a derogatory term. Now the idea is that if you don't follow the crowd of five-star dispensers, you're a tasteless, indifferent shlub."

Signs, Branding, and Cultural Drenching

You may think that creating distinctive consumer brands—Heinz ketchup, Coca-Cola, Band-Aids, and so on—is just a bit of advertising foolishness that has nothing to do with your life or your culture. But you'd be wrong: *consumer brands* are drenched in our culture, and also change our culture.

Branding means creating a distinct image or identity for a product or line of products. This branding aims at making a memorable impression on consumers by promoting brand recognition, loyalty, and preference among the target audience. Branding includes choosing a brand name. The chosen name should be memorable and easy to pronounce and should relate to the product or service offered. It should also be distinctive, making it stand out from competitors.

A brand also needs a visually compelling logo that represents the brand's identity and values is critical. The logo should be easily recognizable and versatile, adapting to different media and formats. Colours play a significant role in brand recognition and emotional engagement with consumers. Brands often use specific color palettes that align with their identity and message. A catchy phrase or sentence that encapsulates the brand's essence, promise, or benefits helps reinforce the brand identity and builds customer recall.

The packaging of a branded product should not only protect the product but also suggest the brand's image and values. It should be attractive and functional, providing information while creating a positive unboxing experience. Brands also need to define their market position, identifying their target audience and telling how they differ from competitors. This information guides marketing strategies and communication approaches.

In marketing, communication is (almost) everything. Brands should communicate consistently across different channels and platforms, reinforcing their identity and values. This consistency strengthens brand recognition and trust among consumers. The experiences customers have with a brand significantly influence their opinion and loyalty. Brands must ensure a positive experience, from the first contact to post-purchase support. Through various initiatives, including loyalty programs, exclusive offers, and engaging content, brands can foster a sense of belonging and loyalty among their customers.

When done properly, these elements work together to create a cohesive and appealing brand that resonates with consumers.

Today, people are even branding themselves, though some researchers claim the practice has gone on for centuries. For example, some claim that Alexander the Great was the first real celebrity in human history. Similarly, they claim the 19th-century German writer Goethe achieved success by using familiar marketing skills to distinguish himself from other authors of his time. Canadian sociologist Erving Goffman (1956) described self-presentation as the intentional and tangible ingredient of identity, thus setting the groundwork for present-day personal branding efforts (Scheidt et al., 2020). What's different today is that personal branding has become an important part of the economy.

And because (almost) all consumer goods are branded, we use them to tell stories about who we are and where we belong in society. In fact, the goods we buy gain cultural significance mainly through branding, which we use to signal our social position. Take, for example, a BMW.

Technically, the BMW is just a car that, like any other car, and transports you from point A to point B. But culturally, a BMW is a ticket into the exclusive club of people who can afford this expensive and stylish car.

BMW markets itself with this exclusivity in mind. For example, BMW launched their small SUV, the BMW X1, with the headline "Embrace the Unknown." With this message, marketers want us to think that people who buy the BMW X1 are daring, travel slightly off the beaten path, and occasionally even break free of conformity. Advertising images of the BMW X1 show the car on an inner-city basketball court, driving along an oceanside highway, or in the desert with a parachutist touching down beside it. Presumably, these are the kinds of offbeat actions (and locations) BMW buyers want to suggest about themselves.

The same principle applies to cheaper items that many more people buy: for example, Lululemon leggings. Why do people pay $100 or more for Lululemon leggings? They cost less than $10 to produce and comparable leggings are available for much less. But people are willing to pay this high price because of the Lululemon brand. The fact that those leggings are from Lululemon—not from Old Navy, say—is seemingly worth a 90 percent premium. People will pay extra to be a part of something unusual, special, and expensive—like Lululemon.

In that sense, brand consumption is a public behavior. It is about manipulating what others think of us rather than merely buying what is cheap and useful. Buying tickets is about belonging to the in-crowd, whatever that in-crowd means to us. The clothes we wear, the coffee we drink, and even the mattress we (privately) sleep on, all mediate our social interactions.

Branding, marketing, and advertising imbue all our purchases with cultural meaning. British sociologist Celia Lury ought to know; she wrote a book on this topic. When Lury writes in her book *Consumer Culture* that consumer products are "culturally drenched," she means our culture has given meaningless consumer objects significant cultural meanings. A Tesla, for example, has come to mean more than a way of getting around; it is a carrier of information about your identity and goals. It shows that you're up-to-date on the latest auto technology, environmentally conscious, and able to afford an expensive electric car. Consumer goods—

like this Tesla—help us compete for status and community membership.

And maybe we can even consider a Tesla to be a "trophy" in the sense we used that word before. In one sense, Tesla is an exception to the general rule that people copy each other to gain acceptance. Tesla pioneered the first highway-ready all-electric car to use lithium-ion battery cells. At first, Tesla customers were few but wealthy. Then, with the introduction of the Roadster model, Tesla stopped trying to steal customers from its automobile rivals. Some think it developed an uncontested market space that (at least for a while) made the competition irrelevant. It created its own "Blue Ocean," a previously unknown market space (Ahmad and Khan, 2019).

Exceptions like Tesla aside, mimicry is at the heart of buying stuff and fitting in. That's why marketers urge you to mimic the crowd. But since fitting in means different things depending on who you are and what group you aspire to join. Fitting into the ultra-orthodox Jewish community of Toronto's Bathurst and Lawrence neighborhood, for example, will look very different from fitting into a community in a low-income neighborhood of Thunder Bay. And fitting in is as much about signaling membership in one social group as it is about signaling a lack of membership in another. So buying is always a two-sided process: signaling where you belong and signaling where you don't.

In his classic book *The Consumer Society* (1970), French sociologist Jean Baudrillard takes this insight even farther—some may even say, takes it too far—and proposes that *everything* you buy is a merely a sign. When you buy a car, a sweater, or a snow shovel, you are buying a sign that communicates something about you to others. Every consumer good sends a message to other people about who you are. It helps you belong to groups you want to join, separates you from groups you don't want to join, and displays your position in the social hierarchy.

Even everyday items like milk, bread, and water can serve as tickets in this sense. Some consumers drink water out of the tap while others drink (more expensive) FIJI water, for example. Same water, different message. And marketers make us feel the need to signal our status even when buying necessities (or basic goods).

Like water, clothing is a basic good, but luxury retailers challenge this—or, at least, persuade us to reimagine a basic good as a status symbol.

In turn, this increases the cost of everything we buy. The luxury clothing industry, already a multibillion-dollar industry, expects to continue growing by nearly 5 percent a year, because people use luxury clothing to send a message. And marketers of luxury clothing achieve this healthy growth by convincing us to reimagine luxury goods as necessities.

Tickets in the Cloud

Let's return to Tamara, our fictitious ticket buyer, to learn more about buying as a means of communication. As we said earlier, Tamara feels better about herself by buying what other people have, and that makes her feel safe and content, whether at work or at home.

Tamara wants to fit in, be popular, and improve her social position, if possible. So, Tamara's buying habits are social, in the sense that her buying behavior is designed to communicate with and influence other people. And that's what many (perhaps most) middle-class buyers in North America are doing. That's why most of us keep buying brands that have cultural and communicative meanings. According to sociologist Juliet Schor, consumption is a "symbolic communicator" that extends far beyond the mere use value of material goods.

We consume information about consumer goods as well as social information through our social media. Going on social media encourages us to compete with one another to consume the best, most exclusive goods. It also encourages us to show the world the best parts of our lives, while hiding the worst, less glamorous parts. And as we scroll through the curated images of other people's lives, we think "If I buy that object or experience, I will be as happy as she is."

With that goal of increasing our happiness in mind, we scroll through our feeds and buy tickets to keep up with "the Joneses," our new online reference group. People use reference groups to assess their own social standing, by comparing themselves to other people like themselves. Your reference group sets a baseline for who you must try to be. Social media heighten the importance of these reference groups by putting them in front of our eyes every minute of every day. As a result, every day, millions of people use social networking sites to decide what clothes to buy, where to eat, and even how to comb their hair.

But some members of our reference group are especially important to us. We're referring to those people we call "influencers," who persuade us how to think, act, and buy. Of all the people we "know," influencers are typically the first to use and display new products and services. And because so many of us watch influencers, brand marketers use influencers to build a strong relationship between their brand and people who may buy it.

You may think that "influencers" are just ordinary people who push themselves into our line of vision and try to sell us stuff, but you'd be wrong. Yes, they are ordinary people, but they don't just try to sell us stuff. They *influence* us to buy stuff. Take the case of Chiara Ferragni, an online fashion influencer with millions of Instagram followers.

When she puts on her sunglasses, she's not displaying the glasses; she's displaying coolness, fun, and flirtatiousness. She isn't selling a consumer item so much as pitching an emotional display. She's telling us that sunglasses like hers encourage the flirtatiousness that we associate with sex and popularity. So if we want sex and popularity, buy those glasses!

The growing presence of social media—and digital technology more broadly—has changed the way fashion brands work and communicate with their customers. Bloggers and influencers come to exercise a hold over consumers far beyond what many brands can achieve themselves. So, fashion companies collaborate with bloggers to promote their products and set trends for the future. And from a fashion consumer's perspective, blogging is one way they can tune in to the fashion industry and build their own personal brand.

Ferragni, who started her career as a fashion amateur, is now a fashion empress. Thirteen years after she launched her blog, Ferragni has more than 27.2 million followers today. She launched a fashion shoe brand in 2013 and has now successfully extended her brand to several other product categories. The result is a new, fast-growing sector of fashion blogger brands (Bazaki and Cedrola, 2023).

In this roundabout way, the influencer can forge a link between a particular brand and a desired lifestyle image. Influencers become influential by walking the fine line between being "just like you" and being significantly cooler, more popular, and more beautiful than you could ever be. Ferragni, for example, posts photos of herself going about her daily activities: waking up, lounging around in her PJs, watching a movie, eating breakfast, and so on. And as a brand in her own right, Ferragni sells goods more convincingly than any skinny, anonymous model on a Milan runway. That's because even though few of us can compete with the runway models in Milan, we can all try to be like Ferragni—an everyday person who looks great.

Yes, in the eyes of most consumers, influencers like Ferragni appear "real" and "genuine." According to researchers, influencer marketing succeeds because followers think influencers have expertise, trustworthiness, likability, similarity, and familiarity (Martensen et al., 2018).

Now, if you've read this far, you may be starting to think about the risks and dangers associated with social conformity. Social conformity, the act of matching attitudes, beliefs, and behaviors to group norms, has been studied extensively in psychology and sociology. Conformity can have benefits, such as promoting social cohesion and cooperation. However, several risks and dangers are also associated with excessive or unquestioned conformity.

When people conform too much, they suppress their unique thoughts, ideas, and identities. This can lead to a loss of self-awareness and individuality. Conformity often discourages innovative thinking and creativity. When everyone follows the status quo, new and potentially useful ideas may not come to the fore. On a larger scale, societies or groups that value conformity over individual thought may become stagnant, failing to evolve or adapt to new challenges or changing circumstances.

The phenomenon of "groupthink" can occur when a desire for group consensus overrides people's desire to consider alternatives, criticize a position, or express an unpopular opinion. This can lead to decision-making errors. When everyone thinks and behaves the same way, it makes the group more vulnerable. From an evolutionary perspective, a diversity of thoughts and actions is safer than uniformity. Feeling compelled to conform can also result in psychological stress, as people may feel pressured to hide or change aspects of their personality or beliefs to fit in.

Blind conformity can perpetuate social norms that are harmful or unjust. Examples include prejudices, stereotypes, and discriminatory practices that people practice in certain settings. Conformity can limit personal freedoms and result in a culture that punishes dissent and discourages independent thought. In strongly conformist societies or groups, people may also severely penalize non-conformity using ostracism, humiliation, or even physical harm.

However, when everyone is doing it, people may feel less personal accountability for their actions. This weakening of personal responsibility can lead to unethical or immoral actions, as seen in historical instances like the Holocaust. Over-reliance on group norms and decisions can create people who become dependent on others for their beliefs and behaviors, limiting their self-awareness and personal growth. Where everyone conforms to the same beliefs and views, misinformation can spread easily, and people may remain ignorant of important perspectives or facts.

To balance the need for social cohesion and the dangers of blind conformity, you need to practice critical thinking. It's also desirable to encourage diverse viewpoints and cultivate an environment where critical thinking is accepted and valued.

Are you wondering how marketers managed to turn our loneliness and need for control into social conformity and large-scale buying? In the next chapter, we will start to answer that question. There, we will discover that consumerism stresses individual consumption over collective well-being, and this even intensifies our isolation and loneliness.

As we will see, the widespread desire for social acceptance and material success, driven by advertising and consumer culture, has increased social comparison, consumerism, and materialism in society. People engage in consumption as a way of gaining approval and acceptance, and giving them control over their lives. Advertising encourages this behavior by exploiting our feelings of loneliness, inadequacy, and need for control.

Chapter Two
All The Lonely People

Shortly after the Second World War, prominent social thinkers in North America and Europe began to write essays, articles, and books about consumerism and mass conformity. This formed part of a general critique of alienation in modern society that went on for decades.

Alienation—an idea often mentioned in sociology, philosophy, and psychology—refers to a sense of disconnection or estrangement. Alienated people feel disconnected from themselves, from others, or from their environment. When connected to consumerism, we usually understand alienation in one of two main ways: as alienation from labor and alienation from true needs and wishes.

In the mid-nineteenth century, philosopher Karl Marx introduced the idea of alienation from labor, writing that workers feel disconnected from the products they create because they don't own or control the means of production. In a capitalist society, laborers have no control over how their product is used or shared, leading to a sense of powerlessness and estrangement. Workers may also feel alienated when mass-producing goods they can't personally afford or that have no personal significance to them. As well, under industrial capitalism, the fragmented labor process has workers only producing parts of the products they make. This leads them to experience a lack of fulfillment and weak connection to the product.

For its part, consumer culture alienates people by pushing them to follow materialistic values, driving a wedge between their real needs and artificially created needs. People feel compelled to buy products not for the utility or joy they bring but for the social status or image they represent.

What makes this theory especially complicated is that many, or even most, people don't know that they're alienated and don't realize that they're buying stuff because they're alienated. Despite their use of consumer products to communicate with others, people struggle to define their identity outside the brands they consume and support. They sometimes fear a loss of self and a reliance on consumer goods to express individuality and worth. And as we have seen, even after gaining material possessions, some people may feel unfulfilled and disconnected, because consumer goods often fail to provide long-term satisfaction or meaning.

This everlasting cycle of consumption and dissatisfaction often deepens feelings of alienation as it doesn't address the underlying need for connection, meaning, and empowerment. Some people feel alienated if they can't achieve their goals, leading to feelings of inadequacy and exclusion. For other people, the focus on individual consumption, rather than collective well-being, contributes to social fragmentation and isolation, weakened social bonds and increased alienation.

For all these reasons, the wildfire spread of consumerism in postwar North America shocked and worried many social critics. And as mentioned, the clearest expression of this shock was the book *The Lonely Crowd* (1950), mentioned earlier. Riesman's goal in this book was to describe different types of social character and discuss how they affect people's actions in different areas of their lives. But where does social character come from and how is it shaped? How do people come to be preoccupied with buying things?

Riesman argues that, throughout history, different societies with different social, economic, cultural, and political structures shaped different types of social characters.

Sociologists and other social scientists use the term *social character* to refer to the personality traits, values, attitudes, and behaviors that are shared by members of a particular society or group. They arise from the social conditions and cultural norms of that society or group.

You may imagine that your personality—anyone's personality—existed when you came out of your mother's womb. But you'd be wrong; it didn't. Personality developed gradually, shaped by the social and cultural environment you live in. In fact, social character represents the internalized expectations of society: the stuff we have learned so well we don't even think about it anymore.

Social character is the psychological counterpart of a society's culture, embodying the emotional and motivational aspects of shared experiences. From childhood onward, society molds us, through influences by our family, education, religious institutions, media, and peer groups. These entities teach us cultural norms, values, and beliefs, which in turn influence our behavior, attitudes, and personality traits.

Social character helps people fit into their society by aligning individual motivations and behaviors with societal needs and functions. For instance, a society that values competitiveness and individual achievement is likely to produce people with strong ambitions and self-reliance. Different societies (or different time periods within a society) can have different social characters based on their historical experiences, economic structures, cultural norms, and other factors.

While social character embodies common traits found in a group, there's always a degree of variation among people. Further, as societies change and evolve, there can be tension between the established social character and emerging new values or behaviors. But mostly, social character prepares people for living in society in the way that the social system expects them to live. Thanks to social character, people learn their roles in society, the goals they must follow, the values they must respect, and the kind of relationship that they must have with others.

Thus, what social character does is to ensure that people will conform to the prevailing cultural system and its expectations. Riesman defines different types of social character as "the way in which society ensures some degree of conformity from the people who make it up" (Riesman, 2001, 5). To understand a social system and its goals and values, one must understand the type of social character it creates (Khandizaji et al., 2021).

The Lonely Crowd discussed three types of people: tradition-directed, inner-directed, and other-directed. The authors claim that in twentieth-century North America, people had switched from being inner-directed to being other-directed. That is, they had become too concerned about how their neighbours lived. People constantly watched their neighbours because they wanted to fit in and be liked by these neighbours. So they became carbon copies of ticket-buying Tamara.

However, as people spent all their effort seeking social acceptance and material well-being, they lost sight of other objectives. They became over-concerned with what to buy and how they appeared to their neighbours. This process was intensified by the branding of merchandise, the advertising of brands, and the use of influencers on social media discuss the process of branding.

Brand Communities, Advertising, and Social Media

Before the First World War, advertising had mainly highlighted the usefulness of a product or service. For example, it would explain to customers not only why they needed a new toothbrush but also why Brand X was the best available toothbrush. Perhaps this was because of price, availability, or density of bristles.

However, advertising changed in the years after the First World War. Between 1925 and 1945, marketers shifted from highlighting a product's usefulness to highlighting its symbolic qualities. Increasingly, marketing turned aspects of personal identity, self-presentation, and social acceptance into central features of an advertised product. So, for example, it may tell you that Brand X toothbrush is the most popular toothbrush, the one preferred by dentists, and the one that people with the whitest teeth use.

Or, consider a Revlon lipstick advertisement from 1943 that showed a woman looking into a small mirror, with copy stating, "Smart women all over the world swear by Revlon." Thus, the advertisement equates Revlon makeup with being smart and being seen as smart. This type of advertisement characterized marketing's so-called "totemism phase," when consumer goods first became *totems*, things that represented sets of social meanings.

In creating totemic products, marketers were endlessly creative in pairing their product with a glamorous or socially admired image. Placing a particular drink or item of clothing next to a surfboard and group of young, healthy surfers, for example, suggested that healthy young people and the young-at-heart enjoyed the item. The product was intended for people who were, or wanted to be, adventurous, energetic, and sexually active. It wasn't made for boring old fogies who had given up having fun.

Similarly, from the 1960s onward, many beer advertisements depicted a happy, attractive heterosexual couple drinking Budweiser or Schlitz in their living room. The unspoken message to viewers was, "Drink this beer, and you too can have a happy life." Perhaps even a happy sex life.

Today, all advertisements encourage people to consider how a particular product will improve their social image and social connections. But of course, some brands are better at this than others. Consider Lululemon's "Sweat Collective." When you buy a Lululemon product, you are buying notional membership in a special group. This group's members are young and fit. They take care of their bodies every day, one CrossFit event or yoga class at a time. Every member or aspiring member of that group is healthy, sensible, and attractive, and wants to be seen as such. What's more, they accept one another as such!

Nowadays, people are more and more aware of the importance of a healthy lifestyle. This has led to the creation of athleisure—a new kind of clothing designed for everyday wear but also fit for exercise. As a company that started by selling yoga products, Lululemon is at the forefront of this trend. It uses health ideology—the ideology that health and happiness are connected—as a tool for business success. Active in both online and offline marketing, Lululemon has expanded its market from North America to Asia and Europe, promoting its ideology and brand wherever it goes (Xu, 2022).

With an example like Lululemon in mind, it's no surprise that historian Stewart Ewen referred to advertising people as "captains of consciousness." They spend their days at work figuring out how to manipulate our desires by creating associations between consumer goods and attractive personal qualities.

And like Lululemon, many brands don't just want us to fit in with the right group; they want to help us find the right group through *brand communities*. Brand communities emerge at the intersection of branded goods and the universal desire for social acceptance. People want to belong to an exclusive group they think uniquely expresses the identity or image they want to project.

But how to create a brand community that attracts people like you? Here's how one brand, Tim Hortons, did it. Today everyone associates Tim Hortons with "truly Canadian" coffee and donuts. Tim Hortons' Instagram account has hundreds of thousands of followers and hundreds of comments per post. All of them pay homage to Tim Horton-ism as a Canadian thing, though the company is today owned by a Brazilian investment firm, 3G Capital.

Brand communities use a wide range of strategies to help people meet their needs for belonging and image management. Consider Sephora's Beauty Talk community. On Beauty Talk, people discuss everything from new fake eyelashes to the care of dry skin. A "conversation" can have upwards of 6,000 people talking about fake eyelashes. Beauty Talk increases Sephora's brand value and customer loyalty, and spreads the word about the brand's products.

Similarly, Lego Ideas, a brand community for Lego users, encourages its members to post pictures of their latest Lego creations. As they communicate with and relate to one another, members strengthen their connection with the brand, building a loyalty with Lego and not its competitors such as Mattel. By engaging in brand communities, people gain a sense of belonging and feel they are among friends. They also forge a close connection with one particular brand.

Brand communities can also form around social causes. For example, if you're aiming at environmental sustainability, you can join eco-friendly consumer circles. People who shop sustainably show one another they can afford to shop at expensive, sustainable, "intelligent," and "socially conscious" establishments. Above all, they can connect with other people who also care about the environment.

For sustainability-conscious shoppers, buying becomes display of "visible compassion" or "conspicuous compassion." Such displays show that you belong to a group of intelligent and socially conscious people who care about the environment. And people who buy in a conspicuously compassionate way want others to see them as caring and knowledgeable about current events.

However, the effort to fit in through buying sometimes backfires. Just think about the psychological effects of social media on young consumers. When people, especially insecure young people, compare themselves to the people they see in advertisements (or on social media), they often feel inadequate. The comparisons may make them worry about not being beautiful enough, slender enough, popular enough, wealthy enough, or exciting enough, among other things.

That's because social media posts usually show people at their funniest, most attractive, and most glamorous. As well, paid media posts show idealized versions of consumer goods and the people using those goods. Facebook and Instagram purposely make it hard for viewers to distinguish between a paid advertisement and a genuine, unpaid recommendation. They often mislead people into thinking the advertisement is an unpaid endorsement.

People of all ages can make themselves unhappy by comparing themselves to others in this way and today, even seniors are joining this lonely band of sad comparers. But older people have much less need for popularity and approval. They are often happier with their lives than young people because they are better at controlling their expectations and emotions. And because they are better at controlling their emotions, seniors can think more logically about buying things.

Now, some may think this is far too simple an analysis of older people and their happiness. Certainly, the U-shaped model of happiness that researchers supported for decades has lost much of its credibility. For decades, researchers had claimed that happiness is highest for people in their twenties, falls to its lowest point in midlife, and then rises again in old age. Researchers often cited this U-shaped model of happiness as evidence for a midlife crisis, or evidence that parenting sucks the happiness out of adult life.

However, researchers now think the claimed U-shape may not be as robust as people often assume, and the research on this may be misleading. In short, we may have been looking at the wrong kinds of data. Cross-sectional studies, based on data collected at one moment in time, are inadequate for drawing conclusions about within-person changes in happiness. As well, cross-sectional evidence of the U-shape in levels of happiness and life satisfaction is mixed: less robust than originally thought.

Meanwhile, longitudinal support for the U-shape in happiness and life satisfaction is also mixed. And when asked to reflect on their lives, older adults often recall midlife as a more positive period. Finally and equally important, the belief in a single path to well-being obscures the diversity in pathways throughout life, as well as its sources (Galambos et al., 2020).

So, at this point, we don't really know how happiness varies over the lifespan. But still, the research on older people is convincing: seniors are less affected by a need for approval than young people are. Advertising, for its part, encourages young and middle-aged people to buy tickets and seek the approval of others. By making them feel lonely and unwanted, it pushes them spend money to make themselves feel better. It produces brand communities, groups of strangers with nothing in common except a desire to share their love of a branded good.

Having read this far, you may be starting to see some dangers and risks associated with marketing-induced loneliness. Loneliness—a subjective feeling of isolation, disconnection, or lack of social engagement—is arguably a significant public health concern today, and you may have experienced it. Prolonged feelings of loneliness can have adverse effects on both physical and mental health.

Loneliness can be both a cause and a result of depression. The two often feed into each other in a cyclical manner. People who feel lonely may also experience heightened states of anxiety, especially in social situations. Researchers have linked loneliness to a decline in cognitive function and an increased risk of conditions like Alzheimer's. Researchers have also linked loneliness to an increased risk of cardiovascular diseases, including high blood pressure and heart disease.

Chronic loneliness can suppress the immune system, making a person more susceptible to infections. Loneliness can lead to raised levels of the stress hormone cortisol, which has known negative effects on physical health. Lonely people may also adopt unhealthy habits such as poor diet, lack of exercise, excessive alcohol consumption, or smoking as coping mechanisms. Researchers have linked loneliness to a range of sleep problems, including difficulty falling asleep, nighttime awakenings, and not feeling rested after sleep. Loneliness can lead some people to self-medicate with alcohol, drugs, or other substances, resulting in addiction and other health problems. Lonely people may have a harder time coping with setbacks or traumas, leading to prolonged periods of recovery or distress. Loneliness can also create a vicious cycle where a person avoids social interactions, further deepening their sense of isolation. Along similar lines, chronic loneliness can lead to feelings of worthlessness or a view that one does not deserve love and connection. Lonely people may become more susceptible to scams, exploitation, or abusive relationships out of a need for connection. Loneliness is a significant factor associated with suicidal thoughts and actions.

Because of all this, some studies suggest that chronic loneliness can be as harmful to life expectancy as smoking or obesity. Occasional loneliness is a natural human experience, so loneliness does not always lead to these undesirable results. However, chronic or prolonged loneliness can be harmful in the ways we have described. Addressing it early through interventions like counseling, social engagements, or community involvement can prevent many of its negative effects.

Given the range and power of loneliness to affect people's lives, it's no wonder that marketers try to harness it to sell branded products. In their endless search for sales, marketers have recognized the importance of portraying their ticket items in ways that reduce buyers' loneliness. One way of doing that is by promoting novel items—items that attract people precisely because they are new and unusual.

In the next chapter, we will talk about the allure of novelty items for lonely ticket buyers. We will see that many social factors influence novelty-seeking. For example, upper-income groups may adopt unique new items to show their fashion sense. Lower-income groups, for their part, may introduce alternative trends that eventually also influence mainstream fashion and buying behavior.

As you will see, in marketing, striking the right the balance between novelty and usefulness is critical. Products need to be novel enough to attract attention but not so novel they appear impractical or alienate potential buyers. The success of a product in the market depends on striking the right balance between innovation and practicality, providing something new while still meeting the users' needs and expectations.

Chapter Three
The Pursuit of Novelty

Consumers can find innovation and novelty appealing for all sorts of reasons. First, innovative products often offer them solutions to everyday problems or improve on existing products in ways that make life easier and more convenient. New technologies may also provide superior performance, expanding what's possible and delivering greater value to their users.

Equally important, owning or adopting the latest products can confer social status and help people feel like trendsetters. Innovative and novel products may help them express their identity, reinforcing their self-concept and how they wish to be seen by others. New products can also stimulate curiosity, offering people exciting and novel experiences that break from routine. The allure of exploring and mastering new product features can be deeply satisfying for consumers.

Often, innovations perform better than older products, allowing users to carry out their tasks more efficiently, effectively, and enjoyably. Sometimes, new versions of existing products offer better quality, durability, or reliability, and give the buyer better value for their money.

Some consumers merely experience the psychological appeal of new products, and FOMO—the so-called Fear of Missing Out. They want to stay current and don't want to miss the latest technologies, and that's what drives their interest in innovative products. For these consumers, owning and using the latest products can deliver psychological rewards that include pleasure, confidence, and accomplishment.

Brands known for innovation, like Apple, can foster loyalty among consumers who value the brand's commitment to pushing boundaries and offering innovative products. As well, effective marketing can create a buzz and anticipation around new products, making them seem irresistible or essential to potential buyers.

So, for some consumers, adopting innovative products is a way to stay relevant and attuned to the future, positioning themselves as modern and forward-thinking. Consumers may even see buying innovative products as an investment in their lifestyle and a way of aligning with new ways of thinking.

Innovation often comes with sleek, modern, and aesthetically pleasing design elements that appeal to consumers' sense of style and beauty. Such new products may also offer unprecedented ways to personalize and customize the user experience.

On the other hand, there is sometimes a natural resistance to innovation and personal change, especially among older or poorer people. For many reasons, they resist what they may view as invitations to disorder in their interactions with a changing environment. They do this by keeping themselves in sensory states that are familiar and expected, given the niche they occupy. As the old saying goes, "If it ain't broke, why fix it?" So, why would they—or people in general—ever be motivated to seek out novelty? Novelty, by definition, is going to produce sensory and physiological states that are unexpected, therefore unsettling and potentially even dangerous.

Yet humans, like other animals, often find play and other forms of novelty-seeking and exploration hugely rewarding. How can we understand this, given the desire we have to minimize the errors we make? The answer is, we don't know. First, no researcher has yet given a persuasive account of *why* it should feel good to engage the world playfully and with curiosity. Second, it remains unclear how the brain works, allowing people to make reasonably correct estimates of the risks they face.

Recent studies of the brain have sought to connect emotional experiences to our ability to reduce errors in predicting the course of future events. People experience negative emotional changes—they feel bad—when they make more errors (and make them at an increasing rate), and experience positive changes in emotion—they feel good—when they make fewer errors in prediction. Fewer errors in predicting the future means a drop in uncertainty, and that is linked to a more positive emotional state. At least that's the theory.

If this theory is valid, it may explain why it feels good to be curious and playful—to experiment with novel objects and novel experiences. The more we experiment, the more we learn about our environment and the less uncertain we are about what may happen next (Kiverstein et al., 2019). When you think about it, this theory is saying that we enjoy things that give us a greater sense of control over our environment. So, consumerism comes back to seeking control over a chaotic environment.

Given this, you may think that everyone loves a new thing, that we are hard-wired to embrace novelty, but you'd be wrong. Many people—and perhaps most people—find innovation and novelty appealing, but not all consumers value them to the same extent. That's why people adopt innovations at different times, some adopting them right away and others waiting years or even decades to adopt them. Early adopters eagerly embrace the new goods and services, while late adopters or laggards prefer to stay with familiar and proven products. Perhaps they are more risk-averse. Understanding these differences is critical for marketers and product developers who want to target and serve different consumer groups.

But, as a rule, in a world we cannot control, where our best chance of survival lies in buying what our neighbours buy, novelty plays an odd role. On the one hand, a novel buy—a new car, kitchen appliance, or item of clothing— runs the risk of alienating our friends and neighbours with its unusualness. On the other hand, a novel buy also offers us the opportunity to stand out: to gain more approval than other people by showing consumer leadership. The trick is to know how much to bend or break the rules of your community.

Wearing transparent clothes or bleaching half of your hair blue may be going too far, turning you into a joke and not a leader in your community. And building a bowling alley in your backyard or developing a special skill in making sushi may be eccentric but not laughable. Buying a Tesla, a Maserati, or a Hummer—that may be the ticket. Ideally, your unusual buy will produce conversation and envy, not hilarity.

To discover how attracted you are to novelty shopping, answer the following twelve statements using the same 5-point scale you used before. Remember to give the statement 5 points if you strongly agree; 4 points if you agree but not strongly; and so on. As before, add up all your points to get your total score on this scale. You are a novelty buyer if you score 48 or more points.

1. I can shift my interests rapidly if I hear about something interesting.
2. I don't mind if things become disorderly so long as I have a good time.
3. I easily make new friendships and see old friends less often.
4. I find surprise to be among the best things in life.
5. I hate being bored and will do almost anything to escape it.
6. I like to do things that thrill me and surprise me.
7. I love to experience things that are new and unpredictable.
8. I often look for new adventures in new places.
9. I often spend money on impulse if something catches my eye.
10. I usually base my actions on intuition, which I trust highly.
11. People I know envy me for my adventures and new purchases.
12. The novelties I buy are fun and all my friends like to see them.

You likely scored higher than 35 on this scale, because we live in a society that admires (and copies) novelty. So, whether you're constantly refreshing your Instagram feed, looking for a new job, or getting that new haircut after a break-up, the lure of novelty is always present. Something new and better is always trying to get into your head.

Take our obsession with Apple iPhones. Every new iPhone model, we learn, brings something different to the table. Apple even released the iPhone 4 in 2010 with the tagline "This changes everything ... again." Seven years later, the iPhone X promised "the future is here" and offered three new features: a slightly slimmer form, a slightly better camera, and no earphone plugs. Whether consumers needed these updates or not was beside the point. They wanted a new iPhone anyway.

RNPs, INPs, and Sensed Novelty

But consumer goods can be "new" in different ways. Some are *Really New Products* (*RNPs*), while others are only slightly or *Incrementally New*

Products (*INPs*). Often, RNPs allow consumers to do things that existing products do not. When marketed correctly, RNPs have the potential to change the market, create new technologies, and change behaviors.

You might wonder why some new products are so successful and some companies outstanding performers in new-product development. Research has identified three "success drivers" in this area. Some companies are effective at identifying the most attractive new features for their products; they do so by listening to their customers and doing their homework up front. A second factor is a company's overall strategic approach to innovation and research and development. Third, success drivers usually include the systems and methods a firm has put in place for managing new product development (Cooper, 2019).

Often, consumers must learn about and adapt their behavior to RNPs. Consider one RNP, the Segway: a two-wheeled, computer-controlled, self-balancing personal transporter. Marketers predicted the Segway would make its first billion dollars faster than any other company in the world, thanks to investors like Amazon's Jeff Bezos. Despite this, consumers bought fewer than 10,000 units in the two years after its release. What went wrong?

The Segway's failure to meet expectations showed that people love hearing about new products, but "really new" ones can frighten them off. Sometimes, consumers are unsure what to expect from an RNP, precisely because it is so new. Their feelings of doubt make them less willing to buy and learn about sometimes expensive products.

At the same time, the novelty of RNPs may result in increased media exposure, attracting more customer attention. This media exposure may encourage consumers to spread word-of-mouth information about RNPs, promoting adoption of the new product.

Unlike high-risk, high-reward RNPs, INPs—Incrementally New Products—offer consumers smaller, more familiar changes. The iPhones we discussed earlier are INPs. With each update, the basic phone design remains the same. Small changes make the phone more efficient and useful, or at least make consumers think it is. The same is true of Air Jordan sneakers, which come in various colours created by collaborating designers. These changes make each pair of sneakers seem unique. However, manufacturers have not altered the basic design of previous models.

With INPs, consumers who are familiar with earlier versions can easily recognize the new features and benefits of the newer versions. So, INPs carry lower levels of market and technological uncertainty than RNPs. Many consumers also prefer INPs because they come closer to guaranteeing safety and need little behavioral change.

Customized consumer goods are another example of INPs. Many industry experts think mass customization is the future of retail sales. Customization allows consumers to enjoy products that are slightly (and enjoyably) unique. Customers can, for example, create their own perfume scent, design a personalized Louis Vuitton handbag, or even customize their own protein bars. These changes create products that differ (slightly) from standard, off-the-shelf offerings. And because they differ, customers enjoy them more and are willing to pay more to own them.

However, customization also considers the need for likeness. Suppose your friend tells you her Nike sneakers were custom-made, so you visit the Nike website and create your own custom shoes. You are unlikely to copy your friend's exact design, no matter how much you admire it. You want something different, so you can stand out—but only *slightly* different. That's because, as much as they want novelty and customization, people put limits on how unusual they want to appear.

Speaking of sneakers, footwear has long served to communicate social status, virility, sexuality, and many other qualities. But how did such a practical, ordinary, and widespread item of clothing come to be a versatile icon of contemporary consumer culture? (Denny, 2021). Perhaps the answer lies in the fact that today almost everyone owns and wears sneakers. And there is a wide, though not infinite, range of possibilities in the ways you can decorate and customize these inexpensive shoes. Typically, customers use customization to blend in or seem like part of a group they want to be part of. To repeat, consumers may seek novelty, but they also seek products that connect them to the group they belong to.

Why We Enjoy Novelty

We should begin by saying that consumers don't always enjoy novelty, and they find some kinds of novelty more appealing than others. For example, buyers are more likely to look for novelty in an aesthetic product like a perfume than in a utilitarian product like a toaster. As well, people who don't mind taking risks are more motivated to embrace novelty by the possibility of profit. By contrast, risk-averse buyers are less likely to look for novelty in the things they buy. The possibility of loss leads them to avoid risks and stay away from untested novelties.

Taste for novelty, or what some people have called "neophilia," is the preference for new and novel experiences. People vary in their degree of neophilia, and their taste for novelty can be influenced by a combination of genetic, psychological, sociological, and environmental factors.

People with certain personality traits, like openness to experience, are more inclined than others to seek out and appreciate novelty. And children raised in homes that encourage exploration, learning, and trying new things are more likely to develop a taste for novelty. Exposure to diverse experiences and cultures can also cultivate a love for new and different things.

Then, if trying new things leads to rewards, people are more likely to seek out novel experiences in the future. Friends, family, and peers who enjoy trying new things may inspire others to do the same. And, as people develop, they often become more open to new experiences. However, cognitive development can influence how people view and seek novelty. People who believe in developing or stretching their abilities and intelligence may be more inclined to seek out new experiences and challenges.

Novelty appeals to people who are naturally curious. They nurture their curiosity through various means like reading widely, traveling, and engaging with diverse groups of people. Equally, people who find their environment boring or monotonous may seek out novelty to stimulate their minds and relieve their boredom. Someone who values learning, growth, and adventure is more likely than average to seek out novel experiences.

Developing a taste for novelty often involves stepping out of one's comfort zone and being open to the unknown. Yet some people form a taste for novelty at a young age. When infants are shown both familiar and novel images, they often prefer the novel ones. This suggests humans have an innate need to learn new things—a quality that many people carry with them into adulthood.

A widespread wish for adventure may also explain some people's fascination with novelty. Their wish for adventure motivates them to behave in daring, risky, and even reckless ways. Some people display their daring by walking a tightrope from one skyscraper to another. Others, risking less danger, travel to foreign countries to sample strange new foods. In their own ways, both types of people are daring. And both types of experience—the rash and the merely unusual—enable customers to raise their *optimal stimulation level* (OSL).

You may think that everyone needs the same amount of novelty, stimulation, and excitement in their lives as you do, but you'd be wrong. People have different optimal stimulation levels, so they need different levels of novelty to work effectively. When their stimulation levels are low, people become bored and seek ways to fill the void. Often, people raise their stimulation level to the preferred or ideal state through novelty seeking. They can also reduce boredom and fatigue by rotating their choices and trying out new products. People with a high OSL are more exploratory and seek more novelty than others, and there is some evidence they may be happier in life.

The term OSL refers to the mental stimulation a person seeks in their environment. This idea is grounded in *arousal theory*, which suggests that people are motivated to achieve a level of arousal that is neither too high nor too low. The ideal or optimal stimulation level varies from one person to another because of differences in personality, developmental experiences, and learned tolerance levels. So, for most people, OSL represents a middle ground between under-stimulation (boredom) and overstimulation (anxiety or stress).

Because it is so novel and provocative, a good place for studying OSL is virtual reality (VR). High-immersive VR environments create a strong impression of reality, and this fact has the potential to significantly change consumer behavior, compared with online shopping. Researchers have already compared consumer choice in the two environments. One is a high-immersive VR environment using a head-mounted display and hand-held controllers. The other is a low-immersive environment showing products as rotatable 3-D models on a desktop computer screen. The results show that consumers in high-immersive VR choose a larger variety of products and are less price-sensitive than consumers in the low-immersive setting (Meißner et al., 2020).

As mentioned, genetic and neurological differences can influence one's need for stimulation. As well, cultural norms and values affect a person's preferences for stimulation. Emotional volatility may affect how much stimulation an individual seeks or tolerates at a given moment. Finally, age may play a role as well, with younger people often seeking higher levels of stimulation than older ones.

Social Factors in Novelty Seeking

Novelty-seekers sometimes practice what sociologist Thorstein Veblen (1857–1929) called *conspicuous consumption*, with the aim of clarifying the boundaries between social classes. Members of one social class want to distance themselves from the next lowest class and to do this, they try to make it harder for the lower class to mimic them. As you may expect, the highest (or elite) class must take this effort to the next level by doing extraordinary things.

To distinguish himself from lower income groups, the "man of culture" (to use the admittedly non-inclusive term Veblen coined) seeks goods and services that appear exceptional, even bizarre—and certainly conspicuous. From this vantage point, it's easy to see how (many) fashion and consumer trends stem from the upper class's need for novelty. Gradually, their tastes and preferences trickle down the social hierarchy, with lower-level positions copying them. But to preserve their distinctiveness, high-ranking people are constantly on the lookout for new trends.

Other classes of people also have an influence over the introduction of novelty into consumer buying. According to some researchers, trickle-up, trickle-across, and trickle-down diffusions all work simultaneously in fashion (Atik and Firat, 2013). For example, some counter-cultural movements use novelty to satirize the materialistic status symbols of the upper classes. Consider "e-girls" and "e-boys," who have gained popularity in recent years on TikTok. E-girls, according to the most visible stereotypes, wear "mesh T-shirts, colorful hair clips, Sailor Moon skirts, and O-ring collars" (Jennings, 2019). These fashion items, while not expensive, are ironic and novel in comparison to how most people dress.

Unlike more traditional shoppers, e-shoppers buy their clothes from alternative online fast-fashion retailers or thrift stores. And despite their opposition to traditional symbols, some of their styles have appeared on Fifth Avenue and in high-end retail stores. E-girl fashion has become a common staple in the fashion industry, with celebrities such as Billie Eilish and Doja Cat adopting e-girl personas. So fashion trends do not always trickle down; they can also climb the social ladder. When this occurs, people who began defying social norms end up creating new ones.

Advertising and Novelty

According to researchers, the main influences on consumers' views of a brand are usefulness and novelty. However, novel advertisements must carry a clear message that is relevant to the advertised product. And while novelty may attract consumers' attention briefly, the product's usefulness produces longer-term brand recall. As well, consumers may value novelty in principle, but they sometimes fear that a too-novel product will lead to social rejection.

Similarly, advertisements that are too novel can be off-putting and even revolting. Excessively distinctive products may drive customers away. As well, the term "new" can mean different things to different people, leaving customers unsure whether a product is new or only slightly new. So, in the consumer world, people want a happy medium between too new and old-fashioned (that is, not new enough). Customers want new ideas, but they don't want too many of them.

In other words, people mainly come to want (and buy) a novel product if that product is also useful. The fate of the Segway tells us that gaining social acceptance for future innovations like self-driving automobiles will likely be more challenging than many anticipate (Clark et al., 2019).

Desire for novelty also varies, with people often seeking it more in aesthetic or pleasure-related products than in utilitarian items. Individual factors like risk tolerance, personality traits, and OSL also influence novelty-seeking behavior. Seeking novelty and innovation can drive progress, spark creativity, and introduce exciting changes. However, the relentless pursuit of the new and untested also carries potential risks and dangers.

If you find yourself drawn to novelty, here are a few of the risks and dangers you should consider:

- Decreased human connection: As new technologies or methods emerge, there may be reduced face-to-face human interactions, which can impact emotional and social well-being.
- Loss of stability: Constant change can undermine the stability of an organization, system, or process. This can lead to confusion, decreased productivity, or operational failures.
- Unforeseen effects: New technologies may have unexpected negative side effects that aren't plain until after widespread adoption.
- Erosion of traditional values: Relentless pursuit of novelty can sometimes lead to discarding traditional methods, values, or practices that have intrinsic worth or long-term benefits.
- Dependency on the new: A constant need for novelty can lead to a dependency where people or organizations feel restless or unsatisfied unless they're continually switching to the next big thing.
- Reduced depth of understanding: Constantly shifting focus to embrace the new can prevent deep mastery or understanding of any one subject, skill, or tool.
- Increased risks: By definition, we have not yet tested the newest thing. We do not fully understand its risks, leading to unexpected challenges or dangers.
- Mental fatigue: Constantly adapting to new things can lead to cognitive and emotional exhaustion, making it harder for a person to make sound decisions or set priorities effectively.
- Resource waste: Trying out new ideas or technologies needs resources. If the novelty doesn't prove useful or feasible, these resources (time, money, and effort) can be wasted.
- Overcomplication: Sometimes, in the pursuit of innovation, solutions can become more complicated than necessary, making them harder to understand, complete, or keep up.
- Economic inequalities: Sometimes, rapid innovations can lead to economic disparities, where people who can't keep up or adapt quickly are left behind.

- Loss of focus: Chasing every new trend or idea can lead to a lack of focus on core goals, missions, or values.
- Short-term thinking: The allure of rapid innovation may lead us to rank short-term gains over long-term sustainability and progress.
- Ethical concerns: In the search for novelty, especially in areas like biotechnology or artificial intelligence, there may be inadequate consideration of ethical implications.
- Over-reliance on technology: While technology-driven innovation is powerful, over-relying on it can make people or societies vulnerable to technological failures or cyber threats.

While these risks exist, novelty and innovation have always been central to human progress. The key is to seek a balanced approach, ensuring that we combine pursuit of the new with a careful consideration of its implications and a respect for enduring principles and practices.

In the next chapter, we will see that consumers increasingly prefer spending money on significant experiences rather than tangible goods. Some experiences, like travel and tourism, need large financial investment. Experiential retail offers its customers more than products, providing unique and memorable experiences designed to build a stronger connection between the consumer and the brand.

We will also see that people who prefer buying experiences over things—so-called *experientials*—tend to be wealthier and better educated than average. They usually belong to middle- or upper- income groups and are often characterized by a pursuit of adventure and outdoor activities.

Chapter Four

The Search for Experiences

You may think that, in a chaotic world like the one we live in, people would want to spend most of their time huddled in bed with the blankets pulled up over their heads. But you'd be wrong. That's not what people want at all.

In this world we cannot control, filled with people we do not know and may not want to know, we look for ways to entertain and distract ourselves. We need to take our minds off loneliness and global calamity. This is the context in which we can best understand the search for new experiences: experiences that will impress or at least interest our friends and gain their approval. How about a vacation in Timbuktu? An afternoon spent skydiving? A summer spent working as roadie with a rock group? These may all win you friends and take your mind off global warming.

With this in mind, many people also seek out *experiential retail*, which refers to shopping for experiences that are all about doing, seeing, and feeling. These shopping experiences range from interactive art displays to live music, lounges, or virtual reality. But why is there such a desire for new experiences? According to political scientist Ron Inglehart, in our post-materialist society, we want to buy things that aren't just things. We want Experiences, with a capital "E."

Seeking Experiences

When you say, "I search for new experiences," you don't sound like someone who wants to stay the same. You're looking for something that is new to you, even if it's not something new to humanity. As a tourist in Europe, you'll see a lot of people taking selfies at popular tourist attractions. They want to brag about their own one-of-a-kind "experience." This is true at the Tower of London, the Bridge of Sighs in Venice, Vatican City, and many other well-known tourist destinations. However, millions of other tourists have done, and will continue doing, the same thing.

In fact, when you're looking for memorable things to do, you often think about what other people have considered important and memorable. Taking a selfie in front of the *Mona Lisa* at the Louvre may not be novel for humanity, but it is novel for you. By photographing your brief encounter with this work of art, you show that you are a successful consumer of global culture and that you belong to the global community of experienced world travelers.

So, this chapter is for you if you've ever taken selfies at the Eiffel Tower or wanted to do something similar. Take the test below to see if you're an experience junkie. Use a 5-point scale to show whether you agree or disagree with each statement. Remember that a "5" shows that you strongly agree, a "4" shows that you agree somewhat, and so on. As before, just add up all your points. You enjoy new experiences if your score is 40 or higher.

I look for interesting and unusual experiences because…
1. They are part of how I've chosen to live my life.
2. I feel I deserve the right to enjoy these experiences.
3. Big experiences show off the kind of person I am.
4. They are in line with the things I value in life.
5. I find big experiences stimulating and interesting.
6. Big experiences improve the quality of my life.
7. Of the recognition I'll get from others.
8. Of the chance to discover what others think of me.
9. In the long run, they are useful and worthwhile for me.
10. They help me fit in with the kinds of people I admire.

Experiences and Happiness

The experiences that bring people pleasure and happiness can vary widely. However, some activities and experiences have repeatedly contributed to people's happiness and well-being. Two activities known to increase well-being are (1) using money to benefit others (that is, prosocial spending) and (2) giving up money to have more time (that is, buying time). Taken together, research on prosocial spending and buying time underscores the value of seeing money as more than a stable life circumstance. Money is also a tool that people use to alter their own happiness levels through creating experiences for themselves (Dunn et al., 2020).

Of course, some experiences don't oblige you to spend money at all. Engaging with family and friends can provide emotional support, companionship, and a sense of belonging, and often this doesn't need a consumer purchase. The same is true of physical exercise. It releases endorphins, which are chemicals in the brain that act as natural painkillers and mood elevators; and exercise doesn't typically need a lot of money. Similarly, spending time in nature and engaging in outdoor activities can reduce your stress and increase your feelings of well-being. These activities may not need a consumer purchase either.

Engaging in artistic efforts, like painting, drawing, writing, or crafting, can also provide personal fulfillment at little or no cost. And we can think of many more things like this. Enjoying music and dance can raise a person's mood and provide an outlet for expression and joy. Learning something new or improving existing skills can provide a sense of accomplishment and boost self-esteem. Engaging with literature can offer escape, knowledge, and perspective, fostering empathy and understanding.

A great many experiences do not cost much money. These include exploring new places and different cultures, which can be exhilarating and eye-opening. Engaging with entertaining or provocative media can provide relaxation and enjoyment, often without much cost. Cultivating interests and hobbies can offer people joy and fulfillment. Practicing mindfulness and meditation helps in reducing stress, anxiety, and depression, promoting inner peace and contentment. Yoga, tai chi, and other mind-body practices can help in balancing emotional and physical health.

Finally, and by no means least, helping others and contributing to charitable or community causes can offer people purpose and connection. Taking part in community events or local groups fosters connections with others and contributes to an encouraging social network. Small, unexpected gestures of kindness can bring joy to both the giver and the receiver.

Experiences of all these kinds teach us who we are to others and how we should see ourselves. And, as we have said, many of these activities need no purchase of goods or services. Indeed, most of the important experiences in our lives do not incur significant expenses.

Consumption through Experiences

On the other hand, *some* important experiences—like travel, vacationing, and tourism—do call for a significant outlay. Beyond that, many people like to spend their money on interesting experiences, not useful or beautiful objects. The Experiential Buying Tendency Scale (EBTS) was developed by marketers to assess how much people prefer enjoyable experiences (Howell et al., 2012). A high EBTS score shows that you have a strong desire for such activities. If you get a high score on this test, you are more likely to be extroverted, empathic, and reward-seeking than average. And if you prefer to buy experiences over things, you probably don't have strong materialistic values. In the words of political scientist Ron Inglehart, you are a "post-materialist." (We will discuss materialistic and non-materialistic values in a later chapter.) And Inglehart ought to know: for decades, he and his associates have been studying people's values and attitudes around the world.

However, you may have a weakness for *impulse buying*. Impulse buying by consumers has received a lot of attention in consumer research. Impulse buying is interesting because it not only responds to various internal psychological factors; it is also influenced by external market stimuli.

Traits (such as sensation-seeking), motives (especially, hedonic motives), consumer resources (especially, time and money), and marketing stimuli are all key triggers of impulse buying. A person's self-control and mood certainly influence impulse buying, as does the consumption context (for example, a brand's identity expression) (Iyer et al., 2020). We will have a lot more to say about impulse buying in a later chapter

Related to experiential buying and impulse buying is experiential retail—buying activity that results in an experience. Most people enjoy experiential retail because it gives them something they can "experience" and also possess.

Some people—men especially—don't like shopping and would find the idea of an immersive retail experience horrifying. "People would hate something like that," they may say. But they'd be wrong. Most people love this immersive experience, largely for its entertainment value.

Experiential retail, often called "retailtainment" or "experience-based retailing," is a strategy where retailers provide a unique, memorable, and engaging shopping experience for customers, rather than just selling a product. The aim is to create an environment where consumers can interact, learn, and connect with a brand or product in ways that go beyond the traditional shopping model.

Key ingredients and examples of experiential retail include interactive displays and installations. These may include touch screens, augmented reality (AR), or virtual reality (VR) stations where customers can visualize products in different scenarios. Retailers may offer in-store classes or workshops. For instance, a culinary store may offer cooking classes, or a tech store may provide coding workshops. Pop-up shops, launch parties, or celebrity meet-and-greets can attract crowds and media attention, improving the brand's visibility. Some stores are organized around a specific theme or idea to immerse the shopper. The American Girl Doll stores, for example, offer cafes, doll hair salons, and theaters for an immersive brand experience.

As well, in-store cafes or restaurants allow customers to relax, eat, and spend more time in the store. For example, some bookstores incorporate cafes where shoppers can read and relax. Customers can often customize their purchases, engraving jewelry, designing their own T-shirts, or personalizing their sneakers. They can use AR to "try on" clothes or makeup without actually wearing them, or use VR to experience a travel destination before booking a trip. Hands-on product testing is especially prevalent in electronics or sporting goods stores where consumers can try before they buy.

Entertainment in these stores might include live music, performances, or even small in-store theatres for product demonstrations or brand-related content. The stores also often include areas where customers can connect with others, share ideas, or just relax. Apple's "Today at Apple" sessions are an example where customers can learn and connect over technology topics in-store.

Several factors drive the shift towards experiential retail. Increasingly, physical stores need to offer something that online platforms can't, and a unique in-store experience can be a differentiator. Younger generations in particular place a higher value on experiences over possessions. These consumers are often looking for memorable moments and stories they can share, and experiential retail provides that.

When customers have unique experiences, they are likely to share them on social platforms, providing free marketing and brand exposure for retailers. As well, interactive experiences can offer valuable insights into consumer preferences and behavior. In turn, marketers can use these to improve products, marketing strategies, and the overall customer experience. In short, experiential retail aims to make shopping more than just a transactional process. It's about creating an emotional connection between the brand and the consumer, fostering loyalty, and driving repeat visits.

Typically, experiential retail offers hands-on, interactive experiences where customers can use or interact with the products. But it requires stores to provide a stimulating and enjoyable environment, often through thematic decor, surrounding music, and captivating visual displays. Stores may also use in-store events, such as workshops, or classes that align with the brand's image and appeal to the target audience.

Sometimes, as mentioned, experiential selling uses advanced technologies like augmented reality (AR), virtual reality (VR), or interactive kiosks to increase the shopping experience. It may also offer services that cater to individual customer needs and preferences, like personal shopping help or customization choices.

Many people like experiential shopping. Often, they remember experiences they enjoyed in the store, which can build stronger brand loyalty and affinity. Engaging experiences encourage customers to spend more time in the store, increasing the likelihood of making purchases. Physical and sensory experiences, absent in online shopping, can foster a deeper connection with products and the brand. Many experiential retail spaces are designed to be social and community-driven, offering a place for like-minded people to connect. Events and workshops allow customers to learn more about the products and how to use them.

With experiential retailing, shopping becomes a source of entertainment and enjoyment. It provides access to in-store exclusives, be they products or experiences, that may not be available online. Often, customers can try before they buy, discovering the look, feel, and usefulness of products firsthand. Positive and engaging experiences foster customer loyalty, encouraging repeat business.

In short, experiential retail is an innovative approach that focuses on offering customers unique and memorable experiences, not just products. By engaging the senses, fostering social interactions, and providing entertainment and educational value, this strategy seeks to build stronger emotional connections with consumers, promoting brand loyalty in a competitive market.

But experiential purchases, including the immersion in experiential retailing, are intangible and short-lived. Yet experiential retail has permeated marketing, nowhere more so than in the tourism industry. Vacationing, visiting amusement parks, touring art galleries, and dining out are just a few examples of experience buying. And when we travel abroad, we gain experiential value from our interactions and experiences in a different country. Making memories through experiences is central to tourism. People travel to have fun, fulfill their dreams, and show off their memories when they return.

When marketers have promoted an experience correctly, people begin to value, want, and enjoy it. Here's one example of a relatively new idea in experience marketing. A "tourism factory" is a working factory that allows visitors to see and learn at the same time. One popular place to visit in Dublin, for example, is the Jameson Irish Whiskey factory. Visitors get to see how whiskey is made and, also, to sample it.

Wine tourism is also growing in popularity around the world. Many people like the experience of visiting a vineyard and sampling the wines produced there. A lecture and wine tasting with a well-known sommelier may even entice some people to try new wines. And in their visits to wine country, tourists look for dining, shopping, and cultural activities that showcase genuine local products and traditions.

Wine tourists want to have a good time while they're visiting. To keep them entertained, wine festivals often include "elements of the spectacular"—shows that entertain people through art, music, and cultural history. Tourists who want to increase their cultural capital look forward to learning about the various types of wine and how wine is aged. Wine tourists with a love of the outdoors often want to sample the natural beauty of the region.

Wealth and Cultural Capital

People with more money and education than average are likelier than other consumers to prefer experiential purchases over material purchases. In short, they are more likely than average to buy non-tangible items such as vacations, concerts, and restaurant dinners.

Then, many of them share information about their experiences online. Social networking sites (SNSs) have greatly changed our means of sharing information about the things we buy. They encourage us to take part in sharing activities and have led to a boost in user-created content. Researchers have found that experiential purchases are likely to be shared through SNSs, because customers hope to gain social approval of their purchase (Zhang et al., 2021).

People whom we may call "experientials" make up only a minority of the consuming public. However, they have a distinctive profile and their number is not negligible. As mentioned, they tend to live well and are members of the middle or upper class. As much as possible, they spend their money on fun activities and new adventures. Experientials enjoy outdoor activities such as swimming, racquet sports, skiing, and hiking. They enjoy riding motorcycles and racing bikes to get the wind in their hair. They are more likely than others to be "foodies," to prefer healthy foods to sugary snacks, and tilt slightly to vegetarianism and veganism. Some say this is because of more educated people having more "cultural capital."

However, most people can only afford to buy experiences that make them happy if their basic material needs are already being met. When political scientist Ron Inglehart said we now live in a post-materialist society, he meant we want to buy experiences more than we did in the past. Compared with the past, we don't have to worry about staying alive because we live in a stable and prosperous country. And we don't have to worry about where our next meal will come from or whether we should flee from an attacking animal.

With many of our old worries erased, we now want to meet new people and discover new things. We can devote more of our time to self-expression, social justice, and saving the environment. Seventy years ago, psychologist Abraham Maslow famously originated the *hierarchy of needs*, an idea that helps explain this post-materialist thinking. According to Maslow, once we have met our basic needs, we can work on achieving our full potential, which includes achieving what Maslow called *self-actualization*. The hierarchy of needs is often depicted as a pyramid with five levels:

1. Physiological needs (basic needs for survival such as food, water, shelter, and sleep)
2. Safety needs (security, stability, and freedom from harm)
3. Love and belonging needs (relationships, friendship, and family)
4. Esteem needs (self-esteem, confidence, achievement, and respect from others)
5. Self-actualization (realizing one's potential, creativity, and problem-solving)

Maslow thought that all people are motivated to fulfill all these needs, though we can only satisfy higher-level needs once lower-level needs are satisfied. His theory has been widely influential in psychology, education, business, and other fields.

So, people with more money and more security—having satisfied their lower-level needs—find buying an experience makes them happier than buying material things. Experiences are self-actualizing. And as we said at the start of this chapter, some activities—especially tourist activities—are especially popular with people who can spare the money and time. Seeking interesting experiences can be enriching and lead to personal growth, new knowledge, and memorable moments.

You may think that the search for new experiences is universally beneficial and risk-free. But you'd be wrong. Even people who seek new experiences find some of them troubling. So, if you are interested in buying new experiences, here are the risks and dangers you should consider:

- Physical danger: Actively seeking adventurous or thrilling experiences, like extreme sports or visiting remote locations, can expose people to physical risks, including injury or even death.
- Financial risk: The need for unique experiences may lead to excessive spending, potentially leading to financial instability or debt.
- Mental and emotional strain: Continually chasing new experiences can become mentally exhausting and lead to burnout. It may also result in feelings of emptiness if the experiences don't provide the expected satisfaction or meaning.
- Neglect of responsibilities: An obsession with seeking new experiences can lead to neglecting daily responsibilities, affecting one's job, relationships, or other commitments.
- Risk of addiction: Continually seeking dopamine hits from new experiences can become addictive, leading to a cycle where one constantly needs more exciting and stimulating experiences to feel satisfied.
- Loss of genuine connection: Seeking experiences for the sake of novelty or for social media bragging rights can result in superficial engagements, missing deeper, genuine connections with people or places.
- Overstimulation: Constantly seeking new stimuli from experiences can make it hard to find contentment in simple, everyday moments, leading to feelings of restlessness.
- Safety concerns: Pursuit of unique experiences may lead people to ignore safety precautions, such as traveling to unsafe areas or trying untested substances.
- Health risks: Some sought-after experiences, like exotic foods or extreme adventures, can expose people to health risks, like food poisoning or altitude sickness.
- Cultural insensitivity: There's a risk of engaging in foreign activities that may be thought disrespectful or inappropriate, leading to misunderstandings or conflicts.

- Environmental impact: Excessive tourism, or seeking experiences in fragile ecosystems, can contribute to environmental degradation.
- Loss of identity: If one's self-worth becomes too intertwined with continually having new experiences, there's a risk of losing sight of one's core identity and values.
- Decision paralysis: The overwhelming array of potential experiences can lead to decision paralysis, where an individual cannot choose or commit to any particular experience.

So, seeking interesting experiences has its rewards, but you need to approach these pursuits mindfully. You must ensure they align with your values, that you don't compromise safety, and that you undertake them for genuine personal enrichment, not external approval.

As we will see in the next chapter, some people prefer to break away from the crowd and follow unusual or niche interests. These are activities of interest to thousands but not millions of other people. Niche marketing addresses the specific needs and preferences of these small, defined consumer segments.

The next chapter will show us that niche marketing tries to serve specific market segments effectively and ethically. The success of this strategy relies on a deep understanding of the niche in question, and the motives of this particular segment.

Chapter Five
Specialization and Niche Buying

Do you like to buy unusual items that help you stand out from the crowd? Or to be more specific, do you like to buy like a small subset of the general population? If that's the case, this chapter is for you. The beauty of niche buying is that it serves all your consumer needs at once. It comes with a defined community of niche buyers, and it often demands lengthy, close attention to detail. What's more, only a few people can enjoy and understand the thrill of getting something rare and special.

Suppose, for example, you become a member of the Canadian Hummingbird Society. You commit yourself to learning about different species of hummingbird, travel to different locations around the world to see rare varieties of the bird, and fill your home with hummingbird-related memorabilia. Doing this will give you a community of like-minded (that is, hummingbird-oriented) friends and provide your neighbours with opportunities for gossip and wonder. Best of all, it will focus your attention away from everything you cannot control.

But how can niche providers make themselves known to their potential customers, and what are the factors that influence customer satisfaction and loyalty of these customers? And how do the smallish businesses that satisfy niche segments survive in the competition with larger businesses like Amazon? Following the Old Testament story, the metaphorical question can therefore be posed: How can David stand up against Goliath?

Customer loyalty, in particular, is necessary for the success of a small company and plays a major role in e-commerce sales and satisfaction. However, other success factors are also moving into the foreground.

Service quality in particular has repeatedly proven to be a key feature of customer satisfaction, which in turn has a positive impact on customer loyalty (Brusch et al., 2019).

To see if you are a niche buyer, respond to the following statements using the same 5-point scale you used in previous chapters. Remember to give a statement 5 points if you strongly agree; 4 points if you agree but not strongly; and so on. As before, add up all your points to get your total score on this scale. You are a niche buyer if you score 40 or higher.

1. People's preferences are always changing.
2. There's no right way or wrong way to describe people: they're complex.
3. I feel like I've passed through many different situations and lifestyles.
4. I know lots of people who are very different from me and my family.
5. Producers are always finding new ways to describe people and serve them.
6. People are always coming up with new needs and new desires.
7. Every day, we change from what we used to be to what we are going to be.
8. What made sense to us ten years ago won't make sense ten years from now.
9. There are many interesting and unusual ways to think about people.
10. New generations of people need new kinds of goods and services.

The term "niche" comes from ecology and refers to a small, self-contained area where species coexist with one another as friends, competitors, or enemies. *Niche marketing*, therefore, refers to a marketing strategy that addresses a specific, defined segment of the market with specific kinds of products or services. This segment, or niche, typically has unique needs and preferences that aren't satisfied by general offerings in the larger market. So, with niche marketing, the focus is on a small, specific group of consumers with distinct needs. Offerings are often designed to meet the unique needs of the target niche.

So, for example, someone with a desire to open a bookstore may decide to sell only mystery books and thrillers. They may think there are enough buyers of these books to turn a profit. So they may name themselves the Mystery Bookstore, stock a wider-than-usual selection of mystery books, and look for ways to build a loyal customer base. For example, they may schedule monthly book readings and book signings by well-known mystery book writers, and perhaps even sponsor a mystery book club that meets at the store.

As the marketing is focused on a small market slice of readers, the potential profits may be lower than one may expect at a general bookseller like Amazon or Indigo. However, niche marketing provides a better opportunity for the business to build close relationships with its customers by developing deep expertise in their niche, increasing their market authority and reputation.

A niche marketing strategy involves targeting a specific, well-defined group of the market with products, services, or marketing messages specifically designed for that group. To research and understand the niche, the marketer may have to conduct market research to understand the needs, wishes, challenges, demographics, and behaviors of the niche market. The goal is to understand what makes this niche different from the mainstream market. The service provider will then create products or services that specifically cater to the identified needs and preferences of that niche market.

In promoting this product, the marketer also will explain the unique benefits that these products or services provide to the niche market. This will mean developing marketing content and messages that resonate with the niche audience, addressing their specific concerns, ambitions, and values. It will also mean identifying where your niche audience spends most of their time.

To build relationships and trust, the marketer will engage with the niche community through social media, events, and other platforms, building trust and setting up the brand as a reliable partner or provider. And finally, the marketer will regularly assess the effectiveness of this niche marketing strategy, adjusting their approach based on feedback and performance data.

Again, examples of niche marketing are easy to find. Consider, for example, vegan cosmetics. Makers of such cosmetics focus solely on vegan, cruelty-free products, targeting consumers who specifically look for ethical beauty choices. Or consider a specialized fitness center that offers programs specifically tailored to the needs of senior citizens, pregnant women, or people in wheelchairs. Other niche companies may specialize in providing sustainable baby clothing and accessories.

Tourism as a Niche Market

One especially obvious example of niche marketing is found in tourism. The first step toward success for a tourism agency is market partition, followed by market targeting. Some agencies focus on particular locations, others on particular types of travel (for example, cruises), and others still on particular segments of the population.

You may imagine that, with the aging of the population, fewer and fewer people are interested in new experiences. That's because the stereotype of old people is that they're set in their ways and unwilling to try new things. But you'd be wrong to think this. With the aging of the population and rise of the Internet, the tourism industry has become more vibrant, blurring the lines between a travel agency and a tourism agency.

On the Internet, people can get (and give) a lot more information about their travel experiences. Many tourists look for personalized services at a reasonable and predictable cost. Some travel agencies specialize in selling boat cruises, other in selling bus tours, and others still in providing expert local guides.

And naturally, the needs of tourists will vary according to many features, including age. The world's population is aging and global demographic changes have resulted in the increased participation of older (or senior) adults in tourism and leisure activities. Population aging, and earlier retirement, have also prompted governments and tourism providers in many parts of the world to identify senior travelers as a priority market. An increasingly healthy senior market segment now has the time and buying power to travel more often. Many seniors want to seek out and experience new, exotic destinations on their "bucket list."

The relationship between food and travel has always been an important aspect of hospitality, destination marketing, and tourism development. This fact has created an emerging niche market that people have called culinary or gastronomic tourism. And recently we have seen a growth in interest in gastronomic tourism as an academic field of study. However there has been little research on the socio-demographics of this niche market, and in particular, on older gastronomic tourists.

In other words, researchers have previously assumed all gastronomic tourists seek a similar experience, so few academics have written about this in the tourism literature.

Recent research suggests that many older gastronomic tourists are experienced travelers who, finally, have the time and money to experience foreign cultures through consuming local food. At the same time, other studies have noted the lessened taste and olfactory sensitivity of older tourists. To avoid any negative effects from a change in diet, and to control existing health problems, some senior travelers prefer to eat familiar foods rather than try out new local cuisines (Balderas-Cejudo et al., 2019).

Place-Making and Place-Seeking

Most tourists start out with a particular destination in mind, and typically, they associate specific places with branded products, companies, or services—and likely experiences. Place-making elements include practices, institutions, physical objects, and representations of location that lead tourists to form mental associations with locations. So, for example, someone visiting Paris may plan to visit the Eiffel Tower, someone visiting New York to visit the Empire State Building, and someone visiting Rome to visit the Colosseum or the Vatican.

Famous branded places like Paris, New York, and Rome typically strive to keep their old and iconic locations alive for new visitors. However, people's mental associations are liable to shift as a location's economic, political, social, and other characteristics change—and as branding experts work to change the public view of the location.

Branded locations like the Eiffel Tower and the Colosseum are places where customers interact with the brand as tourists or visitors. An example of place tourism is Disneyland. Visitors to Disneyland not only enjoy Disney entertainment and buy Disney goods, but also come to meet "real-life" Disney characters and "feel the magic." Exclusive entertainment, living, and dining experiences are also provided on-site, allowing the tourist to experience an entire Disney package of services.

And to repeat, such branding is not limited to Disneyland or other theme parks, or even to famous buildings like the Eiffel Tower. Entire cities, regions, provinces, and even countries try to brand themselves by providing a distinct, almost trademarked experience. Las Vegas, Venice, and Hawaii all follow this approach to marketing. Everyone has some idea of what the experience of Las Vegas, or Venice, or Hawaii, is likely to comprise. And each branded site tries to distinguish itself from the others by providing unique experiences, attractions, foods, culture, and an overall "vibe."

The need to experience a place's "authenticity"—to see and feel it as (imaginary) locals do—is a long-standing tourist motivation and many locations have responded to this challenge. They have created products and services that support their community's brand. Their goal is to project the (imagined) identity and culture of a location while catering to the sometimes foreign desires of tourists. And that's why, even in Paris, Beijing, Moscow and Buenos Aires, you will find a large McDonald's, where lots of foreign tourists eat Big Macs.

Big Macs aside, most travelers have some desire for unique, exotic and genuine tourist experiences. They genuinely want to experience the difference, foreignness, and disorientation that comes with visiting a new, strange place. Research on this finds that experiences of disorientation are good. They influence visitors' view of authenticity across various aspects of cultural heritage tourism, so tourism marketers typically provide for this.

Visitors experience disorientation by traveling outside their usual comfort zone. This disorientation increases their understanding and interaction with the foreign environment and makes their tourism experience feel more genuine. Tourism developers should, therefore, integrate such potentially disorienting activities as wandering in steppe landscapes or exploring unfamiliar culinary traditions into future tourism experiences (Tiberghien, 2020). For people from Japan, for example, even Prince Edward Island can seem disorienting. And just consider how *Anne of Green Gables* has popularized Prince Edward Island with foreign tourists. Despite being Canada's smallest province, PEI attracted over 1.6 million tourists in 2019. The beaches, bike paths, and beloved fictional character Anne Shirley are among its chief attractions. A local paper described the CBC television show *Anne with an E* as the "most significant tourism story for Prince Edward Island by a country mile … in a few decades." So, Tourism PEI spent $160,000 to run advertisements during the show in the hope of attracting visitors.

The television series sparked unprecedented interest in Prince Edward Island. A record-breaking four cruise ships docked in Charlottetown harbor on a Tuesday in 2018, and 11,000 people landed to explore the city. "On a day like today, it becomes an issue… We don't want people standing in line for half an hour," said the Green Gables store manager. The lines were so long the manager had to hire extra cashiers just to keep things moving.

Of course, the tourist interest in PEI is tiny compared to tourism in Venice or Paris, which have experienced congestion, traffic, and pollution as major effects of tourist enthusiasm.

That said, tourism is not the only industry that can benefit from place branding. Consider Saint John, New Brunswick, which has made efforts to brand itself "the retirement capital of Canada," so older adults would consider moving there. Marketing Saint John meant putting an emphasis on the city's quaint, scenic, and quiet features. (The city of Elliot Lake in Ontario has made a similar effort to attract retirees to that former mining community.)

Mindful of the great amount of spending that tourism unleashes, Canada announced a new tourism strategy in May 2019. The goal of this strategy was to move Canada from eighteenth to tenth place in the world as a tourist destination. The strategy highlighted tourism to Indigenous, northern, and rural regions as potential, untapped tourist destinations. These are all regions of Canada that need help with generating economic development.

But will foreign tourists want to visit an Indigenous area, a northern territory, or a village in Nova Scotia, Quebec, or Saskatchewan? For example, will they find satisfaction with the lodgings or food or entertainment in these locations? Consider the issue of food, and the appeal of local Canadian cooking in small communities.

Many marketers rightly highlight local food as a reason for coming to various tourist locations. Foodies are travelers with a special interest in good eating, and look for distinctive food features that include local crops, cooking styles, and food rituals. Of course, other visitors are attracted for other reasons. These may include the natural beauty, historical significance, cultural richness, and recreational possibilities (e.g., hiking) of a particular locale. Will foreign visitors find these in Indigenous, northern, and rural regions of Canada?

The battle for tourist dollars is tough and Canada may have a hard time competing with more settled tourist destinations with long histories and numerous cultural and historical landmarks. Still, each of these destinations is a brand, with instantly identifiable images and name recognition.

Tourism that Is Ethical

Some emerging approaches to tourism include a concern with social justice, equity and rights; inclusiveness and recognition; sustainability and conservation; and governance and participation. Everywhere, we can see a surge of interest in research on justice and ethics that's beginning to guide tourism and sustainability (Jamal and Higham, 2019).

Now, if you've ever seen thousands of tourists leave a tourist ship or line up to see a famous tourist site, you may think they are going to do irrevocable damage to the place they are visiting. But you'd only be partly right. With the growth of international tourism, more and more people have become concerned about the erosion or destruction of the destinations under such the pressure of tourist numbers. One response has been the rise of ethical and responsible tourism. This notion means treating the destination and its citizens respectfully and not harming the environment.

More usually, ethical or responsible tourism refers to tourism practices that are respectful and considerate towards local communities, cultures, economies, and the environment. Responsible tourism stresses increasing the positive contributions that tourism can make in various destinations, while lessening the negative impacts.

This includes lessening the environmental footprint of tourism and encouraging the use of eco-friendly practices, like recycling, lessening waste, and conserving energy. It means showing respect for local communities and cultures, by engaging with and respecting the customs, traditions, and values and ensuring that tourism does not lead to cultural erosion or exploitation. It also includes supporting the local economy by buying local goods and services, whenever possible.

Finally, ethical tourism aims at preserving the environment by protecting the natural habitat, wildlife, and biodiversity in tourist destinations and avoiding activities that cause environmental degradation or harm to wildlife.

Ethical tourists are mindful of their consumption and waste generation. They also safeguard the rights of vulnerable populations, including Indigenous peoples and children. And this, in turn, means preventing exploitation, trafficking, and other forms of abuse. It also means promoting fair labor practices and employee welfare among businesses in the tourism sector.

Ethical tourism has grown more popular in recent years. Compared to a generation ago, many more people today seek a "genuine" experience with "the locals," not a reproduction of the services they can get back home. Nonetheless, some customers continue to prefer Westernized resorts precisely because they do not want to interact with locals who are culturally (and economically) different from them. Linguistic and cultural barriers may also make it hard for tourists to leave Westernized resorts and explore the local area on their own.

The economic side of ethical tourism is also important. Ethical or responsible vacations are often more expensive than other kinds of travel. This means that tourists may have to spend more to ensure good wages for local workers or to use environmentally friendly facilities, and they may not feel able to afford this.

Senior Travelers as Niche Buyers

Because they have so much free time, seniors are especially attractive niche travelers and niche buyers. Seniors who have retired from work have more free time, and often more money to spend, than middle-aged and young working people. So, seniors have become a prime target for the world's tourism and recreation industries. Free of their duties to young children, they are glad to spend their money on travel, personal development, self-education, fun, and entertainment.

What people call "active aging" includes senior tourism but it also comes with niche challenges. Older tourists are concerned about medical care, health care, the location of the accommodation, and the availability of a tourist guide who can speak their native language. Concerns with flight schedules, medical care, availability of a tourist guide, location of accommodation, and mobility conditions vary according to the age of the tourist. On the other hand, experiences with security, climate, comfort, gastronomy, trip price, and local hospitality influence a tourist's satisfaction with their trip (Medeiros et al., 2020).

Compared with earlier generations of retirees, many of today's seniors are in good health and eager to stay that way. Others, realizing their time is limited, want to see the world while they're still healthy enough to do so. For these and other reasons, one survey found that over 80 percent of Baby Boomers have travel at the top of their bucket list.

The tourism industry, like many others, has segmented the senior market into many subtypes. For example, researchers have studied senior travelers in Australia, broken down by age, education, income, and the kind of holiday they prefer. They label their first type of senior traveler as "conservatives." Accounting for nearly half of the Australian senior market, this conservative segment looks for reliable holiday packages. They want to visit famous big cities and receive quality services at a manageable price. They enjoy family-type fun, and though they splurge occasionally, they rarely overindulge.

"Pioneers," a second senior segment, represent about one-quarter of the market. They are active, younger, and more educated seniors who are still seeking new experiences. They want adventure, but within a safe and secure framework. Many are attracted to outdoor, historic, and rural cultural experiences. With an independent mindset, they prefer self-learning and exploration rather than guided activities.

"Aussies," a third segment, represent about 15 percent of the senior demographic. They usually have less formal education and lower incomes than the first two groups we mentioned. Aussies treasure family time during their holidays. They are less interested in the arts, historical events, or cultural attractions, and more attracted to quiet cities and the countryside. In cities they visit, they enjoy cheap entertainment, like the movies. In the countryside, they enjoy picnicking and other family-friendly activities. Aussies often make their own fun, but comfort, security, and familiarity with a holiday destination are essential.

A fourth group, the "big spenders," make up a small fraction of the senior market (about 10 percent). They are wealthy enough to pay for luxury and are looking for nightlife, entertainment, and shopping in the city. They demand high-quality facilities, services, and entertainment and enjoy exclusive retreats that guarantee a high standard of service and fine food.

"Enthusiasts" are the smallest segment in this study (less than 5 percent). They want to have a good time, filled with nightlife and shopping. Security, safety, and quality services are important to them and they are willing to pay a lot of money to get the right experience.

For many senior travelers—for example, the big spenders and enthusiasts in the Australian study—casino gambling is a popular pastime when they travel. Gambling calls for little physical activity or, for that matter, skill. Even seniors with mobility issues can play slot machines. And though their abilities may be declining in other areas, seniors can still feel successful when they win big at the casino. The bright colors, flashing lights, and attractive prizes give seniors enough excitement to disrupt the monotony of their daily lives. Finally, retirees who live alone or see their friends and family less often than they used to can also interact with casino employees, easing the social isolation they may otherwise face.

Though most of the growth in world tourism is centered in major cities and urban locations, remote destinations are starting to look for tourists as well, as we saw earlier. Remote destinations can offer tourists tranquility and accessibility, which some tourists—for example, the pioneers and Aussies in the Australian study—long for.

A study of senior tourism in eleven remote regions of nine European countries focused on the key factors explaining senior tourists' motivations. For senior respondents, an important reason for going on holiday is the possibility of enjoying rest and silence. Safety, nature, historical sites, quality of services, and easy transportation connections are the top five attraction factors for seniors when choosing a destination.

However, remote locations have trouble reaching out to seniors with tourist offers, and trouble promoting local tourist products aimed at seniors. Many lack the financial resources they need to carry out local projects that support the development of senior tourism (Zielińska-Szczepkowska, 2021).

As we noted earlier, niche marketing is a focused marketing approach that targets specific market segments with tailored products and services. In the tourism industry, niche marketing can cater to various groups, including foodies, ethical tourists, and senior travelers, each with its own unique preferences and expectations. The success of niche marketing relies on engagement, deep understanding, effective communication, and continuous adjustment of marketing strategies to serve the identified niche effectively and ethically.

Specialization, in various domains and even in consumer behavior like niche buying, has its benefits, such as deep expertise and catering to specific needs. However, specialization and niche buying carry potential risks and dangers. You need to consider these if you intend to take part in a niche consumer market, especially as a seller of niche goods and services:

- Higher prices: Niche buying, especially in markets with limited suppliers, may lead to higher-than-average prices due to the lack of competition.
- Risk of homogenization: Niche communities or consumers may become echo chambers, reinforcing existing beliefs or preferences and stifling innovation.
- Vulnerability to change: Specialists or niche markets may be more vulnerable to changes in the environment. If the specialized skill or niche product becomes obsolete or demand drops, people or businesses may find it difficult to adapt.
- Limited flexibility: Specialization can lead to a narrow focus, limiting the ability to pivot when needed. For instance, a business that

only sells a specialized product may struggle if there's a disruption in their supply chain or a sudden shift in market demand.
- Reduced understanding: Specialization can sometimes result in a lack of understanding of the broader context. A specialist may not see how their work fits into the bigger picture, leading to potential misalignment with larger goals or values.
- Economic risks: Niche businesses depend on a small, specific market. If that market shrinks or disappears, the business could face severe economic challenges.
- Dependence on only a few clients or suppliers: Specialized businesses may rely on a few of clients or suppliers. Losing a key client or facing a disruption from a primary supplier can be disastrous.
- Skill atrophy: Over-reliance on a specific skill or set of skills can lead to the withering of other skills, reducing an individual's or organization's versatility.
- Loss of diverse interactions: In niche markets, reduced interaction with a broader audience can limit opportunities for feedback, collaboration, and new ideas.
- Economic inefficiencies: Sometimes, specialization can lead to economic inefficiencies. If each entity only produces a narrow range of goods or services, there may be missed opportunities for economies of scale or scope.
- Environmental concerns: Niche products, especially if they have limited demand, may lead to overproduction and waste if not managed correctly.
- Knowledge gaps: Over-specialization in education or professional training may leave people with gaps in general knowledge, making it harder for them to understand or engage with interdisciplinary issues.

So, specialization and niche buying offer the ability to cater to specific needs and achieve deep expertise. However, we must remain aware of the potential pitfalls. Balancing specialization and diversification, and staying adaptable and open to broader trends, can mitigate many of these risks.

In the next chapter, we will discuss a different motive for buying: the desire for trophies. *Trophies* are unique and (usually) expensive goods that symbolize success, superiority, and high social standing. Some people love to get trophies, which range from traditional awards to luxury goods like expensive watches and cars, to show off their achievements and showcase their wealth and status.

As we will see, trophy buying is related to conspicuous consumption, where people buy rare goods to flaunt their wealth and status. Such purchases are not only about getting goods but also about the act of buying, which itself is a display of financial power.

Chapter Six

Trophies

You may have laughed at our description of Timothy and his fascination with trophies. You may even have thought he was an exaggerated fictional character, unlikely to exist in real life. But in fact, there are millions of people just like Timothy, and they live to acquire as many trophies as they can.

Trophies are goods that are unusual and, therefore, usually expensive. Many people enjoy owning trophies because having them suggests you're a boss, a style leader, a smart guy, and the person at the top of the mountain. Trophies say that you are superior to other people and they challenge others to keep up.

Normally, trophies are awards or prizes given to people or groups as a form of recognition for their achievements, success, or participation in particular activities. They are intended to recognize merit, commemorate accomplishments, and provide tangible symbols of success and excellence. Some trophies go to athletes, teams, or clubs for winning or taking part in sports competitions, tournaments, or leagues. Other trophies go to students for excelling in academics, debates, science fairs, or other scholarly activities. In corporate life, some trophies are awarded to employees, departments, or companies for outstanding performance, achieving targets, or significant contributions to the organization or industry.

In these and other cases, trophies recognize and celebrate achievements, providing recipients with a sense of accomplishment. As motivational tools, they encourage people to strive for excellence in various activities. Trophies also act as evidence of past successes and milestones.

In that way, they stand as symbols of excellence, talent, and commitment to a particular activity.

So, people use trophies to send a message. These trophies or honorifics may be medals or ribbons or titles; or they may be Maseratis or Rolex watches. Thorstein Veblen, mentioned earlier, proposed that trophies date back to a time even before humans began to buy goods. He thought that as human societies progress, "the use of trophies develops into a system of rank, titles, degrees, and insignia, typical examples of which are heraldic devices, medals, and honorary decorations."

In our society, many trophies are a display of conspicuous consumption: excessive spending on goods and services to display a person's wealth and social status. To achieve high status in an unequal society, you must (1) buy expensive goods, then (2) flaunt them in public. Brand prominence—the prominence of a brand's mark or logo—is an important aspect of trophy buying, because it signifies the brand's rarity and cost.

People buy trophies like Rolex watches or Bentley automobiles for two main reasons. First, people attach emotional significance to their trophies. Second, they use their trophies to raise their social standing in the community.

Let's consider one example of trophy buying. In October 2019, comedian Ellen DeGeneres shared an Instagram photo of herself in her Beverly Hills home with vintage-watch dealer Jasper Lijfering. In the photo, she has a small smile on her face as she shows off her new buy, a late-1960s gold Rolex Daytona. This special edition of the Rolex Daytona, the John Player Special, is named after a car that raced on the Formula One circuit in the 1960s. Paul Newman, the actor, entrepreneur, and race-car driver, also wears one of these watches in a famous photograph, adding to the cachet of the watch.

Beyond that, note the attention that Lijfering paid to DeGeneres in making this sale. Before DeGeneres bought the Daytona at his Amsterdam shop, Lijfering flew to Los Angeles three times to complete the deal. So, for a handful of good reasons, DeGeneres viewed her purchase as a trophy. In buying this rare, million-dollar wristwatch, DeGeneres was also buying dream-material about F1 auto racing and Paul Newman's mystique.

Consumption in Full View

As we have said, trophy buying is mainly a form of conspicuous consumption and, a century or two ago, "conspicuous consumption [was] a means of reputability to the gentleman of leisure," according to Thorstein Veblen. "Gentlemen of leisure" are men who can afford to take time away from work because they have enough money.

"Gentlemen of leisure" is an old idea but one that still attracts some people, as we see when we consider the appeal of the James Bond novels and the movies based on them. Consider the well-known "oddities" that author Ian Fleming built into the novels. They included luxuries with which Fleming closely associates Bond (down to his favored brand of strawberry jam). Most revealing is the complex interaction between Bond and the story's villain, with its combination of gentility and gamesmanship with murderous intent. In short, the Bond novels present Bond as a conspicuously consuming "barbarian," which is what makes these novels (and the movies they spawned) so entertaining (Elhefnawy, 2021).

To repeat, trophy buying is a display of wealth and leisure. Beyond that, trophy buying is also a display of sacrifice. In fact, all consumer behavior is a display of sacrifices. Whenever they buy something, people give up something they value—money—to get something else they value. They do this because our consumer society values what is difficult to get. That's where money and sacrifice collide.

All commodities are valued in this way, as an exchange of sacrifices. Sociologist Georg Simmel argues in his classic work *The Philosophy of Money* (1907) that objects, whether gumdrops or gold, have no inherent value. Instead, we (as a society) assign them value. In the market for goods and services, people show one another how much they will pay for something, and in this way attribute a value to it.

In this sense, economic life revolves around the exchange of sacrifices, not the exchange of meaningless goods and services. The commodity that demands the greatest sacrifice is the hardest to get and, therefore, the most valuable. Whoever gains this prized possession is admired for his or her supposed sacrifice.

Further, the person who can afford a large sacrifice will be copied by other people who want to be celebrated, causing a whole cycle of sacrificial buys. In short, then, trophy hunting is all about gaining the possession that will elicit the most envy, jealousy, and admiration from those who know about it. And trophy-buying will always need a large sacrifice, even if the person making that sacrifice has a great deal more to spend.

As we've noted, Thorstein Veblen was among the first scholars to study conspicuous consumption. Even though his work is more than a century old, it still helps us understand the relationship between wealth, status, and consumption. For Veblen, a person's reputation directly reflects the money he controls but also the purchases he makes. Thus, "leisure and conspicuous consumption are the foundations of gaining and maintaining a good name" (Veblen, 1925).

Veblen was best known for his critique of capitalism and his analysis of the social effects of economic change. In his book *The Theory of the Leisure Class* (1899), Veblen argued that the leisure class engaged in conspicuous consumption and "conspicuous leisure" to display their social status. Veblen was also a leading figure in the development of institutional economics, which looks at the ways in which institutions (broadly defined to include laws, social norms, and cultural beliefs) shape economic behavior. He emphasized the evolutionary nature of economic change and the importance of understanding historical and social context.

According to Veblen, having a "good name" means having honour, prestige, and esteem in the community—all results that wealthy people are willing to pay for through conspicuous consumption. Their conspicuously luxurious lifestyles distinguish them from the poor, the middle class, and the only slightly wealthy.

Over the twentieth century, conspicuous consumption democratized slightly. The leisure, sporting, and consumer goods industries grew steadily, allowing people from all economic and social classes to take more part in conspicuous consumption. Anyone with time and money to spend could consume conspicuously and acquire trophies. And anyone with trophies could claim to be a member of the privileged social class.

Now, on this matter, Veblen proved to be partly right and partly wrong. In some societies with a hereditary upper class, where bloodlines and "breeding" are taken seriously, having a lot of money does not necessarily gain you access into the highest reaches of society. In this respect, the more traditional England—where bloodlines count for a lot—is different from the less traditional United States—where bloodlines count for little, compared to wealth possessed.

In short, Veblen had failed to recognize the significance of "old money" versus "new money." "Old money" refers to wealth that has been inherited over multiple generations. Families with old money are typically considered part of the upper class, and they often possess not just financial wealth, but social connections, prestige, and influence that have been built up over a long period of time.

Old money families have a long lineage of wealth, often tracing back several generations. They usually have a high social status and are often involved in traditional and prestigious social institutions. Old money tends to be more discreet about their wealth, avoiding ostentatious displays of riches. There is often a strong emphasis on proper etiquette, education, and certain values. Old money families may own historic estates, art, and other valuable items that have been passed down through generations.

Due to their longstanding wealth and connections, old money people and families can have significant influence in social, political, and economic spheres. They often have extensive social networks, and belong to exclusive clubs, schools, and organizations. Old money wealth is typically more stable and less subject to economic fluctuations than new money, which may be earned in one generation. Finally, there can be a perception of snobbery or elitism associated with old money, as these families are sometimes seen as being out of touch with the realities of modern life.

On the other hand, "new money" refers to wealth that has been acquired within one generation, often through entrepreneurship, investments, or other forms of economic success. New money people may be more flamboyant or ostentatious in displaying their wealth, and they may not have the same social connections or cultural capital as old money families.

Supposedly, people with old money have more taste than people with new money, and only people with taste can earn a place in the upper social class. That is because, supposedly, only people with old money have the necessary cultural capital to be classy. The consumer habits of old aristocrats are considered sophisticated and tasteful, while the consumer habits of newly wealthy people may seem tacky, especially in more traditional societies.

Said another way, as the access to trophies trickles down the class ladder, more and more people own the same product, so prestige is no longer conferred on that product. Then, the old aristocrats no longer think a given product—whether a Rolex watch or a BMW—distinguishes them from people with new money. To restore their distinction, they seek different products or newer, more expensive versions to serve as trophies.

This fuels a competition among members of the wealthy leisure class and those at the top set the consumption standard. They specify the amount and type of consumption people need to remain a member of the class. Does that make them narcissists, people who care for nothing more than wealth and prestige?

Some research suggests this is the case: that narcissists are prone to conspicuous consumption and a preference for luxury over mundane products. Through conspicuous consumption, the wealthy establish their distinctiveness and high status. They discover a meaning in life: namely, the enjoyment of unusual goods and experiences. They enjoy the beauty and enchantment of material pleasure. And they signal their sexual desirability. Yet, despite these insights, so far researchers have been unable to clarify the causal flow from narcissism to conspicuous consumption, or from conspicuous consumption to narcissism (Sedikides and Hart, 2022).

How does conspicuous consumption connect with eco-tourism, which we discussed in the last chapter? Most of the previous literature has suggested travelers prefer ecotourism for moral reasons. However, emerging evidence suggests that some tourists look for opportunities to call attention to their social status in making a travel decision. One study compared the relative influence of two possible predictors of ecotourism: a commitment to environmental values and a desire to communicate environmental and social values. Research on a sample of American tourists reports that the desire to communicate environmental and social values had the stronger influence on people's tourism decision (Beall et al., 2021).

This result, though perhaps surprising to us, would not have surprised sociologist Jean Baudrillard, who thought that all buying decisions were communications. Baudrillard is perhaps most famous for his theory of simulation and hyperreality, where he argued that in contemporary society, the distinction between reality and its representation has broken down. He thought that we live in a world of signs and symbols, where representations of reality (like media images, or even Disneyland) have become more real than reality itself, creating a "hyperreal" world. In this context, consumer goods are not just purchased for their utility, but for the social and symbolic meanings they carry, contributing to our identity and status.

In short, Baudrillard was interested in how postmodern societies change the way we understand and represent the world. And in light of his theory of hyperreality, Baudrillard gained notoriety for proclaiming that the First Gulf War was not actually a war in the traditional sense. Rather, it was a media event, a spectacle, and a form of "virtual war" that obscured the real suffering and destruction taking place.

So, if we follow Baudrillard's lead, conspicuous consumption is the only kind of consumption that matters. And conspicuous consumption is an even stronger motivation in fashion than in any other realm, as we see from the work of Ashley Mears, a sociologist, professor, author, and former fashion model. She focuses mainly on the fashion industry, modeling, culture, and consumption.

Her research often explores the intersections of culture, gender, and work, with a particular emphasis on the aesthetic aspects of economic life. In her published works, Mears provides an insider's perspective on the fashion industry. Drawing from her experiences as a fashion model, she explores the industry's dynamics, revealing how beauty is valued and models are selected and paid.

Similarly, her extensive research on the club culture of the wealthy provides a present-day example of competitive trophy spending (Mears, 2020). Within the culture Mears infiltrated, the men at the top of the hierarchy are referred to as "whales"—men who build their reputations by spending extravagantly at exclusive clubs.

During Mears' fieldwork, the whale of all whales was Jho Low, who "spends a million dollars and laughs at everyone… It's as if everyone is beneath him." Club owners value whales like Jho Low not only for the money they spend, but also for the mystique they create among their clientele. They "increase the likelihood that you, too, will witness a grand display of wealth."

Clubs in this fashionable world reinforce the competition for trophy spending on a night out. A significant purchase may provoke the delivery of sparklers or an announcement by the DJ that "Alex from London is in the house, and he just spent $100,000 on Dom [Pérignon]!" The waiters even display empty bottles as trophies so everyone can see how much a party of customers had consumed. Finally, when the "girls" dance, they often remove their shoes—"iconic, red-soled Louboutin's"—and put them next to the empty bottles (Mears, 2020).

"Celebrities" are lower in the clubs' pecking order than "whales." Clubs typically don't make as much money from celebrities and they often have to lure celebrities to the establishment with complimentary drinks. Even further down the trophy list of customers are "mooks"— wealthy tourists and businessmen whose tables produce between $1,500 and $3,000 per night, the greatest source of a club's profits.

The Insider Crowd and Brand Prominence

You may think that any item can be a trophy, if it is accompanied by the appropriate ritual—typically, a public trophy-granting ceremony. But you would be wrong. Today, consumer trophies don't need a public ritual or ceremony. They only need brand prominence. Brand prominence, the esteem people grant to a brand's mark or logo on a product, is the key feature of trophy owning and trophy buying today.

Consider Canada Goose, a manufacturer of expensive parkas. Canada Goose jackets cost well over $1000 and feature a large, distinct logo on one arm, signaling the individual has lots of money to spend. Oddly, you can buy a Canada Goose parka at Galeries Lafayette in downtown Nice, France. Likely, no one is buying a Canada Goose jacket (rated to −25° C.) on the warm French Riviera, at least not to help them face bitter winter winds. They are buying them to own them and say they own them.

How do trophy products deal with other public concerns, like environmental sustainability? For Canada Goose, a key communication concern is *greenwashing*. Public discourse on environmental responsibility and sustainability continues to pressure corporations to improve, especially those that have been portrayed as key contributors of environmental harm. Greenwashing is a strategy that companies adopt to engage in symbolic communications with environmental issues without substantially addressing them in actions. With Canada Goose, some researchers question whether businesses can "go green" in good faith. It is unclear if corporate responsibility and environmental responsibility can ever be reconciled. To answer this question, we need to be a lot clearer about the intended effects and unintended effects of corporate greenwashing (Gacek, 2020).

Along similar lines, consider the development and sale of Hummer SUVs. No doubt, the Hummer H2 (marketed from 2002 to 2009) was a distinctive trophy vehicle. According to one early review, "there is no mistaking the Hummer [H2] for anything other than a Hummer" (New Car Test Drive, 2002). It was positioned to be a trophy purchase. With a base price of slightly more than $50,000 US, it announced to the world that you could afford to buy a lot of gasoline (and were indifferent to the environmental impact).

Marketers were optimistic about potential sales of the vehicle. Dealers "will be swamped," *New Car Test Drive* reported, "with only about 40,000 of these to sell." GM even asked dealers to build a distinctive Quonset hut adorned with a 10-metre-tall "H" to sell the H2.

In a study of Hummer sales, researchers noted two waves of Hummer H2 buyers. The first group of buyers were early adopters, buying a Hummer within six months of its release; the second group of buyers followed later. Dealers estimated the early adopters, or first wave buyers, had annual incomes of around $360,000 US. In keeping with the Hummer H2 being a trophy purchase, "the first-wave buyers hunted down H2s with a feverish avidity equaled only by zealous sports fans."

As previously stated, the purpose of a trophy is to signal superiority over others in the community. "It wasn't enough for many of the wealthy clients to get their hands on a … Hummer H2, they wanted to beat the other customers," the article continues. Dealers told researchers that some customers would bribe them to get their vehicle first.

The appeal? The Hummer H2 projected an image of safety and power, unsurprising given its history as a military vehicle and its enormous size. It also gave many owners the sense of superiority they desired from a trophy purchase. "It looks like it's all steel and it's going to take some punishment," one respondent noted. Some respondents reported that their Hummer H2 prompted sexual encounters. One hip-hop celebrity took the phone numbers of two women he met while driving around Los Angeles. Another buyer who described himself as ugly got a date with a "beautiful woman" while stuck in traffic. So, it isn't all about money in this Hummer H2 case history.

That said, when it was first released, the Hummer H2 was less expensive than many other trophy vehicles. For people who valued what the Hummer represented, much more than the price made it a compelling buy. In fact, many Hummer H2 buyers saw the lower price as a benefit when compared with a more expensive car.

What this shows us is that trophies sometimes achieve a high value because of their back story, not merely their cost and rarity. The back story of Hummer is that it is warlike and aggressive, as well as expensive. So, people who want to a warlike and aggressive image will pay extra for such a vehicle, environmental sustainability be damned!

In some respects, "trophy wives" are like Hummers. They are valuable, in part, because of their rarity and expense, but also because of the message they communicate about their "possessor." The term "trophy wife" is often used disparagingly to describe a younger, attractive woman who is married to a typically older, more financially secure man. Acquisition of a trophy wife implies a woman's primary "value" is her physical appearance and social charisma—perhaps also her ability to bear children—rather than other qualities such as intellect, empathy, or shared interests.

In Australia, the football trophy "WAG" (Wife and Girlfriend) is fast becoming an iconic figure and a critical part of Australian football branding. Commodification of the WAG reportedly benefits the Australian Football League (AFL) as a business and bolsters players' masculine image. The WAG fits well with traditional narratives about gender embedded in football culture. In Australian news media, the WAG is represented as a trophy wife; this representation functions to reinforce the dominant masculinity of her male partner (Marks, 2019).

Of course, the term "trophy wife" carries sexist and ageist connotations, because it reduces the woman in question to an object or "trophy" to be shown off. It also implies she doesn't bring other, equally important qualities to the relationship. And because of the sexism implied by the term "trophy wife," the term "trophy husband" is used less. A "trophy husband" is typically a younger, attractive man married to an older, more financially successful woman. This term also suggests the man's primary value lies in his physical attractiveness and ability to improve his partner's social status. It does not depend on his other personal qualities or contributions to the relationship. It also implies the man may not be as successful or ambitious as his wife. This implication may perpetuate harmful gender stereotypes about the roles and expectations of men and women in relationships.

These ideas of "human trophies" bring obvious problems. They reduce complex human beings and relationships to superficial qualities, ignoring the depth, diversity, and multifaceted nature of people and their partnerships. They reinforce harmful gender and age stereotypes, which can perpetuate bias and discrimination. Use of the terms disrespects the people involved, degrading their worth and the contributions they make to their relationships. And such terms reduce the dynamics of these relationships to transactional or superficial partnerships, while ignoring the many reasons people choose to be together. That said, Veblen recognized that one sign of great wealth was the ability to buy the services of a remarkable servant or retainer and waste (and devalue) these services. Indeed, *conspicuous waste* was one prominent feature of what Veblen called conspicuous consumption.

If you are someone who seeks trophies, you should be aware that trophy-seeking comes with risks and dangers. Seeking and buying trophies, to display as status symbols, can come with the following risks and dangers you should consider:

- Financial strain: Gaining trophies often comes at a high cost. Spending beyond your means can lead to significant financial strain or debt.

- Superficial approval: Relying on external symbols for confirmation can lead to a superficial sense of self-worth, where your identity and self-esteem are heavily tied to material possessions.
- Relationship strain: Others may see a strong focus on trophy acquisition as arrogance or superficiality, which can strain your personal and professional relationships.
- Loss of authenticity: Overemphasis on getting trophies can lead to choices not aligned with your true values or needs, resulting in a loss of authenticity.
- Mental health impact: The pressure to preserve or improve your status through trophy acquisition can lead to stress, anxiety, or depression, especially if you feel you are not living up to societal expectations.
- Obsessive behavior: For some, the need for trophies can become an obsession, where the constant need for more or better possessions dominates your thoughts and actions.
- Cultural insensitivity or appropriation: In some contexts, trophies may be items of cultural significance. Getting these without understanding their origins can be seen as cultural insensitivity.
- Legal risks: There's a market for fake trophies. Accidentally buying fake items can result in legal ramifications or financial losses.
- Risk of theft: Expensive trophies or status symbols can make you a target for theft, leading to potential financial and personal safety risks.
- Opportunity cost: The money spent on getting trophies could be invested elsewhere, potentially yielding better long-term benefits, whether in terms of financial returns, personal growth, or societal contributions.
- Environmental concerns: The production and acquisition of trophies can sometimes have significant environmental impacts, from resource extraction to production to transportation.
- Depreciation: Many trophies, especially those bought as status symbols, can fall in value over time.
- Lack of fulfillment: Despite owning trophies, you may find that such possessions don't bring lasting happiness or fulfillment, leading to feelings of emptiness.

- Ethical implications: Some trophies, like animal heads or skins, may be sourced unethically, involving issues like animal cruelty, exploitation of workers, or unsustainable practices.

Seeking trophies as markers of success or status is deeply ingrained in many cultures, but you should consider the potential pitfalls of such pursuits. Finding a balance between celebrating achievements and seeking genuine, intrinsic fulfillment is a key to avoiding many of the dangers associated with trophy-seeking behavior.

It's easy to confuse trophies with luxuries, because both trophies and luxuries tend to be rare and expensive. However, in the next chapter we will explore the unusual or unique features of luxuries. *Luxuries* are non-essential goods and services—often associated with wealth, comfort, and indulgence—that everyone wants. These items are characterized by their quality, price, aesthetic appeal, exclusivity, and status. They may include expensive cars, designer apparel, premium homes, and jewelry. As we will see, many different kinds of people are aspirational luxury buyers.

Chapter Seven
Luxuries and Luxury Buyers

You may think that luxuries are merely goods whose prices have been marked up to impress potential consumers. They may even be unnecessary goods and services that are highly desired by wealthy people. But you would be wrong, in part. Far from being merely expensive, luxury goods are often more comfortable, enjoyable, or indulgent than less luxurious brands—at least, in the eyes of their buyers.

Examples of luxuries would include expensive cars that are produced with premium materials, display superior craftsmanship, and often have a brand name associated with status and wealth. Luxuries would also include apparel and accessories from famous fashion houses, often handcrafted with exquisite materials. Other luxuries would include expensive homes in prestigious areas, often with extensive amenities and unique architectural designs. And of course, luxuries would include expensive jewelry and watches: pieces crafted by notable brands or designers, often using precious metals and stones.

In the past, people typically bought luxuries with cash, but today more people buy luxury goods on credit, something that can lead them into significant financial debt. What are the behavioral effects of being under debt stress, you may wonder? Using a survey and three laboratory experiments, some researchers find that debt stress leads to sensed status demotion—a fear of status loss. This, in turn often increases a consumer's intention to buy more luxuries—a counterproductive behavior that is commonly seen among less rational consumers (Wang et al., 2020). Such a response to debt stress also suggests a buying addiction, where the consumer is unable to resist continuing to buy, despite debt.

Of course, not all luxury goods are purchased. Some are received as gifts from family, friends, or associates. And some luxury goods, like designer clothes, watches, or cars, are purchased secondhand at a lower price than new items. Some art pieces, jewelry, and collectibles are bought at auctions, where interested buyers can bid on them.

Some luxury items, like art or real estate, may increase in value over time, making them not just purchases but also investments. However, luxury buying can be risky. The luxury market has many fakes. Ensuring the authenticity of a luxury product is critical, as fake items lack the quality and craftsmanship of genuine products.

As mentioned earlier, some luxuries are merely totemic objects—trophies—and not valuable things in themselves. Think of diamonds. You can't eat diamonds. You can't live in them or use them to cure an illness. They are merely signifiers of wealth, valued because we have agreed to value them. They have a rare quality—hardness—that we have agreed to value, though other things are harder, and we rarely (if ever) need a diamond's hardness for practical purposes.

This elevation of something meaningless to the status of a widely desired luxury is widespread in our culture. Our consumer society is full of goods and services that are unnecessary and even useless that we, nonetheless, have agreed to treat as valuable. This fact merely reinforces the view of many social critics that we live in a society where everything comes down to approval and belonging. Hundreds of millions of people—people like us—lead their lives in pursuit of increasing their "likes" through luxury buying.

Do you enjoy buying (or thinking about buying) luxuries? If so, this chapter is for you. To see if you qualify as a dyed-in-the-wool luxury buyer, respond to the following ten statements using the same 5-point scale you used in previous chapters. Remember to give the statement 5 points if you strongly agree; 4 points if you agree but not strongly; and so on. As before, add up all your points to get your total score on this scale. You enjoy trophies and luxuries if you score 40 or more points.

1. People need to pamper themselves more often than we are willing to admit.
2. Treats and luxuries are basic needs for people who can afford them.
3. I would buy myself something special every day if I had the money.
4. I admire people who treat themselves to gifts now and then.
5. Some people are too strict with themselves, denying themselves pleasure.
6. There's nothing wrong with buying luxuries on credit now and then.
7. I often feel like I can't wait another minute until I eat something delicious.
8. I think that I need more treats and luxuries today than I did five years ago.
9. I'm going to buy myself something special even if other people don't like it.
10. Going without treats and special events is not living at all: it's being dead.

Status and Luxury

As noted, luxury purchases are communication tools. They broadcast messages about our wealth, "good taste," luxurious lifestyle, and other qualities you nay wish to project. However, newly rich people—nouveau riche—often go overboard in their buying of luxuries. Consumption by newly wealthy people may be conspicuous in ways that old aristocrats find tacky. Seeing this, people with "older money" may seek newer, more expensive versions or different products.

The pervasiveness of luxury marketing worsens this problem for people with old money. Increasingly, merchandisers label products of all kinds and prices as "deluxe" or "premium." Some refer to this as "masstige," a term for mass-produced products that are marketed as prestigious. *Masstige* is a portmanteau of "mass" and "prestige." The term is used to describe goods priced above those typically available from mass market retailers but still more affordable than luxury items.

Masstige products occupy a niche between the mass market and prestige products, offering a sensed higher quality or more aspirational brand image without the hefty price tag associated with traditional luxury.

Compared with mass-market goods, masstige products often offer better quality materials, handiwork, or performance. And like luxury brands, masstige brands often invest in building a prestigious image, making consumers feel they are buying something special. While offering a sense of exclusivity, masstige products are still accessible to a broader consumer base because of their more affordable pricing. These brands are often sold in conventional retail outlets and not just in exclusive boutiques.

Typically, these products target middle-income consumers. Such consumers are willing to pay a little extra for products that offer better quality or a prestigious brand name but perhaps cannot afford high-end luxury goods. Brands in this category often use marketing strategies that highlight the premium qualities of their products, their special features, or the cachet of owning the brand. And they do this without positioning themselves out of reach for average consumers.

One researcher claims that masstige products especially appeal to people with "dark" personality traits such as narcissism, Machiavellianism, and psychopathy. He reports that, among big-selling luxury products, only Porsche, Rolex, and Mercedes can (also) be classified as masstige brands.

Surprisingly, the research finds a significant correlation between Tesla buying and all three "dark" personality traits, which the researcher credits to the public image of Tesla's CEO, Elon Musk. Further, he also reports a connection between psychopathy and the perception of coffee as a masstige product. Finally, the researcher reports that voting behavior—like consumer behavior—links to certain dark psychological tendencies. Allegedly, Machiavellianism predicts extreme voting behavior of all kind and psychopathy predicts right-wing voting behavior (Müller, 2023).

Another equally surprising piece of research asserts that masstige goods influence two important aspects of peer popularity: status and warmth. The purchase of luxury items makes the buyer appear colder to observers. However, the purchase of masstige products gives consumers the benefits of status without incurring the social cost of lower perceived warmth (Ho et al., 2023).

In case you are wondering about this, other research has shown that rich people are popularly stereotyped as competent but cold, while poor people are stereotyped as incompetent but warm (Fiske et al., 2019).

Many cosmetic brands in the masstige market offer products that are priced higher than the brands available in drugstores but priced lower than high-end luxury cosmetics. Thus, they offer quality and packaging that feels premium at an attractive price. Similarly, masstige clothing and accessory brands provide stylish, trendy items made with better materials and design than fast fashion, but at prices lower than designer labels. And in home decor, some masstige brands offer well-designed, durable pieces that are more exclusive and higher quality than those available from mass-market retailers, yet still reasonably priced.

In short, masstige products appeal to the many consumers who aspire to premium or designer goods but find the cost of luxury items prohibitive. These consumers are often willing to pay a premium over mass-market prices for items that offer extra quality, style, or brand prestige. This makes the masstige market a profitable one for brands that can successfully position themselves here.

But in this marketing environment, brands traditionally considered "luxuries" must distinguish themselves. Often, they do so by highlighting their superior quality. However, the sheer number of self-proclaimed luxury brands may frustrate these efforts. Marketers occasionally promote certain luxury products through exclusive, small-circle events. These products may even be hidden in a physical retail setting, forcing customers to ask for them.

You may think that, in keeping with the conventional rules of economics, when the price of a good goes up, people buy less of it. Not so with "snobby" customers. When the prices go up, they buy more. So, when marketers target such customers, they price their products differently. The demand curve slopes *upward*: a higher price produces more sales. Women's cosmetics provide an example: as the price rises, so does demand, at least among women who are snobs and want other women to know what they are buying.

Luxury and Social Inequality

As Veblen told us over a century ago, consumption reveals our social status and the consumption of luxury goods signals a position of privilege. So, wealthy people (and people who aspire to appear wealthy) engage in conspicuous, luxurious consumption, sometimes going into debt trying to copy those at the top of the status ladder. Their need to appear successful drives their demand for "communicative" consumer goods like luxuries.

However, even some low-income consumers buy luxuries, when they can, because they want to avoid the stigma of appearing poor. Research has shown that in a society with high income inequality, people are especially likely to seek higher status. Researchers in one study manipulated the perception of high versus low income inequality to see its effect on imagined buying behavior. Doing so, they found that a sense of high income inequality increased the pursuit of luxurious (positional goods) among people with low social status, producing aspirational consumers. A sense of high inequality had no effect on people with high social status (Du et al., 2022).

Positional goods are products and services that people value mainly because they signal status, wealth, or a particular social standing. The value of positional goods is derived not just from their inherent qualities, but significantly from their scarcity and the prestige they confer upon their owners.

Positional goods are often scarce or limited in supply. This scarcity is what helps to uphold their high status and desirability. For a good to serve as a status symbol, it needs to be visible or known to others. This is why luxury cars, designer clothing, and large houses are classic examples of positional goods. The value of positional goods depends on how they compare to the goods possessed by others. Owning a luxury car is more valuable in status if few others in your community have one. Positional goods serve as a signal to others about one's wealth, success, or social position. These goods often confer a sense of exclusivity, as not everyone can afford or access them.

Examples of positional goods include luxury car brands like Ferrari, Lamborghini, or Rolls-Royce, as they represent wealth and status. Owning a large, expensive home in a prestigious neighborhood serves as a status symbol. Clothing brands like Chanel, Louis Vuitton, or Gucci are often used to signal wealth and taste. Degrees from prestigious universities can be considered positional goods as they can confer status and open doors to high-status social networks. Being a part of exclusive clubs or societies can also be a positional good.

The pursuit of positional goods can worsen social inequalities, as it can lead to a society where people are constantly striving to one-up each other in terms of status and material possessions. Resources may be inefficiently allocated as people invest in positional goods instead of more productive or socially beneficial activities. Further, the constant pursuit of positional goods can contribute to a sense of dissatisfaction and a "keeping up with the Joneses" mentality, which can negatively impact people's mental well-being.

Understanding positional goods is important, as it sheds light on consumer behavior, social dynamics, and the allocation of resources in a society. Efforts to mitigate the harmful effects of the pursuit of positional goods involve fostering values of sustainability, community, and well-being over materialism and status.

Despite the harmful effects of positional buying, an estimated 40 percent of Americans (and an unknown but likely comparable percentage of Canadians) are aspirational buyers in this sense. They buy luxury items whenever they can, and hope to buy more of them in the future.

Aspirational consumers are drawn towards products, brands, and lifestyles that symbolize a high socio-economic status or level of achievement, success, or sophistication. They are motivated to buy products mainly for the symbolic value and status they confer. They have a strong need for upward social mobility and seek to align themselves with brands and products that reflect a successful and ambitious lifestyle.

Aware and conscious of brand differences, they are attracted to those brands people view as prestigious, high-quality, or luxury. They are keen on projecting a certain image or identity, and the products they buy play a significant role in crafting this.

Aspirational consumers are also influenced by advertisements, celebrity endorsements, social media influencers, and peer groups that promote high-end products. Though they do not belong to the wealthy class, they are willing to spend significant amounts on premium products and services. They often even sacrifice in other areas of spending to afford these items.

Aspirational consumers often buy designer clothes, handbags, shoes, and accessories sported by celebrities or popular in high-end fashion circles. High-end smartphones, smartwatches, and other gadgets from prominent and premium brands are also popular among these consumers. So are luxury beauty products, perfumes, and cosmetics. Aspirational buyers often want to own luxury or sporty auto brands that signify status and success. And whenever possible, aspirational consumers also invest in fine dining, exotic destinations, wellness retreats, and high-profile events or concerts.

Understanding aspirational consumers is critical for all marketers, as this demographic can be a profitable target audience. They are willing to pay a premium for products that align with their ambitions and also influence the buying decisions of their peers. Successfully appealing to their wishes and ambitions not only drives sales but also improves a brand's image and loyalty in a wider consumer base. Crafting a brand narrative for this group often means stressing exclusivity, sophistication, and the promise of a grand lifestyle.

However, efforts by lower-income consumers to appear wealthy (or upwardly mobile) may sometimes backfire. They may be better off in the long run if they save their money or spend it on education, housing, and health care.

The aspirational desire for luxurious status symbols begins in childhood. Children from all socioeconomic backgrounds learn about the signs of success and prosperity. Poor children, like all children, want to be accepted by their peers. And by the age of 14, they are already making purchases. Some of them engage in "compensatory consumption" to compensate for low self-esteem.

Compensatory consumption refers to consumer behavior that aims to offset or relieve feelings of inadequacy, low self-esteem, or failure in some aspect of life. Essentially, people engage in compensatory consumption to improve their feeling of self-worth and project an image of success or contentment to themselves or others. Such buying is also driven by a need for social approval and acceptance, in which consumers seek to present an image that is admired or envied by others.

Occasionally, consumers use compensatory consumption to cope with negative emotions, stress, or dissatisfaction with life. Buying luxury goods is, often, one telltale sign of compensatory consumption. Someone may buy an expensive car, designer clothes, or luxury accessories to project an image of success and wealth, even if their income does not align with this image. They buy items recognized as status symbols, such as the latest technology gadgets, to fit in or be seen as trendy and up to date. Similarly, people may splurge on vacations, dining at fancy restaurants, or attending high-profile events to feel accomplished or create memories that make others envy them.

In an era of social media, people often compare their lives with others, leading to feelings of inadequacy that they try to compensate for through consumption. As well, advertising and marketing strategies often play on consumers' insecurities and desires, prompting them to buy products that promise status or happiness. Societal norms and expectations about success, beauty, and lifestyle can drive people to engage in compensatory consumption to meet these goals.

However, compensatory consumption is risky and liable to backfire. For example, people who live in a wealthy neighborhood are more likely to be dissatisfied with their income than people who live in a less wealthy neighbourhood. Doubling the number of (say) Ferraris and Porsches in the neighbourhood would have the same negative impact on people's happiness as a 5 percent drop in their income. They would be happier with their own cars if they lived in a less posh neighbourhood with fewer luxury cars.

On the other hand, living in a disadvantaged neighborhood can be stressful too. That stress accumulates over time and undermines a person's health. Research shows that exposure to neighborhood disadvantage results in greater negative emotion, less positive emotion, and more compassion, compared with exposure to wealth. In all cases, people's reaction depends on their sensitization to prior experience (Hackman et al., 2019).

Today, four out of every ten Americans (and likely Canadians) are "aspirational" luxury consumers, meaning they value luxury goods but don't buy them often because they can't afford them. When they do buy them, it is to reward themselves for their hard work. This has been a common trend among Baby Boomers who think they have too little time to themselves and need occasional pampering.

As we have said, to attract aspirational buyers, some luxury brands launch budget or masstige offshoots. They want to expand their reach beyond the small number of traditional wealthy customers. However, in doing so, they risk alienating their original customer base. Wealthy consumers who bought the brand to distinguish themselves from the masses may now be buying the same brand, if not the same product, as the masses.

You may think this problem would doom the providers of luxury products, forcing them to choose between a small but wealthy luxury market and a large but non-wealthy non-luxury market. But you would be wrong, because the marketers have figured out a way around this problem.

To avoid losing their loyal customers, marketers price their entry line luxury products higher than competing brands. For that strategy to succeed, so-called entry lines must deliver the key brand values and extras people associate with the brand in question. When these conditions are met, the entry lines of well-known luxury brands become regarded as semi-luxurious brands themselves.

Off-price retailers provide another way that aspirational buyers can get luxuries or semi-luxuries. American off-price retailers have now moved into Canada and the off-price segment for apparel is Canada's fastest-growing retail channel. For example, off-price retailer sales in Canada grew from $2.39 billion in 2015 to $3.24 billion in 2019. This less expensive luxury alternative allows consumers of various social classes to dress like the wealthy.

But even some wealthy people think certain luxuries are too expensive and the price is unjustified. Luxury brands often try to compensate by pampering the customer. Many luxury consumers are looking for a special or remarkable retail experience, as well as a remarkable product, when they shop. When shopping in a store, they want "extras" like bottled water or glasses of champagne, and luxurious packaging.

Luxury brands also rely on their employees' "emotional labor" to make customers feel good. Doing *emotional labor* means managing your emotions to accord with organizationally defined rules and guidelines.

Projecting the right manner or appearance is needed to produce the proper state of mind in customers. In service-oriented professions, including luxury retail, this often means expressing positive emotions that align with the expectations of the clientele, even if these emotions are fake.

So, for example, luxury retail employees may have to exude enthusiasm, warmth, and politeness in a way that creates an inviting and exclusive shopping experience. They may also need to suggest sophistication, elegance, and knowledge about luxury lifestyle to align with the brand image and customer expectations. And they must do all this even if the employee is not feeling enthusiastic themselves.

Employees in luxury shops engage do emotional labor to build rapport with wealthy clients, showing an interest in their lives, remembering personal details, and anticipating their needs. Strong customer relationships are especially critical in the luxury segment, as this clientele often expects personalized service. Wealthy buyers are loyal to sales associates who understand their preferences and taste.

When luxury customers are dissatisfied or difficult, retail workers must effectively manage their own frustration and respond with patience, empathy, and professionalism. Salespeople also have to embody the aspirational lifestyle associated with the luxury goods they are selling. They need to appear successful, refined, and content, since this may encourage customers to associate the product with a desirable lifestyle and status.

However, constantly managing and performing emotions can be mentally exhausting, so all this emotional labor comes at a cost. It can be draining and lead to burnout, stress, and dissatisfaction among employees. People in the luxury retail sector may need training in emotional intelligence, relationship management, and stress reduction to navigate the demands of emotional labor successfully.

Women and Luxury Spending

When given the choice, women prefer luxury brands significantly more than men. What's more, women are more picky about luxury buying than men. One research project was conducted to examine how men and women differ in their perceptions of e-luxury service quality. For male luxury consumers, reliable ordering and delivery was the only dimension that impacted e-satisfaction. For female consumers, reliable customer service, personalization, trust, and entertainment value were other critical dimensions that influenced their e-satisfaction. The findings of this study showed that male luxury consumers are goal-oriented and pay most of their attention to the information that helps them complete their purchase. However, female luxury consumers evaluate a wider range of service features when buying luxury fashion goods online (Kim, 2019).

In general, evolutionary psychology suggests that women tend to desire men who own luxury products, and men will buy such goods to improve their mating choices. What's more, these gendered dispositions intensify under conditions of resource scarcity.

Research tested this hypothesis across three studies, using cues suggesting the onset of an economic recession. Their goal was to manipulate participants' perceptions that financial resources were scarce. One such study revealed that, after being primed with recession (versus control) cues, women (but not men) rated opposite-sex targets who owned luxury brands as more attractive. The second study found recession cues increased men's, but not women's, need for luxury brands compared with budget brands. Finally, the third study showed that, under conditions of resource scarcity, men seeking short-term, sexual relationships had the greatest desire for luxury products (Bradshaw et al., 2020).

This research also showed that women's desire for luxury also intensifies under conditions of scarcity. This is turn intensifies men's determination to acquire and supply such luxury items, for purposes of mating.

No wonder, then, that spending on luxury goods in the United States alone can reach $525 billion per year, with women's products accounting for more than half of this total. Female consumers report that, compared to non-luxury brands. luxury brands make them feel unique, raise their self-esteem, and heighten their status. No surprise, then, that in most markets and product categories, the price of luxury brands aimed at women is significantly higher than that of the luxury brands aimed at men.

As mentioned earlier, women are also more likely than men to flaunt luxury items when they are around other women. In their minds, such conspicuous consumption discourages other women from chasing their partners. In their minds, looking good deters other women from stealing their mate.

Women are especially likely to value wealthy-looking men if they have been primed with concerns (or cues) about poverty and economic recession. "Recession cues" are signals in the economy, market, or consumers' behavior that suggest a coming or continuing recession. A recession is a significant decline in economic activity across the economy, with two or more consecutive quarters of negative growth in real GDP.

In a study we mentioned earlier, recession cues caused women to rate men who owned luxury items as more attractive than other men. And for men, recession cues increased a desire to own luxury goods rather than budget products. In general, during times of scarcity, women seek men who show signs of wealth. Men are aware of this and, when possible, buy luxury items that will make them appealing to eligible women.

With this in mind, certain brands have set up themselves as especially luxurious and coveted. But what is it about these brands that makes them so special? All luxury brands have image, symbolism and prestige to some degree, and brands with charisma build on these to produce extraordinary levels of buyer attachment and motivation. But how do luxury brands convince consumers they have charismatic personality, and what are the charismatic characteristics they claim to have? (Ashill et al., 2019).

Brands with charismatic personalities are often recognized for their distinct identity, a strong emotional connection with customers, a rich history, and a consistent brand narrative. Some luxury brands that can be said to possess a charismatic personality include Rolex watches—watches that allegedly tell a story of heritage, innovation, and craftsmanship. Their association with notable personalities, sporting events, and philanthropic efforts adds to their allure. Similarly, Louis Vuitton, founded in 1854, has long been associated with luxury, travel, and craftsmanship. Their iconic monogram and luggage pieces, as well as collaborations with artists and designers, give them a charismatic presence in the fashion world. And Coco Chanel's legacy has set up the Chanel brand as an epitome of elegance and timelessness. With signature pieces like the little black dress and the No. 5 perfume, Chanel has secured its place as an iconic luxury brand.

For its part, Ferrari has long represented speed, power, and luxury. The brand's association with Formula One racing and its prancing horse logo gives it a charismatic personality that appeals to car enthusiasts and luxury aficionados alike. Then there's Gucci. Known for its innovative fashion, rich heritage, and the double G logo, Gucci often collaborates with contemporary artists and culture influencers, adding modern charisma to its historic roots.

Tiffany & Co.'s brand has long been associated with love, commitment, and luxury. The signature Tiffany blue box is instantly recognizable and evokes feelings of romance and elegance. With its origins in saddle-making, Hermès has grown to become a symbol of French luxury. Birkin and Kelly bags have already reached cult status, adding to the brand's charismatic aura. Recognized for its impeccable craftsmanship, innovative technology, and luxurious design, Bentley has long been a symbol of prestige in the automotive world.

Finally, Cartier, the "jeweler of kings," is synonymous with luxury, romance, and royalty. Their pieces are timeless, and their signature panther motif is instantly recognizable. Then there's Burberry, with its distinctive tartan pattern and trench coats. Burberry has a rich British heritage and is known for its combination of classic and contemporary styles.

These brands, and a few others, have successfully combined their history, craftsmanship, and innovative approaches to remain appealing over time. In this way, they have created for themselves what some people consider a charismatic personality. Now, you may think the notion of a product having a "charismatic personality" is ridiculous. Only people have personalities, charismatic or otherwise. But, in fact, both marketers and consumers think some branded products *do* have a personality. In their eyes, buying luxury goods can offer a sense of prestige, superior quality, and unique craftsmanship. However, if you are inclined to buy luxury goods, you should keep in mind several risks and dangers that are associated with the possession of luxury items, however charismatic:

- Financial strain: Luxury goods often come at a high cost. Spending a significant portion of one's income on luxury items can lead to financial instability or debt.

- Fake products: The luxury market is rife with fakes. Unwittingly buying a fake luxury item can result in financial loss and disappointment.
- Depreciation: Some luxury items, like cars, can depreciate rapidly. This means they lose their value over time, which can be a concern if one views the purchase as an investment.
- Theft or robbery: Owning luxury items can make one a target for theft, especially if they are flaunted or not stored securely.
- Obsession with image: Over-reliance on luxury goods to boost self-esteem or project a certain image can lead to an unhealthy obsession with outward appearances and neglect of inner values.
- Risk of scams: The high demand for luxury goods makes buyers susceptible to scams, such as fake online luxury retailers or fraudulent deals.
- Ethical concerns: Some luxury goods carry ethical issues associated with their production, such as the use of animal fur, exploitation of workers, or environmental degradation.
- Peer pressure and social comparison: Being in an environment where owning luxury goods becomes a status norm can lead to unhealthy social comparisons and pressure to "keep up with the Joneses."
- Emotional distress: The fear of damaging or losing a luxury item can cause anxiety. Additionally, the initial pleasure of acquiring a luxury good may be short-lived, leading to feelings of emptiness or the desire for more.
- Opportunity cost: The money spent on luxury items could be used elsewhere, such as investments, experiences, or charitable causes, which may offer more lasting satisfaction or benefits.
- False sense of superiority: Ownership of luxury goods may lead some people to develop a distorted sense of superiority or right, affecting personal relationships.
- Economic volatility: The value of certain luxury assets, like high-end real estate or art, can be affected by economic downturns, leading to potential financial losses.
- Overspending and debt: The desire to own luxury items may lead

some people to live beyond their means, incurring significant debt, which can have long-term financial effects.
- Cultural misunderstandings: In some contexts, flaunting luxury goods may be seen as insensitive, especially in areas where there's significant economic disparity or dire poverty.

In short, luxury goods can offer enjoyment and a sense of accomplishment. However, such purchases should align with one's broader financial, ethical, and personal goals. In the next chapter, we will delve even deeper into the enchanting mysteries that are luxury brands.

Chapter Eight
Luxurious and Trophy-worthy Brands

As we have seen, people prefer certain brands over others and consider them luxuries if they are widely coveted. With this in mind, marketers devise strategies to raise their brands to a preferred status by making them "prominent." The more prominent a brand is, the more likely people will want it, seek it out, buy it, and praise it to one another. And the more likely they will pay luxury prices to own it.

Brand prominence refers to the extent to which a brand is seen or recognized in the marketplace, highlighting its visibility and standing out from the competition. A prominent brand is one that is easily recalled and recognized by consumers, often holding a significant market share in its category. Brand prominence is critical for businesses as it helps in attracting customers, fostering loyalty, and driving sales.

Achieving brand prominence means defining the brand's unique value and positioning it in the minds of consumers so it is associated with specific qualities, emotions, or benefits. This involves understanding target audiences and their needs, preferences, and opinions. It also means achieving consistency in branding elements like logos, colors, fonts, and messaging across all marketing channels.

Consistency reinforces brand identity and helps build a strong, coherent image in the market. Social media help to build brand recognition and foster community around the brand, as do celebrity endorsements. So the marketer has to collaborate with influencers or celebrities who resonate with the brand and its target audience. These partnerships can enlarge brand exposure and credibility.

In short, achieving brand prominence needs a strategic, multifaceted approach that combines various marketing tactics and continuous effort. A prominent brand not only attracts attention but also sets up a deep connection with consumers, building trust and loyalty that drive long-term success.

More than anything, achieving brand prominence means marketers need to understand how consumers see and rank available products. Since people don't always know what those views and rankings are, marketers need to tell them. Marketers need to tell consumers what the most popular soap is, the most economical way to travel, or the most delicious frozen pizza. Consumers, whose concern is social comparison, need to know what other people think and what they are choosing. Again, the job of the marketer is to tell them. So, achieving brand prominence means telling potential customers what the buying norms are, in an otherwise confused and confusing society.

Happily for marketers, customers and potential customers are rarely able to challenge the claims that marketers make. Most consumers—and especially those who are in a hurry or desperate for acceptance—will first try the brands that marketers have made the most prominent, or most normal-seeming.

Marketers often use influencers and celebrities to make a brand seem not only prominent (and normal) but also desirable. And in their present-day marketing efforts, companies have increasingly abandoned traditional celebrity endorsers in favor of social media influencers. But what is the effectiveness of using influencer endorsements compared with traditional celebrity endorsements?

A recent research project studied the impact of celebrity compared to influencer endorsements on advertising effectiveness: that is, on attitudes toward the advertisement and product, and purchase intention. The research also examined two potential mediators underlying this relationship: identification (sensed similarity and wishful identification) and credibility (trustworthiness and expertise).

Overall, the results showed that participants identify more with influencers than celebrities, feel more like influencers than celebrities, and trust influencers more than celebrities. In all, the results show the value of using influencer endorsers over celebrity endorsers, and the importance of highlighting similarity, identification and trust in this process (Schouten et al., 2020).

More than celebrity and influencer promotions are needed, however. Images must be created to interest and excite potential buyers. Slogans and memes are needed. Marketing claims need to speak to people's underlying concerns: to their powerlessness, loneliness, pessimism, and meaninglessness, among other things.

Products, to succeed, must claim to increase people's sense of power or competence, their popularity, their prospects for advancement, and their sense of purpose. And none of this is easy. To take an everyday item and make it distinguishable from competitors—even remarkable and widely desired—takes ingenuity. Above all, it calls for fantasy, and we will discuss the uses of fantasy in a later chapter. In short, the marketer must promise people things the product can't actually provide. In other words, marketing demands lying or, as we may say more charitably, wishful thinking.

But, in the end, what distinguishes one brand from another? How easily can one point to an object and tell where it came from and how much it cost?

Brand Distinctiveness

As we said in earlier chapters, brands that do well in the market often have a distinctive logo, name, or slogan. For example, most people recognize the big Nike "swoosh" on a T-shirt. However, subtle branding, using a small, discreet logo, means that only the elite can tell the difference between "trashy" and "classy" brands (Han et al., 2010). These cues allow people to feel they're part of an elite group, in on a "secret" that other people don't know about.

So, expensive brands rarely have branding as prominent as less expensive brands (Berger and Ward, 2010). One piece of research on branding studied 120 pairs of sunglasses that ranged in price from very cheap to very expensive, with luxury sunglasses costing more than $500 a pair. It found the most expensive sunglasses were the least likely to have an easily visible branded logo on them.

A study of handbags discovered a similar pattern. From this, the researchers concluded that inconspicuous luxury consumption is a way to identify people who are "in the know." These are people whose taste is refined enough to distinguish between a pair of cheap, low-quality sunglasses and expensive, high-quality sunglasses. They can also distinguish an expensive bag from a cheap bag, based solely on the quality of the product and not the logo or other brand identifier. These shoppers are part of an elite group who engage in quietly conspicuous consumption.

For some high quality products, branding may be unnecessary. Consider a recent trend in the United States: the purchase of trophy trees, as reported on by the *Wall Street Journal* in 2021. Wealthy people pay tens of thousands of dollars or more to have fully mature trees transplanted onto their property. One provider of this service takes clients on a trip around south Florida in search of desirable trees. The seller then mediates the transaction (often by making an unsolicited offer to the tree's owner), and arranges for the tree to be moved to his client's property. Often large trucks, barges, and cranes are needed to transplant the tree.

In buying an extraordinarily expensive tree, the consumer is buying a piece of history. Rather than waiting for decades to pass, the homeowner can effectively buy time by transplanting an older tree from somewhere else. Many transplanted trees also evoke an exotic setting, such as a patch of Tuscany that can be transported to Los Angeles.

You may think this purchase of "vintage" trees is an absurd and disgusting display of wealth by people with too much time and money on their hands. And maybe you're right about that. But you'd be wrong to think this is the only example we can find of such behavior.

In most ways, this is the same as the story behind the rare and vintage watch Ellen DeGeneres bought and we discussed earlier. People who buy trophy trees (or trophy watches) are looking for a compelling story to tell their friends and dinner guests. As the newspaper story noted, it took eighteen months to find and transplant a 150-year-old olive tree from Tuscany to Los Angeles.

As you may imagine, the total cost of doing so was extraordinary. And this process of tree-finding and transplanting would have been good for at least twenty minutes of conversation at a fancy dinner party. So, what are the roots of this desire for luxury at almost any cost. At least one scholar thinks the answer lies in romanticism.

The Role of Romanticism

The English writer Colin Campbell (2018) thinks modern luxury consumerism stems from Romanticism, a philosophical and artistic spirit that swept through Western Europe in the nineteenth-century. Campbell holds a Ph.D. in marketing and has contributed significantly to understanding how consumers make purchasing decisions, their responses to advertising, and the cultural factors that influence their behavior.

Campbell has studied how brands tell stories and create narratives that resonate with consumers, influencing their preferences and purchasing decisions. He has also delved into the impact of social media on consumer behavior, exploring how online platforms shape perceptions, attitudes, and behaviors.

Campbell states that "Romanticism is characterized by a desire to experience in reality those pleasures created and enjoyed in imagination." The objects we romanticize often take on a dream-like quality based on our beliefs surrounding the product. In turn, these beliefs are often created by advertising.

In other words, modern consumerism is hedonistic—pleasure seeking—and in that sense, arguably a good thing. However, Romanticism in our society is locked in conflict with another central concern of modern society: asceticism (Campbell et al., 2020).

Asceticism refers to a lifestyle characterized by abstinence from various kinds of worldly pleasures, often with the aim of pursuing spiritual or religious goals. Ascetics may refrain from activities such as eating flavorful foods, wearing luxurious clothing, engaging in sensual pleasures, or even leading a typical familial or societal life. They do this all in the pursuit of personal enlightenment, self-discipline, spiritual growth, or religious merit. Ascetic practices can be found in many religious traditions. Christianity, Buddhism, Jainism, Hinduism, and Islam all have traditions or sects that emphasize ascetic practices.

In Christianity, ascetic practices are associated with monastic life, where monks and nuns may take vows of poverty, chastity, and obedience.

Spiritual growth and religious merit are common motivations. However, people can also practice asceticism for personal discipline, to cultivate resilience, or to attain specific goals or insights. And even outside traditional religious contexts, some people adopt ascetic practices to challenge consumerism, reduce environmental impact, or for health and wellness reasons.

It's important to understand that asceticism isn't about self-punishment but rather about attaining a deeper understanding, spiritual growth, or closeness to a divine entity. The practices and reasons can vary widely among and within different religious or philosophical traditions.

Another dynamic in luxury-buying is the need for something new, as discussed by Simmel and Veblen. This model assumes that ideas of what is fashionable trickle down from superior to inferior classes in society. Luxury brands, though not unknown to the rich, will—after they trickle down—be new to many people who are less rich. But why do so many people in our society become fixated on buying luxurious, costly goods, to the point that they become "aspirational buyers" (Campbell, 1992)?

This fixation on buying luxurious, costly goods makes us wonder how some people become so fascinated by this activity. And that, in turn, leads us to the study of children and parenting.

The Role of Parenting Styles

Parenting styles influence whether a child will become a luxury buyer, preoccupied with materialism and seeking costly, unusual goods. In rich families, children learn the consumer role quickly because they have more buying opportunities with larger allowances or access to a credit card. But children can also learn materialism in poor families, through watching their parents' compensatory spending and hearing envious stories about the wealthy.

Beyond that, children also learn in imitative or reactive ways. When parent-child relationships are poor, children often resort to conspicuous consumption to feel worthwhile (Gudmunson and Beutler, 2012). Conversely, good parent-child relationships reduce conspicuous consumption. And a loving mother, seemingly, has more influence on a child's conspicuous consumption than does a loving father.

Compensatory buying patterns refer to consumer behaviors people adopt to compensate for their own self-perceived flaws or failings, often as a way to heighten their self-esteem or social status. Children learn these patterns through various channels. First, children watch and copy their parents or caregivers. If parents engage in compensatory buying, children may do so as well. The need to fit in with peers may also drive compensatory buying. For instance, a child may want particular brands of clothing, gadgets, or accessories that are judged popular or prestigious among their friends.

Social and cultural expectations instill in children a sense of what's valued or considered successful, leading them to view compensatory buying as a way to meet these standards. Accordingly, some companies target children with ads suggesting that owning certain products will make them happier, more popular, or more successful.

Interestingly, compensatory buying surged during and just after the COVID-19 pandemic. During the pandemic, traditional brick and mortar stores closed temporarily, making it impossible for people to shop. This deprivation evoked feelings of frustration and anger in consumers. Once stores reopened, consumers went shopping even more enthusiastically to ease their negative feelings and make up for lost time.

Some of this was so-called "revenge buying." Research shows that eliminating behavioral freedom impedes buying, which in turn drives consumers to recover from this deprivation by buying hedonic products when they are again able to do so. Besides working as a compensatory performance, revenge buying is a therapeutic performance: a way for consumers to improve their mood and well-being through the purchase of desired goods (Atalay and Meloy, 2011).

After disruptive events that awaken negative feelings, people often experience an uncontrollable and irresistible desire to buy (Lins and Aquino, 2020). Online platforms are full of influencers and advertisements promoting materialism, creating an environment where compensatory buying of luxuries is normalized. And many consumers justify their purchases as gifts to themselves to compensate for the period when they were deprived of shopping opportunities (Lins et al., 2022).

Children with low self-esteem may use compensatory buying as a way to feel better about themselves or heighten their social status. Other children who are more often rewarded with material possessions may learn to use buying as a way to self-soothe themselves or celebrate.

Are there ways to prevent or reduce pathological buying? Yes, there are several. Teaching children to understand media content critically can help them resist advertising pressures. Parents can also model healthy consumer behaviors, discuss advertising tactics, and explain the difference between needs and wants. Schools and parents can foster self-esteem, emotional control, and resilience in children, reducing their reliance on compensatory buying.

In the end, children learn compensatory buying patterns through a complex interplay of social, media, and psychological influences. But through mindful parenting, education, and open communication, caregivers can help their children develop healthy consumer habits.

The Role of Gender

As we have seen, women are more likely than men to buy luxury items, and are more thorough when they do it. However, both men and women spend on luxury items, though for different reasons. Women buy luxury items to feel good about themselves and to hold onto romantic partners. Men buy luxury items to attract female attention.

For example, men are more likely than women buy luxury cars for this purpose. Now, you may think that middle-aged men buying luxury sportscars is pathological or, at best, laughable. Yet, a great many people—men especially—would say you're wrong. Owning a fancy sports or luxury car is extremely stimulating, even for middle-aged men. One study revealed that men's testosterone levels increased significantly after they drove an expensive sports car; these levels decreased significantly after driving an old family sedan (Saad and Vongas, 2009). The location and visibility of the drive (whether a busy downtown area or a semi-deserted highway) moderated this response. Men's testosterone levels were most likely to increase when they drove their sports cars in busy downtown areas where young women could see and admire them.

Men try to attract a mate using conspicuous consumption because it apparently works. Consider the following experiment: Researchers photographed an attractive male and female couple in one of two cars (Dunn and Searle, 2010). One was a "high-status" car (a Silver Bentley Continental GT), and the other a "lower status" car (a red Ford Fiesta ST). They showed photographs of the couple to male and female participants and asked them to rate the models' attractiveness.

The results? Male participants thought the couple was equally attractive whether seated in the Bentley or in the Fiesta. However, female participants found the male model significantly more attractive when riding in the Bentley than when riding in the Fiesta. Conclusion? Wealth makes men look more attractive to women.

So, men consume luxury products conspicuously to attract a mate and signal their value as a mate. As well, men say they would rather buy a conspicuously luxurious car than an inconspicuous nonluxury car, apparently because a luxury car increases their feelings of social status, especially in the context of intrasexual competition (Hennighausen et al., 2016).

Another study showed that males tend to rate a man with a conspicuous luxury car more as a rival (and potential mate poacher) and less as a friend. They also saw him as superior on various mate-value characteristics, such as attractiveness, intelligence, ambition, and status; and rated him as more oriented toward short-term mating. In sum, these findings suggest that conspicuous consumption of luxuries by men may also serve a function in male–male competition (Hennighausen et al., 2016).

The use of such ideas drawn from evolutionary psychology is debated among marketing scholars. Some praise it, others see it as promoting ideas that are patriarchal, politically incorrect, and generally problematic. However you view matters, evolutionary psychology does focus on deep-rooted explanations for human behavior. Unlike many marketing theories, it tries to explain the deeper "why" behind our purchases, showing how they yield evolutionary advantages in reproduction (Otterbring, 2021).

Such research does not prove women are genetically hardwired to prefer Bentleys over Fiestas, but it suggests women are inclined to favor mates with money over mates without money. Many women still seek out high-income mates even if they have good jobs and good incomes of their own. They learn these mating aspirations as members of our culture, and, though seemingly paternalistic, these views also uphold traditional views of gender.

If you recognize some of yourself in the things we've discussed in this chapter, you may want to consider the issues associated with buying luxuries to attract mates. Acquiring luxury goods to impress potential mates or peers can lead to a range of risks and negative results, both tangible and intangible. Some of these risks and dangers include:

- Financial strain: Overspending on luxury goods can lead to significant debt, especially if one is living beyond their means. This can risk future financial stability and goals.
- Superficial relationships: A relationship based mainly on material possessions may lack depth and genuine connection. Such relationships can be fleeting and may not provide emotional or psychological satisfaction.
- Stress and anxiety: The pressure to uphold an image of wealth can be stressful. The constant need to acquire the latest luxury items to keep up appearances can lead to anxiety and feelings of inadequacy.
- Distorted self-worth: Tying self-worth to material possessions can lead to a distorted sense of self. You may start evaluating a person's value based on what they own rather than who they are.
- Identity crisis: A continuous focus on external approval can lead to an identity crisis. People may struggle to understand their true selves without the veneer of luxury.
- Depreciation and loss: Luxury goods, like cars or tech gadgets, often depreciate over time. The investment can result in a significant loss if one decides to sell the item later.
- Risk of theft or robbery: Displaying or flaunting luxury goods can make one a target for theft or robbery, leading to potential personal danger.
- Peer pressure: The desire to fit in or be accepted by a certain social group can lead to unhealthy peer pressure, pushing one to make decisions that may not be in their best interest.
- Neglect of important aspects of life: A focus on materialism may di-

vert attention from other important aspects of life, such as personal growth, relationships, health, and well-being.
- Mental health issues: Always seeking the best item to purchase next can contribute to mental health issues such as depression, anxiety, or obsessive behaviors.
- Economic vulnerability: Spending large amounts of money on luxury items can leave people economically vulnerable, especially during financial downturns or personal emergencies.
- Social isolation: If one becomes excessively concerned with status and luxury, it may alienate friends or family who do not share the same values.
- Consumerism and environmental impact: Excessive consumption can contribute to environmental degradation. Many luxury goods, especially fast fashion or tech items, have significant environmental footprints.

It's natural to want beautiful or luxurious things, and they can sometimes bring genuine joy or satisfaction. However, we also need to consider the underlying motivations and potential consequences of such pursuits.

Trying to acquire more and more luxuries, for whatever purpose, can launch a person on what we might call a "trophy treadmill." They may then find themselves in a cycle of competitive consumption, where purchases, often luxurious, serve as trophies to represent social status. We will discuss this treadmill in the next chapter.

Chapter Nine

The Trophy Treadmill

Consumers may find themselves on a *trophy treadmill*—a cascading effort to buy more and more trophies—because of what we will call the "snob effect" and the "envy premium." Both lead people to compare themselves with others and fight to keep (or improve) their position in the pecking order.

Competitive consumption turns us all into caged hamsters on a treadmill. You may not think of yourself as a caged hamster on a treadmill. But if, like Timothy, you buy things for their trophy value, you've put yourself in this unenviable situation. Some of your expensive, luxurious purchases may provide momentary pleasure and even enchantment, but you can never be certain of winning the battle for social supremacy.

But why does your position in the social hierarchy matter so much? We can offer at least three answers to this question. First, holding a high-status position may give you a sense of control, and even a feeling of power. Second, it may give you the sense that you are accepted, admired, and approved of. Third, holding such a position may give you the impression that you set the standards for other people. And if you set the rules, you can never fall outside the rules. In short, holding a high-status position not only makes you a member of a community: it makes you the ruler of that community.

Of course, the problem with holding a high status position is that you have a lot to lose. When you're at the top, you can't improve your status, only lose it. What's more, you become the object of envy, and some people will resent you—perhaps, even hate you—for the status you have amassed. So, it will take constant effort to keep your high position. As a consumer, you will always have to be on the lookout for new luxuries and trophies to buy and new records to set in your community.

Luxury and trophy buying often means paying an envy premium. But most consumers are willing to pay more for products that make others envious.

Envy is an emotion that arises from social comparison. It signals that you are outperformed by another person or group of people, which makes you feel painful inferiority. The word envy itself originates from the Latin *invidere*, which means to "gaze maliciously." Yet, it is hard to identify or admit to envy, partly because of a range of other negative emotions, such as hostility, resentment and rejection, that often accompany envious feelings. Envy may sometimes trigger admiration that motivates you to "do better." However, most subjective, historical and philosophical accounts speak of envy's negative effects.

Not surprisingly, many people view envy as a social taboo, something to avoid. Only recently has evolutionary psychology shed new light on the emotion nobody likes to feel, much less think or talk about (Milic, 2019).

What marketers call an *envy premium* refers to the extra amount that consumers are willing to pay for a good that excites their envy and is seen as desirable or enviable by others. This term is often used about luxury goods, exclusive services, and high-end brands that carry social status and prestige.

Now, you may think that paying this extra amount of money is ridiculous—something only a fool would do. However, millions of consumers do this every day. The envy premium may not be based on the inherent value or quality of the product, but it is based on the status and recognition it confers on its owner. Products with an envy premium are often seen as signs of wealth, success, or a particular lifestyle that others may admire or envy. And many people are willing to pay extra for this.

Here's how the envy premium works: Consumers pay the envy premium to distinguish themselves from others or to gain social approval and admiration. The envy premium can also reflect a consumer's ambition, where owning a particular product is seen as achieving a personal or social milestone. And it's not just about conspicuous consumption.

Sometimes, consumers may take genuine pleasure and satisfaction from owning products envied by others.

Consider two taglines that capture this envy premium: Cartier's "the art of being unique," and Bottega Veneta's "when your own initials are enough." This envy premium varies depending on who owns the item being desired. On the one hand, the owner may be someone higher in the social hierarchy, whose position you think is well-deserved. You're more likely to be envious of—and pay a premium for—a product that person owns. We buy new products to keep up with those we consider to be socially superior to us.

Another measure of marketing success is the so-called *bandwagon effect*, which encourages people to buy what other people are buying—especially other people with high status. The bandwagon effect is a psychological phenomenon where people do something mainly because others like themselves are doing it, regardless of their own beliefs and preferences.

In the context of luxury buying, the bandwagon effect can significantly influence consumer behavior in several ways. One reason people buy luxury items is to improve their social status. If they see others in their social circle, or even celebrities, flaunting luxury goods, they may feel inclined to buy similar items to preserve their status. When many people are buying a particular luxury brand or product, it's often seen as possessing a high value. Even if the intrinsic value of the item doesn't change, its perceived value can increase because of growing popularity.

The bandwagon effect can create a sense of urgency among potential buyers who fear missing out on a trend. This may prompt them to make purchases they hadn't previously considered. As we've said before, humans have an inherent need to fit in and belong. Owning and showcasing luxury items that others possess can provide a sense of belonging or alignment with a particular group or class. Luxury brands often use well-known people to promote their products. When consumers see these figures endorsing luxury products, they become more inclined to buy them, thinking it will align them more closely with those figures or lifestyles.

Once someone has made a luxury purchase, receiving compliments or acknowledgment can serve as a reinforcement, increasing the likelihood of making similar purchases in the future. In thriving economies, people usually buy more luxury products. Seeing others indulge can give people a false sense of financial security, leading others to splurge, thinking it's a social norm. In some societies, rapid economic growth and increasing disposable incomes may lead to a surge in luxury buying. As more people buy luxury items, the bandwagon effect intensifies, causing even more people to make similar purchases.

The bandwagon effect isn't the sole determinant of luxury or trophy buying. Individual preferences, financial capability, brand loyalty, and other factors can also play significant roles. However, the bandwagon effect is an important cause of buying behavior. So, too, is the so-called *snob effect*—the wish to avoid and reject the behavior of people you don't want to associate with. In this case, consumers want goods and products that are exclusive, rare, or expensive, because owning such items signals status, wealth, or a distinctive lifestyle. The snob effect influences people to pay higher prices for goods seen as prestigious or not accessible to everyone.

Because of the snob effect, products with limited availability or accessibility are more attractive to consumers than other products. Limited-edition items, luxury brands, and products that are hard to get often carry this allure. Consumers seek products that help them distinguish themselves from others, signaling a higher social status, more refined taste, or even a unique personality.

The snob effect is closely related to conspicuous consumption. Consumers influenced by the snob effect are less repelled by high prices than other consumers may be. The high cost of a product may even heighten its appeal, serving as a barrier that prevents others from buying.

Therefore, high-end brands in fashion, automotive, or jewelry often benefit from the snob effect. Consumers are willing to pay a premium for the status and exclusivity associated with these brands. As well, high-priced memberships, premium travel services, and exclusive clubs and resorts also draw snobby consumers looking to distinguish themselves from the masses. Obviously, the snob effect contributes to social stratification and inequality, as people use consumption to define and set up social boundaries.

Some wealthy people even reject consumer goods that are popular with lower- or middle-income people. Instead, they seek out rare, exclusive items that set them apart from the crowd. The snob effect is rooted, at least in part, in the wish to stand out. Snobs—people with a strong need for uniqueness—are drawn to scarce consumption (such as dining at a five-star restaurant).

Marketers therefore promote luxury and trophy products through exclusive, small-circle events to capitalize on the snob effect. They may even hide their high-end products, forcing customers to ask for them specifically. When companies target snobbish customers, they price their products differently, typically raising the prices.

To preserve an image of scarcity and exclusivity, many luxury companies destroy excess stock rather than selling it. According to the *Wall Street Journal* (Dalton, 2018), "destroying unsold inventory is a widely used but rarely discussed technique that luxury companies use to maintain the scarcity of their goods." Burberry, for example, destroyed £28.6 million worth of unsold inventory in 2018. Similarly, "We do not like to sell our goods in discounted stores," said Nicolo Ricci, an executive from the luxury clothing brand Stefano Ricci.

All trophy buying is about satisfying the snob effect, but it may not require good taste or what sociologists call cultural capital. Sometimes, it doesn't even require much money. But it's always about inciting envy. Consider events like motorcycle rallies and NASCAR races. These gatherings are known for their drunkenness, fighting, and sexual undertones. Despite the crowds, traffic, heat, and noise, such mega-spectacles provide people with trophies of enjoyment (Krier and Swart, 2016). Attendees at such events focus on hunting and displaying trophies, rather than spontaneous enjoyment of the staged event. Trophies here work as distorting mirrors in which viewers conflate a trophy owner's experience of legendary pleasures with their own vicarious or *surplus enjoyment*.

In this way, mega-spectacles produce and promote envy-inducing legends and ritually load trophies with three forms of potential envy. These include status trophies (envy of symbolic prowess), action trophies (envy of imaginary risk-taking) and trophies of *jouissance* (envious yet repressed desire for libidinal pleasure).

In short, mega-spectacles do not directly please their attendees, but provide them with trophies of surplus enjoyment that disturb and disrupt the pleasure of others. So, for example, a photo of yourself standing next to your favorite team's pit at a NASCAR race suggests you had special access. It connects you to the tribe that supports that particular driver.

Trophies of *jouissance* are intended to instill envy by showing how much fun you allegedly had at the event. "*Jouissance*" is a French word that refers to pleasure or enjoyment that is extreme or excessive, sometimes so intense that it borders on pain or discomfort. In a broader, non-academic context, *jouissance* can just mean joy or bliss.

So, for example, two researchers report having watched photo opportunities with "scantily dressed, tattooed, or body painted waitresses and barmaids … [b]lending the roles of wait staff, model, and sex worker" at a motorcycle rally (Krier and Swart 2016). Now, that's bliss for you.

Or consider how this same principle applies to loftier cultural events. For example, in 2012, New York's Museum of Modern Art displayed one version of Edvard Munch's painting, *The Scream* (four versions exist). It was placed on the same wall as Vincent Van Gogh's *The Starry Night*, which is part of the permanent collection. Many viewers bypassed *The Starry Night*, instead crowding in front of Munch's masterpiece to take a selfie with it. After taking their trophy picture, they left the room. In the end, the gallery had increased its attendance figures by hosting the temporary exhibition of *The Scream*, and theyt did so by capitalizing on the force of eny.

Along similar lines, consider the Shanghai Symphony Orchestra, which saw its ticket sales increase when it switched from Asian to Western music. The symphony realized that, to draw in crowds, it needed to associate its concerts with refined taste, which meant adding more Western classical music to its programs. It also started a one-on-one volunteer service targeting VIP ticket holders. Before the show, the volunteers showed VIP ticket holders around the theater and explained the history and significance of the music they were about to hear. Once the concert began, the volunteers remained with the ticket holders and pointed out key elements in the music.

What these examples show is people's eagerness to gain and display cultural capital, and the tendency of people with cultural capital to spend money on cultural trophies and experiences.

Purchases of Experiential Value

In contrast to the value gained from material purchases, experiential value—which we discussed in an earlier chapter—is something a customer gains from the direct use of goods and services. But experiential consumption is mainly possible once people have met their material needs.

Some marketers capitalize on experiential consumption by incorporating an experiential ingredient into shopping. There, as we mentioned earlier, some marketers use augmented reality to transform the mundane into something enchanting. For example, augmented reality may present a live-action image of you huddled over a new Apple computer, explaining some computer function to a gorgeous young model. Now, you may think that putting on a pair of goggles and experiencing a consumer item in augmented reality is fun but, essentially, a waste of time. Still, techniques of augmented reality have been found to increase a consumer's intention to buy the product portrayed.

Beyond that, many consumers seek out retail environments that provide memorable experiences because they provide an escape from daily routines. As well, consumers are more likely to make impulsive buys in such places, especially if the goods for sale are high-priced luxury items.

However, experiential marketing is not limited to luxury goods, and even some high-end banks have adopted such a strategy. Soft lighting creates calm in the open spaces of the SEB Bank's offices in Frankfurt, Germany, for example. Customers can listen to soothing music while sipping cappuccinos at the in-house café. Similarly, both the Gucci and Chanel stores in Tokyo have an in-house restaurant, so hungry customers don't have to leave the store for a bite to eat. Ferrari provides a two-day "driving experience" seminar designed to bridge the gap between one's driving skills and a Ferrari's performance abilities. And tourism has always been about creating memories through experiences. Many tourists travel in search of adventure, to fulfill their fantasies, and finally, to brag about their experiences. All these examples show how marketers have used the power of experiences to sell more goods at a higher price.

According to at least one author, conspicuous consumption has changed dramatically since Veblen's time. *The Sum of Small Things: A*

Theory of the Aspirational Class by Elizabeth Currid-Halkett (2017) explores the shifting nature of status and consumption among the upper-middle class in present-day society.

Her book introduces the idea of an *aspirational class* whose consumption patterns and lifestyle choices reflect their values and ambitions rather than their economic capital. Currid-Halkett notes that, in this group, we see a notable shift from conspicuous consumption (spending on visible luxury goods) to *inconspicuous consumption* (spending on intangible goods and experiences).

This aspirational consumer group is identified by its consumption of education, health, travel, and other intangibles, supposedly valuing knowledge and cultural capital over material wealth. Members of this aspirational class are said to collect and signal their status through knowledge and cultural experiences, which can be as exclusive and divisive as material wealth.

Currid-Halkett divides inconspicuous consumption into three categories. The first category saves people time through the purchase of childcare and domestic services. The second is experience-based, such as a night at the opera, while the third is "important" consumption, including education, health care, pensions, and personal insurance.

The cost of some items consumed inconspicuously can be quite low. For example, Currid-Halkett discusses Essie Weingarten's sheer nail polish shade, "Ballet Slippers." This colour is understated for nail polish, but it has become "de rigueur ... for a specific group of women in Beverly Hills, New York's Upper East Side, and London's Kensington." The late Queen Elizabeth herself wore the colour, with her hairdresser seeking a bottle from Weingarten in a letter "complete with Royal seal."

Ballet Slippers is an example of what Currid-Halkett refers to as "information cost inconspicuous consumption." However, a second kind of consumption she calls "cost-prohibitive inconspicuous consumption." This category includes childcare, health care, and college tuition, all of which significantly improve the quality of life for people who can afford it "while simultaneously reinforcing and retrenching existing class lines."

The book lumps a widely diverse group of people into the aspirational class, so this term may be too broad or vague to be useful. After all, not everyone who values education and health does so for status reasons. More important, the aspirational class she describes enjoys a degree of economic and cultural privilege that lets them put the highest priority on inconspicuous consumption. In that sense, the book may not fully recognize the economic constraints that many people face, and which influence their consumption choices every day.

Then too, the very idea of an aspirational class may unintentionally suggest this group is homogeneous. Putting all these consumers into the same category potentially oversimplifies people's varied and nuanced values, beliefs, and behaviors. And while the book analyzes changing consumption patterns, it values aspirational consumers more highly than other kinds.

What we can all agree is that, in a prosperous consumer society, people at every income level have an ample opportunity to consume. And owning cultural capital allows even people with low incomes to display their consumer knowledge to the best advantage.

Earlier in this chapter, we discussed envy at some length, and if you recognize some envy in your own behavior, you may want to consider the risks. Envy, the emotion that arises when one wishes for the qualities, achievements, or possessions of another, has been recognized since ancient times as a potentially destructive force. So here are some risks and dangers associated with envy:

- Decreased well-being: Constant comparison with others can lead to dissatisfaction with one's own life, reducing overall happiness and well-being.
- Strained relationships: Envy can harm your relationships, as you may harbor resentment towards the person you envy, leading to mistrust, gossip, or even sabotage.
- Mental health issues: Persistent feelings of envy can contribute to depression, anxiety, and feelings of inferiority.
- Damaged decision-making: Being driven by envy can cloud judgment, leading to decisions made out of spite rather than genuine interest or benefit.
- Reduced self-worth: Measuring self-worth based on comparison

with others can lead to feelings of inadequacy and low self-esteem.
- Loss of focus: Being preoccupied with what others have diverts attention from one's own goals and priorities.
- Financial strain: Trying to "keep up with the Joneses" can lead to unnecessary spending and financial strain.
- Maladaptive behaviors: To relieve feelings of envy, some people may resort to maladaptive behaviors like substance abuse, overeating, or other forms of escapism.
- Physical health issues: Chronic envy and the stress associated with it can lead to physical health problems, including headaches, digestive issues, and even cardiovascular problems.
- Decreased productivity: Spending time brooding about what others have can lead to procrastination and a decline in your productivity.
- Aggression and hostility: Some studies suggest that envy can lead to aggression towards the envied individual, whether in subtle or overt forms.
- Moral dilemmas: Envy can lead to unethical behaviors, such as lying, cheating, or stealing, in efforts to level the playing field or get ahead.
- Loss of authenticity: Trying to copy or outdo someone else can lead to choices that aren't aligned with one's true self, resulting in a loss of authenticity.
- Stunted personal growth: Instead of focusing on self-improvement, an envious person may spend more time lamenting what they lack, stunting their personal and professional growth.

So, envy is a natural human emotion, but we need to manage it constructively. Reflecting on the underlying causes of envy, practicing gratitude, and focusing on self-improvement are some strategies to mitigate its negative effects.

In the next chapter, we will look at *materialism*, which is the pursuit of material goods in the hope they will provide happiness. People display materialism in different ways, and their buying habits often reflect deep needs for belonging and approval. We will also examine the idea of *relative deprivation*, which is the sense of being deprived in comparison to others, leading to feelings of discontent and frustration. This outlook affects people' life satisfaction, consumer behavior, career choices, and economic decisions, as people often base their choices on comparisons with others rather than absolute standards.

Chapter Ten

What is Materialism?

Some people say that our buying is motivated by a commitment to materialism—the belief that money and material goods are more important than anything else.

For some, materialism is merely an extension of the beliefs of people like Tamara, Anton, and Timothy. But as we have seen, it can take different forms for different people: a search for novelties, luxuries, experiences, and so on. As we have also seen, materialism can grow out of different motives: a need for belonging (Tamara), for praise (Timothy), or for fulfilment (Anton). In all instances, however, materialism is a product of social life, with social roots and social effects.

You may think that only a few superficial people would harbor such superficial thoughts. But hundreds of millions of people think this way, and what's more, their way of thinking has historical roots in the rise of capitalism and Protestantism. At least, that's what the great German sociologist Max Weber has told us.

In the early twentieth century, Weber introduced the idea of the *Protestant ethic*. By this, he meant a set of beliefs, norms, and behaviors that promoted capitalism. These included sobriety, thrift, hard work, and a dedication to gaining rewards in the human world (not in heaven.) People with a Protestant ethic sought evidence of God's favor, not worldly pleasure for its own sake. Yet, many people today view worldly success (and the acquisition of material rewards) as proof of unusual merit. Thus, paradoxically, materialism as it is practiced today is both a pursuit of possessions for their own sake and a wish to prove (and display) one's exceptional merit—perhaps even blessedness in God's eyes.

From this standpoint, materialism is a demonstration of earthly success in the lifelong competition for status, wealth, approval, and power. People act like materialists because they want to display their success, not because they think that money and material goods are more important than anything else. And as we noted in the last chapter, many people are aspirational materialists: people who have not yet achieved material success but aspire to it. Their goal in trying to appear like materialists, and therefore as successful individuals, is the same as everyone else's: a wish for acceptance, status, approval, envy, and eventually power.

As we have seen repeatedly, displaying material goods helps people to gain approval and acceptance from others, even if they have bought those material goods on credit. And some materialists enjoy buying things more than they enjoy using them. They are drawn in by the excitement of buying things and think doing so makes people like them more. They are enchanted by the prospect of gaining social acceptance and approval, if only they can buy their way into the select circles they want to occupy. But to repeat, for these people and other materialists, consumer goods are merely a means to a social end.

Before we say more about this topic, let's see how materialistic you are. To begin, take a piece of paper and write down the numbers 1 to 10. Then, for each of the following statements, write down how much you agree or disagree with it, using the same 5-point scale we have used up to now:

1. Buying things gives me great pleasure.
2. I admire people who own expensive homes, cars, and clothes.
3. I have fun just thinking of all the things I own.
4. I like people who have expensive cars or clothes.
5. I like spending money on many different things.
6. I worry about people taking my possessions.
7. I would love to buy things that cost a lot of money
8. I'd be much happier if I could afford to buy more things.
9. I'd rather spend time buying things than doing almost anything else.
10. It bothers me that I can't afford to buy all the things I like.

If you agree or strongly agree with all the statements, giving you a total score of 40 or more, you have very materialistic views (Richins and Dawson 1992). And if you disagree with many of these statements, scoring less than 40, you are not a materialist. But what does it mean to say someone is a materialist?

Materialism Defined and Explained

Materialism can refer to many ideas, depending on the context in which the term is used. However usually, it describes a preoccupation with material or physical concerns. *Consumer or acquisitive materialism* refers to a value system and lifestyle characterized by an emphasis on getting and consuming material goods. People with this outlook draw their sense of identity, satisfaction, and life's purpose from owning and amassing physical possessions.

Critics argue that all forms of materialism lead to a superficial understanding of the world: one that neglects the importance of subjective experience, spirituality, and moral values. So, when discussing the materialist lifestyle, critics often point to the emptiness, isolation, social inequality, and environmental degradation associated with materialist consumer cultures.

To some, materialism signifies low self-esteem or depression. To others, materialism is merely the result of assimilating a culture that gives top billing to consumption and possessions. Whatever the reason, critics see all the negative features of being materialistic.

As we have noted throughout this book, people's levels of materialism vary. Timothy, our trophy buyer, never tires of buying things to impress people. Anton obsessively buys things to cheer himself up. Tamara repeatedly buys things to win social approval. Their buying habits all reflect a need for belonging and approval from other people. And they are all exhibiting different versions of materialism, flowing from different sources.

The most important thing to know about materialism is that it comes with negative connotations: most social thinkers consider materialism to be a bad thing. In fact, many sociologists of the nineteenth century pointed out the materialism and associated immorality of city life.

Today's researchers are beginning to test this argument quantitatively. One recent research project even claims to have established an empirical (that is, a data-driven) connection between materialism and immorality.

The study found that on seven out of eight measures, there was a higher incidence of materialism and immorality (or, at least, crime and deviance) in large cities than elsewhere. The causal connections among urban residence, materialism, and immorality remain unclear, however, and more research is needed. However, the researcher suggests that cities tolerate more immorality than do rural areas, so people expect and tolerate rule-breaking in urban centers (Okulicz-Kozaryn, 2022).

Psychological Foundations

But in what sense is materialism evil or immoral? And if we have reasons to criticize materialism, how do we explain why so many people gravitate towards this way of life?

Some believe that materialism results from psychological issues such as low self-esteem, depression or anxiety, and social insecurity. This would square with the high rates of materialism observed among teenagers, since low self-esteem is especially common among adolescents. People's self-esteem usually improves as they get older, though parents and other adults also have the power make it better or worse. Timothy, our adult trophy hunter, has never been able to overcome his immature need for approval through buying. For people like him, retail therapy is an immediate response (though not an effective long-term solution) to emotional pain.

Similarly, people who are socially insecure like Anton try to attract the attention of others by buying and displaying possessions. But consumption does not improve their state of mind. Happiness research shows that material possessions do not help people with low self-esteem. Our self-esteem is largely determined by how we feel about ourselves in our early years, when we form our values and sense of self-worth. Low self-esteem cannot be remedied through buying things.

A Social and Cultural Problem

Materialism, according to one school of thought, is a social and cultural issue, not a psychiatric or developmental one. It holds that we are materialistic because society has taught us to be. So in that sense, personal problems such as depression and shopping addiction are private displays of larger societal issues. But changing a person's psychic state is easier than changing a society where what's "normal" is mentally or spiritually distressing. We live in a society that values owning things, and where people compete for money rather than cooperating, let alone sharing the wealth.

The economic competition all around us benefits a few while harming the majority. Materialism consumes us with the need for more, and our consumerist society is to blame for compulsive shopping. As we will see in a later chapter, people develop a shopping addiction because capitalism forces us to alternate between two life modes: working and shopping. Society teaches you not only to earn as much money as possible, but to spend as much as possible too.

Our culture does *not* encourage saving, and with poor consumer education, money management is a recurring issue among youth. Budgeting, saving money, paying on time, managing credit card debt, and knowing one's net worth may all be hard for the person who has received no consumer education. Materialism discourages prudence and encourages compulsive and impulsive buying, topics we will discuss in later chapters. As suggested, compulsive buying is a major issue for people who don't know how to manage their money, such as teenagers. So, materialistic people usually have more money worries than other people because they tend to overspend, then worry about how to pay their bills.

You learn the values of materialism as a child. In fact, you learn to shop and spend money the same way you learn to speak and interact with others: through example, practice, and reward. And the learning of consumer patterns happens early. For example, many children learn to recognize the golden arches of McDonald's before they can recite the alphabet.

Materialism can take many forms, as we have seen, and people like Tamara, Timothy, and Anton all have different reasons for being materialistic. Yet, all of us associate materialism—putting a high priority on earning and buying—with wealth, power, and happiness.

People in prosperous countries like Canada are less concerned about merely surviving than they are about leading a pleasant, comfortable life. They place a high value on belonging, independence, self-expression, and some degree of self-determination. They also claim to care about social justice and the environment, though these are secondary concerns.

Yet we live in an economically unequal society, and even when the economy performs well, only the people at the top benefit significantly. The continued increase in social inequality leads to a continued increase in social comparisons; and when people feel they are doing worse than others, they become angry and upset. They begin to experience what sociologists call relative deprivation.

Now, you may think that how people feel about their lives is a result of whether they are *actually* rich or poor, overprivileged or underprivileged. But that's not the case: how people feel about their lives instead depends on how they compare with other people they know. Said another way, relative deprivation makes a lot more difference to people's thinking than absolute deprivation.

Relative deprivation is a sociological term used to describe the experience of being (and feeling) deprived of something to which people feel entitled. This deprivation is relative rather than absolute, meaning it's based on *perceiving* disadvantage when comparing oneself or one's group to others. It is not an absolute or objective measurement of deprivation.

As noted, relative deprivation is grounded in social comparisons. People or groups come to sense they are worse off compared to a reference group, which can be either specific people, social categories, or even a self-imposed standard. The feeling of deprivation arises not merely from envy but from a sense of injustice or unfairness about the difference between one's situation and that of others. This experience of relative deprivation often leads to frustration and discontent, which may trigger different reactions, ranging from self-improvement efforts to resentment, aggression, or movements of social protest.

Two researchers recently carried out a series of seven studies on relative deprivation. They explored how personal relative deprivation influences zero-sum thinking—the belief that one person's gains can come only at other people's expense.

They found that personal relative deprivation fosters a belief that economic success is indeed zero-sum, and that this is true regardless of the participants' household income, political ideology, or subjective social class. The more people see themselves as being unfairly disadvantaged, compared with others, the more likely they are to view the world as unjust, and to think that economic success is determined by external forces beyond one's control (Ongis and Davidai, 2022).

Different types of relative deprivation exist, though only a few are directly relevant to consumer behavior. When a person compares themselves to others in their reference group and feels they are worse off, they experience *egoistic* relative deprivation. This may affect their self-esteem, happiness, and life satisfaction. But when members of a group collectively feel that their group is disadvantaged, compared with other groups, they experience *fraternal* relative deprivation. This can lead to social unrest, protests, and even revolutions.

To repeat, relative deprivation is not based on objective conditions but on opinions of how one's situation compares with others'. Relative deprivation is greatest when a person feels they are falling far behind others in their quest for material well-being.

This is a powerful theory, but we should note some defects in it. First, as noted, it neglects objective conditions of deprivation or inequality, focusing excessively on people's perceptions. Second, it does not predict how people will respond to this sense of relative deprivation. Some people may engage in social action, while others become demoralized or resigned. So understanding relative deprivation is critical for analyzing discontent, but we need to employ the theory carefully, considering its limits and the complexity of human behavior.

Materialism and Fetishism

Some people who live in consumer societies fetishize the goods they buy. A *fetish* is any object that consumers use to replace social relationships. For Marxists, *commodity fetishism* is the tendency to see consumer goods solely in terms of their market value, not in terms of the human labor that went into making those goods. Said another way, we can use the term fetishism to describe how consumers are captivated (enchanted or possessed) by the things they buy.

The idea of commodity fetishism was introduced by Karl Marx in his seminal work, *Capital*. According to Marx, in capitalist economies, the social relationships between producers are hidden. Thus the *value* of a good seems inherent in the commodity itself, rather than resulting from the labor involved in its production. This mystification of "value" hides the social relations in capitalist production. In capitalist societies, the social relations between workers and employers are largely hidden, and we pay more attention to the relations between commodities themselves. The market, where commodities get their value, seems to be a natural and self-regulating entity, not something built on labor and exploitation.

Commodity fetishism of this kind leads to "reification," where abstract social relations between people are expressed as properties of things (commodities). This confusion makes capitalism seem natural and unavoidable, rather than a historically specific mode of production. And under conditions of commodity fetishism, consumers focus on the end products (commodities) and their exchange value in the market. To repeat, they often remain unaware of, or indifferent to, the conditions of production, labor exploitation, and environmental degradation involved in creating these products.

We see such fetishism all around us. One researcher asks us to think of the soccer ball as an illustration of this idea. Specifically, he views the manufacture of the World Cup soccer ball through the lens of commodity fetishism, and the journey that football makes to become a commodity. He specifies three aspects of this journey. These include a *symbolic* fetishism of the World Cup ball in the build-up to tournaments, around which ritual activities are performed. Then there is a *scientific* fetishism in the corporate marketing of footballs, where marketers dispute the best way to capitalize on soccer events. Finally and most recently, we see a *corporate* fetishism in the form of (claimed) corporate social responsibility.

All three aspects of commodity fetishism tend to fragment and confuse our understanding of the contradictions between profit and social justice. And all three obscure the nature of exploitation in the industry that produces footballs (Kennedy, 2023). So, what may seem like a simple sporting event is actually an object lesson in capitalist mythology.

However, some academics think materialism can be useful. If materialists build their sense of identity by buying things that make them feel good, who's to say there's anything wrong with that? They're just sending other people a message about who they are. Besides, people can achieve their materialistic objectives in a large variety of ways. They should be free to communicate their status and identity through their possessions (Shrum et al., 2013).

From this perspective, materialism is nothing more than (as Baudrillard told us earlier) a means of signaling our social identities and social goals to other people. Material possessions reveal and tell the world who we are. The things we own reveal our social class, gender, status, and membership in other social groups. Using consumer goods in this way is fine, even if it discourages people from developing other, more personal ways of expressing and communicating about themselves.

Since, in reading this chapter, you may have discovered you are inclined towards materialism, here are some risks and dangers you should consider. Personal materialism, or putting an excessive value on material possessions and the relentless pursuit of them, can have negative results for people and societies and here are a few of them to consider.

No matter how much one gets, there's always something newer, better, or more luxurious. This continuous need to get new things can lead to everlasting dissatisfaction with what one has. Many studies have found a correlation between high levels of materialism and high rates of anxiety and depression. People who give the greatest importance to their possessions may neglect their personal relationships. They may even value other people based on what they own rather than who they are. In family life, disagreements over finances, purchases, or values can lead to increased tension in relationships. Beyond these dangers, consider a few other risks associated with materialism:

- Debt: A strong desire to have the latest and best can lead to excessive spending and debt.
- Financial insecurity: Overemphasis on buying can lead to inadequate savings for emergencies, retirement, and other future needs.
- Hollow pursuits: An excessive focus on material goods can overshadow deeper pursuits in life such as personal growth, spirituality, and helping others, and divert attention from non-material growth opportunities like education, skill development, or cultivating hobbies and passions.
- Misaligned values: You may begin to equate self-worth with net worth, leading to a distorted sense of self and purpose.
- External approval: You may seek approval of yourself through your possessions, tying your self-esteem to the goods you own.
- Loss of authenticity: You may buy things to fit into certain social molds or expectations rather than being true to yourself.
- Happiness (or lack of same): After one reaches a point where basic needs are met, added material wealth does not significantly contribute to happiness. Getting more will not make you happier.
- Media influence: Constant exposure to advertisements and media portrayals of "ideal" lifestyles can distort your sense of normalcy and what's important in life.
- Addiction: The dopamine rush from buying something new can become addictive, leading you to shop compulsively even when it's not in your best interest.
- Overconsumption and resource depletion: Materialism can drive overconsumption, leading to increased waste, environmental degradation, and the exhaustion of Earth's natural resources.

Material possessions can undoubtedly provide comfort and convenience, but an excessive focus on them is harmful. You will do better finding a balance and giving top priority to values that foster genuine happiness, personal growth, and deep connections.

In the next chapter, we will look at the use of enchantment to sell goods. Despite the disenchantment of living in a rational, scientific, secular society, modern people still seek enchantment, often through consumer goods. Advertising plays a critical role in creating enchanting narratives around products, promising magical transformation, emotional fulfillment, and a blissful escape from reality. Products that promise to transcend the mundane or the rational are attractive to consumers, so enchantment becomes a potent advertising tool.

Chapter Eleven
The Search for Enchantment

So far, the motives for consumer buying have sounded cold-blooded. Sure, you want power, approval, acceptance, and admiration, so you buy a bunch of stuff that other people hold in high regard. What's important is giving the illusion that you are successful, sociable, and worth knowing.

With that in mind, you may be wondering why we are only halfway through this book. The answer is, because we are only halfway through explaining why people buy stuff. Many researchers think there is a whole lot more to consumerism than that. For example, they think consumer buying is about *enchantment*—the emotional excitement that comes from feeling under the magical spell of pleasure.

Many scholars argue that consumerism is *supremely* about enchantment and choice. One researcher even asserts that, philosophically, marketing is a core ingredient of the modern capitalist society. Marketing has the power to improve a person's experience of life by giving them meaning and purpose. In the end, marketing helps us define the human condition and the possibilities available to us in a free, enlightened world (Negulescu, 2021).

No wonder, then, that many people report significant emotional experiences around shopping. As we will see in a later chapter, some people even fall in love with their possessions. Other people dream about things they own or hope to own. And some people imagine themselves in fantastic situations where their lives are transformed by something they have bought.

As an example, consider what it means to own a red sports car, allegedly a fantasy item for many middle-aged men. According to this fantasy, the possession and use of such a car is thrillingly erotic. It is so erotic that men's testosterone levels increase when they drive a sports car, especially where they can be seen by young women. (As we noted earlier, this is the finding of a study by two psychologists!)

All this suggests the pursuit of material pleasure through consumer buying is not cold-blooded at all. It is an almost magical process in which we grant at least some of our possessions an aura of enchantment.

Manufacturing enchantment is necessary because, in present-day societies, we have lost much of the magic, fantasy, and wonder people experienced in preindustrial societies. In a world like ours, where science is the norm, magic, spells, and other supernatural forces usually seem unnecessary. Yet modern people still seek out enchantment wherever they can.

So, advertisements try to create a world where things work differently than they do in reality. Many advertisements show people being overjoyed after buying something. Narrative transport like this, where "Buying product X will leave you feeling overjoyed," immerses you in a fictional or imagined world. We routinely see enchantment stories like that in advertisements for luxury goods, because in that case marketers need to motivate people to spend a *lot* of money.

To repeat, advertising routinely taps into the power of enchantment to sell goods and services. "Enchantment" here refers to the process of captivating an audience by creating a sense of wonder, allure, or desire. To do this, many advertisements use compelling narratives that appeal to audiences. Beautiful imagery, striking visuals, and pleasing designs can create a mood or feeling that connects the viewer to the product. For instance, a car advertisement may use sweeping shots of the vehicle driving through breathtaking landscapes, enchanting viewers with freedom and adventure.

In short, marketing narratives are mini-stories that all have a happy ending. The plotline: Your life sucks. You buy product X. Your life becomes wonderful.

Marketing tries to excite all our senses with these narratives. For example, a magnificent or exciting soundtrack may be used to set the tone of an advertisement. A well-chosen song or background score can evoke strong emotions and memories, heightening the advertisement's enchanting effect.

Often, advertisements tie products to ideals like success, happiness, or societal approval—the happy endings that most of us desire. For instance, luxury-brand advertisements may show scenes of luxurious lifestyles, suggesting that their product is a gateway to such a life. On the other hand, some advertisements create a sense of mystery or allure around a product, making viewers curious and enticing them to learn more.

So, marketers try to tap into strong emotions, whether it's the joy of family moments, the excitement of adventure, or the comfort of nostalgia. Emotional resonance of this kind can make a product or service seem more desirable. Then there is the role of the celebrity: when a respected or admired figure endorses a product, it is more enchanting to people who trust that figure's judgment. Tapping into popular culture or a timely event can also make advertisements more relatable and captivating. For example, advertisements that play on current memes, trending topics, or universally recognized cultural moments can enchant audiences by seeming up-to-date and relevant.

Finally, and most relevantly, in times of stress or difficulty, advertisements that offer an escape from the everyday can be especially enchanting. This can be through showcasing exotic travel destinations, luxury experiences, or even just simple, comforting moments. More recent advertising focuses on personal stories, individual experiences, and inclusivity.

By showcasing a diverse range of people and experiences, brands can enchant viewers by making them feel seen and represented. Products that promise cutting-edge technology or new experiences can enchant consumers by making them feel they are accessing the future or something previously thought impossible.

In essence, enchantment in advertising revolves around creating connections—whether emotional, aspirational, or cultural. By forging these connections between the product and some happy ending, advertisers make their products and services not just desirable, but seemingly magical or transformative.

For all these reasons, the famous dichotomy Max Weber drew between enchantment and disenchantment is hotly disputed today. Cultural perspectives on technology adoption and consumption, up to now, have tended to be cognitive, instrumental, and individualistic—to focus on rationality, efficiency, and profitability. However, now it is possible to consider an alternative desire-centered, future-oriented, and culturally grounded alternative model of technology called the Disenchanted Enchantment Model (DEM). Researchers who do so argue that desire is at the heart of (even) our enchantment by technology, whose emotional fulfilment (they say) is temporary, skeptical, and ironic. The reason people buy present-day technology arguably centers on desire, wonder, and expectation, no less than when they are buying a piece of jewelry or a vacation trip (Belk et al., 2020).

If all this is true, we may have to revise Karl Marx's famous claim that "religion is the opiate of the masses." Today, consumer buying is the opiate of the masses. Today, consumer goods help us achieve the enchantment and dreamlike fantasy that we once sought in religion. We look for comfort and solace in our enchanting buys, and often we find it.

Do you look for magical enchantment in the things you buy? To see if you do, respond to the following statements using the same 5-point scale you used in previous chapters. Remember to give a statement 5 points if you strongly agree; 4 points if you agree but not strongly; and so on. As before, add up all your points to get your total score on this scale. You are longing for enchantment if you score 40 or more points.

1. I like products that are beautiful and spellbinding.
2. I always look for products that give me pleasure and delight.
3. I feel that some things I buy are magical in their beauty.
4. I try to buy things that have a spiritual quality to them.
5. Some products almost hypnotize you with their beauty.
6. I take delight in the most beautiful things available for purchase.
7. Some things you can buy are mysteriously attractive.
8. I wish there were more products for sale that are enchanting.
9. I like to daydream about the magical beauty of some products.
10. I always admire people who own beautiful, unusual objects.

The Pursuit of Enchantment

According to one of sociology's founders, Max Weber (mentioned earlier), as rationalism and secularism took hold of modern life we lost the magic, fantasy, and wonder preindustrial societies possessed (Hanke et al., 2019, 2020). During the Age of Enlightenment, which lasted from roughly 1650 to 1850, rationality and science largely displaced religion as a source of knowledge about the world. The Scientific Revolution made it possible for people to study and prove the causes of things in a rational, dispassionate way that needed no magic or enchantment.

Thus, Max Weber's idea of "disenchantment" refers to the transformation of the Western world from a preoccupation with mysterious and magical thinking to more rational and secular thinking. This shift was closely associated with the processes of modernization, rationalization, and secularization that took place during and after the Enlightenment.

In this context, "disenchantment" describes a rejection of supernatural and mystical explanations of the world. Instead, we are encouraged to understand the world through scientific, rational, and empirical means. One key aspect of disenchantment is the process of rationalization, which structures social life around reason and logic. Disenchantment also refers to the decline of religious belief and the retreat of religion from public life. In this process, secularization leads to a worldview where phenomena are no longer explained through religious or spiritual means but are instead understood as natural.

All this implies the disenchanted world is a place where phenomena are predictable and controllable. Science and technology help humans to understand and manipulate the world in unprecedented ways, leading to advances in medicine, industry, and other fields. So disenchantment brings about increased control and understanding of the world. However, it also leads to a loss of a sense of mystery, wonder, and deeper meaning.

For Weber, the disenchanted world is characterized by routine and mechanization, which may lead to feelings of alienation and emptiness. Perhaps that is why Weber famously described the disenchanted world as an "iron cage" of rationality. So, rationalization creates efficiency and order. However, it also traps people in a system of bureaucracy and rational-legal authority that is dehumanizing and constraining.

As we have already noted, some critics have argued that disenchantment is not universal or unavoidable. Many societies continue to incorporate religious, magical, or spiritual understandings of the world alongside rational and scientific viewpoints. Some scholars even suggest that modern societies may experience processes of "re-enchantment." This occurs when new forms of spirituality, meaning, and wonder emerge within or alongside a rationalized and secularized social order.

And here, we have to side with Weber's critics. Most modern people still have room for enchantment and irrational behavior. For example, some people find happiness in gambling, where the odds of winning or losing are unpredictable. Many people cross their fingers hoping for "beginner's luck." Others look to popular culture for magic. They find their escape in characters, plots, and events in science fiction, cartoons, and video games. By traveling to faraway fictional places and marveling at glamorous fictional people, people see things that aren't possible in our rational world. You can make characters appear and disappear, fly through the air, and always enjoy happy endings.

Now, you may think that no one in their right mind would spend time thinking about characters that appear, disappear, fly, and always enjoy happy endings. After all, that's not how life actually works, you may say. Yet, precisely because life doesn't work that way, people are enchanted by stories in which life *does* work that way.

In their search for happy endings, consumers increasingly look to advertising and consumer buying for satisfaction. We can rely on advertising to create enchantment for us: a world where things do not work as they do in reality. In this fantasy world, things follow rules that are gentler and fairer, or more exciting and mysterious. In fact, some researchers think marketing can even shape the real world.

Consider here the example of AI (artificial intelligence.) Are new technologies driving us towards dystopia or utopia—or something in between? People hold various views about the likely effects of AI: call those views dystopian (black magic), utopian (white magic) or "dualopian" future (grey magic). Today, the net effect is squarely in the grey, but some think that marketers have a unique power to leverage AI and robotics developments for good (Letheren et al., 2020).

And because enchantment gives people what they want, it is an effective advertising tool. People want to escape reason and science. Any product that promises to take someone beyond the boundaries of cause and effect will capture a buyer's attention. Even people who do not believe in the promise of a break from cause and effect will be drawn to enchantment because it is so appealing. The prize is so large that even a small chance of success is a good thing.

How does the creation of advertising enchantment work? Which parts of the cause-and-effect chain should a marketer omit to create an enticing advertisement? Sixty years ago, Vance Packard's classic book, *The Hidden Persuaders*, discussed what people wanted but didn't always get in reality.

Vance Packard (1914–1996) was an American journalist, social critic, and author best known for his books that critiqued consumerism, planned obsolescence, and the influence of the media on society. *The Hidden Persuaders* (1957) was perhaps Packard's most famous work. In it, he delved into the use of consumer motivational research and other psychological techniques by advertisers to manipulate the public into buying products. He discussed how advertisers appealed to consumers' subconscious desires and fears to promote their products.

Packard reminded us that the things we want out of life but don't always get include emotional security, reassurance of worth, ego satisfaction, creativity, love objects, a sense of power, roots, and immortality. So, as a first guess, we can say that an advertisement will enchant you if it can deliver any one or two of these things that you cannot always or even usually get in reality.

Enchantment is especially good for selling items to children, because they have an even looser grip on reality and its discontents than their parents do. That is why children make especially good consumers.

Advertising Enchantment

It's normal to dream and even to daydream, and all of us do it. In our dreams, we imagine worlds that don't follow the normal rules of cause and effect. Advertisements are dreamlike stories that marketers feed our subconscious mind with the goal of getting us to buy something. Certain advertisements excite us because they deal with issues that we haven't thought about fully but want to deal with anyway. Some advertisements excite us because they offer images of sex, risk, danger, popularity, and excitement that we normally avoid or can't get enough of.

In dreams, people often show up in distorted shapes, but some of these shapes are universal—obvious in pictures and myths from around the world. Psychoanalyst Carl Jung (1875–1961) called these universal shapes *archetypes*, and some marketers have realized that using these archetypes in fantasy advertisements is a good way to make money. Jung wrote that archetypes (stories and characters that resonate with us in our subconscious mind) help us understand how we act.

Jung was a Swiss psychiatrist and psychoanalyst who became one of the most significant and influential figures in the history of psychology. The school of psychology Jung developed, analytical psychology, stressed the importance of the individual psyche and the personal quest for wholeness.

Jung developed the idea of the *collective unconscious*, which refers to the part of the unconscious mind that is shared by all of humankind. It is the reservoir of our experiences as a species. And like Freud, Jung thought dreams were a window into the unconscious. However, his approach to dream interpretation differed significantly from Freud's, focusing more on symbols that connect personal experiences to universal archetypes.

Jung's theory of psychological types led to the development of the popular Myers-Briggs Type Indicator (MBTI). Jung proposed that people can be categorized based on their preference of general attitude (extraversion vs. introversion), perception (sensing vs. intuition), and judgment (thinking vs. feeling).

Unlike many thinkers of his time, Jung felt spirituality was a critical component of mental health and sought to integrate it into his psychological theories. Jung introduced the idea of synchronicity, which refers to meaningful coincidences that cannot be explained by cause and effect. He saw these events as evidence of a deeper order or principle in the universe.

In Jung's thinking, archetypes are universal symbols, themes, or images that arise from the collective unconscious and are expressed through myths, religion, art, and dreams across different cultures and historical periods. The collective unconscious is different from the personal unconscious, which is unique to each person. Archetypes are seen as timeless and universal symbols and themes that recur in human cultural expressions. They are not learned or gained through individual experiences but are inherent in the human psyche, present at birth.

Archetypes can show up in various forms, including myths, religious symbols, fairy tales, and dreams. These expressions may vary culturally but all stem from the same universal archetypical themes.

Consider some common archetypes, and you will easily see how they may be used in advertising. The *hero* is characterized by courage, determination, and the pursuit of a great quest. Heroes often undergo significant transformation or growth during their journeys. The *shadow* represents the darker, unconscious side of the individual, embodying chaos, disorder, and the unknown. It is often projected onto others or externalized as a dangerous or evil force. The *anima* represents the feminine side of the male psyche, while the *animus* represents the masculine side of the female psyche. These archetypes embody qualities and characteristics associated with the opposite gender.

The *wise old man* archetype embodies wisdom, guidance, and mentorship, often serving as a guide or counselor to the hero in myths and stories. The *mother* archetype represents nurturing, care, fertility, and protection, often symbolized by mother earth, goddesses, or maternal figures.

Archetypal images and themes are widely employed in literature, art, and film analysis—also, advertising—to explore our thoughts, wishes, and dreams. However, some critics argue that Jung's idea of archetypes is too vague, subjective, and difficult to empirically test or corroborate. Others contend the idea of universal symbols may oversimplify cultural differences and variations in symbolic expression and interpretation.

Nonetheless, we can see archetypes in mythology, fiction, and, if we're being honest, branding. Motivational theory says marketers should try to get people to buy something by appealing to their emotions and even to their subconscious. Using archetypes for this purpose helps connect a product to the consumer's wish to buy the product.

Storytelling is also considered an important instrument for cultural brand strategy management. The effectiveness of brand storytelling is grounded in *narrative transport* and *archetypal psychology*.

To illustrate how this works, consider a recent experiment. For a functional product (mineral water) and a symbolic product (perfume), two researchers designed four storytelling scenarios, using four main archetypal categories as defined in the relevant literature. In one part of the experiment, consumers were randomly shown one of the four brand stories or one traditional promotional scenario. The scenarios were presented in a series of commented drawings. After viewing the brand stories, the participants were asked to reveal their thoughts and feelings about the products.

The experiment found that—for both functional and symbolic products—the use of archetypes can elicit specific feelings towards brands, though the narrative persuasion system works differently according to product type (Ganassali and Matysiewicz, 2021).

Consider, as an example of this, three prominent archetypes in Jung's universe: the hero, outlaw, and magician. These archetypal characters all break the rules and take risks, usually to make the world better. The hero sometimes breaks the rules to defeat the bad guys. The outlaw breaks rules that he doesn't consider important; in effect, he is a rebel, and rebellion is sometimes useful. And the magician uses his sacred knowledge to make the world work even better. These archetypes all fit into the "mastery" part of consumer motivation theory, but they lend slightly different coloring to different products. In particular, there is a great divide in popular thinking between a "hero" and an "outlaw."

In *The Hero and the Outlaw: Building Extraordinary Brands through the Power of Archetypes* (2001), authors Margaret Mark and Carol S. Pearson argue that to make brands significant, advertisers should use more of these archetypes. Mark is a strategic consultant and branding expert who has held leadership positions in major branding and communication companies. Pearson is a scholar and author known for her work on archetypes and their role in personal development, leadership, and branding. Together, they delve into how brands can leverage the power of universal archetypes to build a strong, genuine identity that resonates with consumers.

The book offers insights into how understanding and aligning with these archetypal images can lead to more effective and impactful branding. By using archetypes, you get into people's minds and connect with deeper personal needs and wants than you can with the product alone. To sell their products, marketers should use rule-breaking archetypes to show that breaking the rules can be a good thing for consumers personally.

The Power of Sex

Sexual imagery in advertising is the use of sexually suggestive images, symbols, or themes to promote products and services. Anything that evokes the power of erotic fantasy is likely to fascinate buyers. But advertisers must be careful about the sexual content they show. Even though sexual imagery can be appealing, most advertisements only show hints of it. Images, colours, music, and words are used to make people think that if they buy certain things and services, sexual enthrallment will follow.

Does a sexual approach help to sell a product? An eye-tracking experiment was conducted to gauge how the use of sexual appeals impacts visual attention to competing components of the ad: the model, product, advertising copy and the logo or brand. In this experiment, the sexual element took the form of partially clad, decorative female models.

Now you may think that the ad containing a scantily, attractive model would draw the greatest attention from viewers, and as a result would produce the greatest sales. And both men and women did direct more attention to the models in advertisements that used sexual appeals than to the models in non-sexual advertisements. However, the sexual element did not increase overall attention to the *product* advertised. What's more, viewers paid little attention to the advertising copy and the brand when sexual appeals were employed. Finally, this sexual distraction was more pronounced for men than for women (Cummins et al., 2021).

In short, this experiment showed that advertisements that contain sexually attractive models certainly catch the eyes of men. However, these men are unlikely to remember the product or buy it.

The use of sexual imagery can be polarizing, and it's important to understand the rationale, implications, and criticisms associated with it. As we have just seen, sexual imagery attracts attention, which is critical in the crowded and competitive advertising landscape. The provocative content can make consumers more likely to notice and remember the advertisement. But it does not make them remember the product advertised, or the alleged merits of that product.

Sexual content has been used in advertising for many years, driven by the adage "sex sells." This approach has its proponents and critics. However, there are conflicting values and concerns associated with the use of sexual content in advertising.

By associating a product with sexual imagery, advertisers aim to suggest that using the product will make the consumer more desirable or that the product itself is desirable. Most especially, marketers understand that sexual arousal is a primal urge—especially in men—and by using sexual images, they are trying to harness that powerful arousal. But how does sexual arousal stack up against (or in connection with) other kinds of arousal?

A study that compared sexual arousal with hunger made clear how elemental is the appeal of sexiness in advertising. Research had already shown that people's financial decisions are influenced by sexual (versus neutral) stimuli. Exposure to sexual stimuli makes men, more than women, eager to spend money immediately, take financial risks, and "show off" their wealth. But hunger is also known to influence financial decisions, such that hungry (vs. satiated) people are more likely to display financial impatience (choosing smaller-sooner over larger-later monetary rewards).

In the present study, researchers examined the moderating roles of participant sex and hunger in the association between sexual stimuli and financial impatience. They found that exposure to sexually arousing (vs. neutral) advertisements makes men more financially impatient than women, and hunger further enhances this effect. Hungry men become more impatient in their monetary choices after viewing sexually arousing advertisements, while women do the opposite (Otterbring and Sela, 2020).

So sexual content may appeal to certain demographic groups (e.g., young and middle-aged men), especially if the product itself is related to sex appeal, personal attractiveness, or intimate relationships. For this reason, some brands use sexual content to provoke or create controversy deliberately. This can lead to increased media coverage and word-of-mouth, extending the advertisement's reach beyond its first audience.

However, many concerns have been expressed about the use of sexual content in advertising. There's a significant concern that sexual content in advertisements can perpetuate harmful stereotypes, objectify people (often women), and present unrealistic standards of beauty. In many cultures—for example, in Middle Eastern Islamic cultures—overtly sexual content is seen as inappropriate or offensive. Advertisements with such content can alienate or upset potential customers in these cultures. As well, repeated exposure to sexual content (in any culture) can lead to desensitization, where viewers become less responsive or more indifferent to such content over time.

If the sexual content is not seen as relevant to the product, it may confuse consumers or be viewed as a cheap tactic, which could undermine the brand's credibility. Sexual content may also not be suitable for all audience segments, especially younger viewers. This can lead to criticism from parents, educators, and advocacy groups.

In the last ten years, there's been a push in many markets for more responsible advertising that avoids unjustified sexual content, especially if it objectifies women or is not relevant to the product. Brands are becoming more aware of the broader societal impact of their advertisements and are often choosing content that is inclusive, empowering, and respectful. However, like any advertising strategy, the effectiveness of sexual content varies based on execution, product, target audience, cultural context, and other factors.

As noted, sexual content in advertising may be directed at particular demographics, typically younger and presumably more sexually active audiences. Products related to beauty, health, and romance more often use sexual imagery, as it's seen as more relevant for these categories.

However, here are a few warnings about the use of sexuality in advertising. Depending on execution, the use of sexual imagery can either improve the brand image by making it appear modern and bold, or damage the image by making it seem crass and exploitative. Sexual imagery may grab our attention, but, as noted, viewers often remember the imagery more than the brand or product, leading to ineffective communication. Reactions to sexual content vary widely across different cultures and communities, and what's acceptable in one context may be offensive in another.

Beyond that, critics argue such advertising may contribute to an environment where sexuality is trivialized or commodified. Using sexual imagery raises ethical concerns, especially about the exposure of underage audiences to inappropriate content. Also, presenting idealized and sexualized bodies can contribute to body dissatisfaction and negative body image among viewers, leading to various mental health issues, including low self-esteem and eating disorders.

So, sexual imagery in advertising must be used judiciously and ethically. Advertisers need to navigate this sensitive area carefully, weighing the potential benefits against the risks of alienating or harming audiences.

With these criticisms in mind, we see an increasing presence of "femvertising" in the media: an advertising style that highlights women's talents, centers themes on pro-woman messaging, and counters stereotyping. This is a way of changing the role of women in mainstream advertising, and of moving the discussion away from stereotyped and sexually exploitative portrayals of women.

The major factors leading to the growth of femvertising include activism around the better representation of women in advertising and an increasing awareness of gender stereotyping. Other significant influences are brand activism; a widespread criticism of corporate and commodity feminism; and an increasing scrutiny of gender role representations by regulatory bodies (Varghese and Kumar, 2020).

Advertisements for couples' vacation getaways are among the many products that still use sex to advertise their product. The advertisements suggest couples will rediscover their romance and sexual zeal if they go on these trips. However, even advertisements for clothing, personal hygiene, and high-end cars can also contain sexual messages. Often, they include women, since men have traditionally viewed women as sex objects that can be acquired and enjoyed along with the advertised product.

Narrative Transport

Marketers are most effective when they use narrative transport—elements of the grotesque and the fantastic—to make their stories more powerful and effective. Usually, it's good to use images that make the familiar seem strange, and the non-familiar seem familiar. Grotesque or offbeat advertising imagery has a lot in common with works of art because the artistic quality of the image makes people unable to look away.

Narrative transport means immersing people in a story to the extent they are transported into the narrative world. In advertising, narrative transport is a potent tool used to engage consumers emotionally and cognitively with a brand through storytelling.

Advertisements that use narrative transport often tell a compelling story that elicits emotional responses from viewers, making them feel connected to the characters, events, or situations depicted. When consumers are "transported," they temporarily suspend disbelief and accept the story as if it were real, which helps in creating a deep emotional and cognitive engagement with the narrative.

Consumers may identify with the characters in an advertisement, experiencing their emotions and adopting their perspectives. This, in turn, fosters a strong connection with the brand or product being promoted. Immersing people in a narrative reduces the likelihood they will reject the advertising message, which makes them more receptive to the product being advertised.

How do the copy writer, art director, and other members of the creative team achieve such results? First, they promote narrative transport by crafting stories that evoke strong emotions like joy, sadness, excitement, or nostalgia. Second, they develop characters with whom the target audience can identify or empathize. Third, they immerse the target audience by employing compelling visuals, soundtracks, and voiceovers that contribute to the atmosphere and mood of the story increases immersion. Finally, they promote engagement with a clear and coherent storyline.

As part of the branding, the creative team often crafts narratives that embody the values, identities, or lifestyles they wish to promote, engaging consumers through relatable or aspirational stories. When introducing new products, advertisers create narratives around the innovation, uniqueness, or benefits of the product, positioning it within a story that resonates with potential buyers.

The experienced marketer makes viewers feel like they are inside the advertisement. In this way, the narrative transports the consumer to a place they've never been before. Doing so calls for the use of imagery that makes people feel something and makes them pay attention to the story itself, rather than the product. Sometimes, fine art is used to make a luxury brand more seem more important by appealing to people who value such paintings or sculpture.

A multisensory experience can also make a brand seem more interesting. Research suggests that aroma or scent may help to evoke emotions and memories—to transport the consumer into another state of consciousness. Unconsciously, but powerfully, the scent of a product affects how a customer feels about his surroundings and makes him want to return to the place (perhaps, a store or hotel) where they smelt it. This can be useful in marketing homes or hotels, for example.

In a book titled *Culture and Enchantment* (1993), author Mark A. Schneider argues that enchantment comes from a sense of wonder when we can't fully explain an event. "Enchantment is a normal part of our lives, and it doesn't go away with the rise of science." Instead, he says, "it exists (though often unrecognized) where our ability to explain the world's behavior is limited, that is, where neither science nor practical knowledge seem to be of much use."

However, there are dangers and risks associated with leaving yourself open to enchantment by consumer goods and consumer spending. If you have discovered you have some inclination in that direction, here are a few dangers you should consider:

- Overspending: Being constantly drawn to enchanting products can lead to spending beyond your means.
- Amassing debt: Using credit cards recklessly or taking out loans to

afford enchanting consumer goods can lead to significant debt.
- Materialism and happiness: Research suggests that a preoccupation with material goods, even enchanting ones, can be inversely related to life satisfaction and well-being.
- Temporary satisfaction: The first thrill of an enchanting new buy often fades quickly, leading to a cycle of buying more to chase that fleeting feeling.
- Waste production and resource depletion: Buying more than you need leads to more waste, contributing to environmental degradation, while overconsumption means faster depletion of natural resources.
- Status anxiety: The wish to keep up with societal standards or reference groups can lead to anxiety and a feeling of inadequacy.
- Shifting values: A society that glorifies consumerism may value people based on what they own rather than their character or contributions.
- Sedentary lifestyle: A preoccupation with certain consumer goods, like electronic gadgets, may encourage more screen time and less physical activity.
- External approval: Relying on consumer goods for self-worth can be precarious. Such a basis for self-esteem is external and can be shaken by trends or financial instability.
- Loss of authenticity: You may feel pressured to conform to certain lifestyles or images presented by media and advertising, leading to a loss of personal authenticity.
- Reduced savings: Overconsumption may divert funds from savings, investments, or more important financial goals.
- Physical clutter: Continuously buying can lead to a cluttered living space, which may be linked to increased stress.
- Mental clutter: Being preoccupied with consumer goods can clutter one's mind, detracting from more important pursuits or experiences.
- Technology dependency: Over-reliance on enchanting consumer tech products can make you feel helpless without them.
- Loss vulnerability: The more you are attached to consumer goods, the more distressing it can be if those items are lost, stolen, or become obsolete.

In summary, consumer goods can be sources of convenience, entertainment, and even identity to some extent. However, an excessive enchantment with them can have negative effects. So you have to pay attention to your consumption habits and the underlying motivations behind them.

As we will see in the next chapter, some people fall in love with their possessions. This form of love affects how people buy, use, and discard their property, in ways that make them feel elated and happy. It also suggests that people fall in love with brands when they identify with them or feel a sense of community around them, fostering loyalty. As we will discover, for some people the love of possessions can be as enjoyable, passionate, and flexible as many human relationships.

Chapter Twelve

Possession Love

Some people are so attached to buying things that they experience *possession love*, meaning they fall in love with something they own. Such possession love influences how we buy and use our favorite items. It also has an impact on how we feel about ourselves and what we own.

Materialism does not just make consumers more likely to love brands, it also alters the way they relate to them. Specifically, *brand love* is associated with loving brands you currently own rather than wishing for brands you can't afford. But materialism is not just associated with loving brands; it is also strongly associated with loving money. Finally, there has been an active debate over whether brand love applies to a wide variety of brands or just a few. This research finds that consumers love a wide variety of brands, if they love any brands at all (Ahuvia et al., 2020).

Consumers can develop strong emotional attachments to the things they have bought. This attachment or "love" can show in various ways and is driven by multiple factors. For example, items bought during significant moments in life—such as engagement rings, first cars, or souvenirs from a memorable trip—can carry deep emotional value. Over time, these items become more than just objects; they symbolize memories, experiences, or relationships.

Consumers may also develop a fondness for products that consistently meet or exceed their needs. A reliable gadget, tool, or appliance can become a cherished possession because of the convenience and comfort that it offers.

Objects that are visually pleasing, such as art, jewelry, clothing, or even well-designed everyday items, can be sources of joy. Over time, consumers may grow attached to these items because they add beauty or style to their lives.

Some purchases play an important role in how people see themselves and how they wish to be seen by others. For example, someone may cherish a particular fashion item, musical instrument, or book collection because it resonates with their personal identity. Items that have been used often and for an extended period can evoke a sense of comfort and familiarity. This can apply to anything from a favorite old sweater to a well-worn sofa.

Sometimes, the attachment to a possession is more rational. For example, items seen as investments can be deeply valued. They can be valued financially (like a piece of real estate or a collectible) or in time and energy (like a plant that has been nurtured for years).

Some brands excel at storytelling and fostering a community or lifestyle around their products. Apple, for example, has customers who are loyal and have a deep emotional attachment to the brand. The brand narrative can make consumers feel connected, not just to their purchases, but to the broader brand ethos. Vintage items or items that remind people of their past can be sources of nostalgia. This emotional connection can imbue objects with value beyond their inherent utility or cost. Items that are custom-made or display exceptional craftsmanship can also be especially cherished. The uniqueness and attention to detail can make the owner feel a deeper connection to the item.

It's worth noting that not all purchases lead to this kind of attachment, however. The development of such emotional bonds depends, to some degree, on the possessor's personality, values, experiences, and the context in which the item is used or gained. However, whenever consumers do "fall in love" with their purchases, it highlights the intense ways in which material objects can intersect with human emotion and experience.

People fall in love with a brand when they identify with or feel a sense of belonging because of it. People who love particular brands tend to like other people who love that same brand. With these findings in mind, brand-love researchers propose ways for marketers to make their products more human to entice people to own and be loyal to them.

People are especially likely to love the pets they own, and perhaps someday they may even come to love human-seeming robots in their employ. Two researchers (Banks and Edwards, 2019) tested a scale to measure the social distance people want from robots. This may seem like a reach, but when you reflect on the growing sophistication of artificial intelligence, such a concern may not be unreasonable.

Here is the social distance scale the researchers used for this purpose:

SOCIAL DISTANCE SCALE ITEMS

Item	Maximum Score*
Physical Distance	
I would be in the same country with them.	5
I would be in the same city with them.	4
I would be in the same building with them.	3
I would be in the same room with them.	2
I would stand next to them.	1
Relational Distance	
I would accept them as my servant.	5
I would accept them as a casual acquaintance.	4
I would accept them as a buddy.	3
I would accept them as a close friend.	2
I would accept them as a significant other.	1
Conversational Distance	
I would participate in small talk.	5
I would chat together about our favorite hobbies.	4
I would share an inside joke.	3
I would discuss the most important things in life.	2
I would share a deep secret.	1

*Higher numbers mean people want more social distance.

Interviewing people about their willingness to interact with robots, the researchers found some are strongly and consistently pro-robot. Others are strongly and consistently anti-robot; and many are in the middle, taking a "wait and see" position. The researchers conclude that "this metric promises to be a useful tool for evaluating and comparing … degrees of understanding and intimacy" between people and robots.

But why did they bother to do this research, you may wonder. Here's how the researchers explained their goal (Banks and Edwards, 2019): "Degrees of social distance likely influence one's willingness to adopt a particular technology into one's everyday social life and [interact] with robots. Of relevance to social robots, social distance is influenced by social cues in robot appearance and behavior. Distance is minimized when robots call humans by names and use casual or familiar speech and hold more positive attitudes toward robots in general."

You may read this and think the effort to humanize robots is preposterous: it will never work, and even if it worked, it would never sell people on treating machines like people. But in fact people already treat machines (particularly complex ones) like people, giving them names and talking to them (though usually when no one else is around).

So to get consumers to try, then adopt new robotic technologies, we need to make the robots as humanlike and approachable as possible. If we can get the robots to speak to their users in casual and intimate ways, we are more likely to seal the deal. So now we're trying to measure "degrees of understanding and intimacy" between people and robots, and we're not that far from present-day reality.

What Is This Thing Called Love?

But what exactly is love? For millennia, poets, philosophers, and scientists have tried to define love. We throw the word around a lot today. You may love your mother, but you may also love your shoes. In this chapter, we'll look at what it means to be smitten by something. To calculate your possession-love score, respond to the following statements on the same 5-point scale you used in previous chapters. If you strongly agree with the statement, give it 5 points; if you agree but not strongly, give it 4 points, and so on.

Now, consider a specific product you own and enjoy ("item Y") and express your agreement or disagreement with the following statements:

1. Just thinking about it "turns me on."
2. I cannot imagine anything else I own making me as happy as item Y does.
3. I enjoy running my hands over the outer surface of item Y.
4. When I cannot be around item Y, I find myself longing to see it.
5. The day I bought item Y was a dream come true for me.
6. I know details about item Y that wouldn't interest most other people.
7. I work to make sure item Y is always looking its best.
8. I enjoy spending time on item Y.
9. I am always interested in learning more about item Y.
10. I can't imagine ever selling item Y.

Just add up all your points to get your score. You have feelings of possession love toward Item Y if you scored 40 or more points. But what exactly does that mean? Let's look at the reasoning behind this scale.

Two researchers who were interested in learning more about possession love examined the three major ingredients of love: motivation, emotion, and understanding. Then, they asked a group of male bikers how they felt about different types of love between people to find out how human and possession love differ. Doing this, they discovered bikers love their motorcycles in ways people love one another. That is, they show passionate, possessive, and selfless feelings of love toward their bike (Shimp and Madden, 1988).

And as with human love, brand or possession love can turn to hate if it fails to satisfy. One study finds that consumers facing brand failure suffer negative emotions and then plan to retaliate (or take revenge). Brand love positively moderates the link between failure severity and negative emotions—the "love becomes hate" effect. Meanwhile, brand love negatively moderates the link between negative emotions and retaliation intention—the "love is blind" effect (Zhang et al., 2020).

In other words, if you love a particular brand but your current version of that brand is disappointing you, you may decide to retaliate. But you are less likely to "retaliate" against the manufacturer than if you had hated that brand or felt neutral towards it at first.

Various Types of Love

With a growing understanding of the emotions we invest in our possessions, researchers are beginning to study the problems that come with having a lot of things. These include how we buy, use, and discard our favorite stuff; how marketing affects possession love; and how possession love affects consumer well-being.

Even though this research has grown rapidly, we still do not know everything we need to know about it. That's because people have so many kinds of love. Possession love is often proportional to how long you've had the possession, and what that possession may be. Besides, each type of possession love is important at different stages of the buying-and-owning process. For example, you may love something more when you first buy it than when you've had it for twenty years.

One survey of French respondents examined the words consumers use to describe their relationships with the brands they adore. In doing this, they came up with eleven different dimensions of love. Interestingly, the dimensions of love in France proved to be different from the dimensions of love discovered by researchers in the United States. Apparently, cultures vary in the ways they experience and express love.

But this should not surprise us. Love is a multifaceted emotion that can show in various forms and intensities, even within a single culture. Over time, scholars, psychologists, and thinkers have tried to classify and understand these different kinds of love.

There are many widely recognized types of love. *Agape* is selfless love, often associated with spiritual and religious contexts. It represents love that is given without expecting or even wanting anything in return. *Eros* is passionate or romantic love; it often encompasses both physical attraction and deeper emotional connections. *Philia*, or caring love, is often referred to as "brotherly love." Philia applies to the deep connection found in close friendships. It's about the platonic affection and mutual respect shared by friends. Other forms of love include *storge*, the love shared by family members, such as the bond between parents and their children, or between siblings. *Pragma* (or enduring love) is long-term commitment, including the compromises people make to ensure a relationship lasts. It's built over time between long-term partners and represents dedication and shared goals. *Ludus* (or playful love) is often experienced in the early stages of a romantic relationship, and is characterized by flirtation, teasing, and playfulness. Finally, *mania* is a form of love that's intense and often characterized by extreme feelings and obsession. It may show as intense jealousy, insecurity, or possessiveness.

So what is possession love? In the most direct examination of possession love, two researchers studied how people felt about the cars, computers, bicycles, and firearms they owned (Lastovicka and Sirianni, 2011). They discovered that people who are in love with a product take care of it, and even buy more products and services for it.

For example, someone who adores a laptop may buy accessories to improve its appearance and usefulness. The closer these things are to living things, as you may expect, the more you want to primp them and improve them. Possession love can be lighthearted and enjoyable, but it's not erotic, and it lacks the commitment that comes with long-term love or infatuation.

People who are in love with their computers or guns, for example, are open to having relationships with similar products: additional computers, more powerful guns, and so on. Polygamous relationships with multiple guns or serial marriages with one beloved computer after another are examples of this type of love in people's lives. In possession love, both polygamy and serial monogamy are free to thrive.

Infatuation can be a problem in personal relationships, but it isn't as dangerous in relationships with an inanimate object. "You're stunning!" a guy may say to his new Ferrari. "I can't think how gorgeous you are! The sleekness of your body! I must be with you!" Like the first few days with a new boyfriend or girlfriend, the first few days with a new car may make you feel you're in love. But love of a possession doesn't mean forever, and there is no obligation to divide up your property if you split.

Brand Affiliations

When we "fall in love with" a brand, we are more likely to buy it and engage with it. People fall in love with a brand when they see it as distinct from other brands and especially when they are part of a group of people who share positive feelings about it. It's easy to fall in love with a brand if the product is one-of-a-kind, special, or scarce: a Maserati, Rolex watch, or bottle of Macallan 25-year-old scotch.

People who study possession love are also interested in how people feel about being a part of a brand community and how they interact with other members of that group. A customer who falls in love with a product or brand can easily become a loyal member of that community. The "brand lover" need only imagine themselves as one of many people who adore and use the product.

According to research, marketing managers should strive to create a sense of community with their customers. People are more likely to buy from a company if they like and trust it. Formal brand communities are an excellent way for marketers to foster community. They can, for instance, create online groups. Advertisements or event sponsorships reveal who the brand's users are and what they have in common. Organized, branded events may be a good way to foster such a community. For example, Lululemon, an athletic clothing company, offers free yoga classes both online and in its stores.

To have *brand passion*, a person must be familiar with the brand and have faith in it. When we are passionate about a brand—indeed, passionate about anything or anyone—we do two things: think about it a lot, and think about it positively. In other words, brand passion is a mental state characterized by excitement, infatuation, and even obsession with a brand. It's like having a crush on a product.

Brand passion plays a key role in improving word-of-mouth discussion of a brand, and in increasing our willingness to pay a premium for the brand. It may also increase brand loyalty, brand advocacy, brand community engagement, social media support, price insensitivity, and purchase intention.

People who love a brand are more likely to buy it again and again, compared with people who just think a brand is good. Anthropomorphism, or giving human characteristics to things that aren't alive, is a major factor in why we love a brand. When we anthropomorphize brands and fall in love with them, they become more relatable and thus more lovable.

Research shows that when brand attachment and brand passion are compared, brand passion usually has the greater effect on purchase intention. However, brand attachment increases a consumer's willingness to buy everyday products (e.g., a particular brand of toothpaste), while brand passion increases a consumer's willingness to buy a higher-cost product (e.g., a particular brand of handbag). This makes brand passion a more prominent predictor of the purchase intention of high-involvement, high-cost shopping brands (Gilal et al., 2020).

Self-congruence is another way to think about the similarities and differences between consumer–brand relationships and social relationships. For example, in both cases, we love relationships that display what we see as our best characteristics. And in both cases, liking the relationship a lot—especially liking the quality of the relationship—is very much like loving it. We are likely to think about it, talk about it, and want to explore it.

Now, remembering the robots we discussed earlier, you may think that possession love is even more preposterous than talking to a robot. How can someone *love* a car, a guitar, a necklace, or a bar of pricey soap? It's impossible, you may say. But it happens.

Basing their work on research in the area, marketers have devised four strategies to anthropomorphize their products in ways that make people want to own and be loyal to them. First, a product or brand should speak about itself in the first person. People are more likely to fall in love if they hear first-person slogans like "Hello, I'm your new Apple Watch." Second, they should make the product resemble a human being, as much as possible. This method has already been used in the automotive industry, where manufacturers often design the front of a car to resemble a person's face. We discussed this earlier, in connection with human-like robots.

Third, marketers must try to ensure their brand has a distinct personality and create a distinct set of brand features to show this. Which computer is cool? Apple or Dell? Marketers may use testimonials or celebrity spokespeople, with the goal being to reflect their personalities in the brand. Fourth, marketers should connect with customers through social media. They could, for example, create a Facebook page that interacts with (and listens to) people.

Does Consumerism Improve Social Relations?

Often, our materialism prevents us from getting to know and care about other people, which makes us even more materialistic, compounding the loneliness problem. Materialism and loneliness feed off each other.

On the other hand, some materialistic people buy things they think will improve their chances of attracting a mate. That's why some men refer to their car as a "chick magnet." They expect to attract a mate, and often they succeed. As we've noted before, in one experiment the researchers discovered that when men drive a high-priced sports car, their testosterone levels rise, compared to when they drive a low-priced family sedan. However, men react differently depending on where they are driving and how visible they are to other people. Are they on a busy downtown street or a lonely highway? Driving a sports car on a busy downtown street is the most erotically stimulating choice. When a man drives a high-end car, he anticipates that women will see him as more powerful, desirable, and sexy.

Possession love also can be passed down through generations, becoming a source of bonding across generations. We see this in the treatment of so-called family heirlooms. Using interviews collected from the owners of the heirlooms, one researcher examined relations between the owner and object, as well as their practices of storage and presentation.

The preservation of family heirlooms provides a particular channel of existence for family memory, and plays an important role in framing family identity based on ancestry (Sokolova, 2013). Most important, perhaps, heirlooms serve an important role in rituals which preserve the cohesion and identity of a family (Curasi, Price, and Arnould, 2004).

Heirlooms, objects passed down from one generation to another, are often valued for their historical, familial, or sentimental significance rather than their monetary worth. Some common heirlooms that families collect include jewelry; engagement and wedding rings, in particular, often become treasured family heirlooms.

However, many other kinds of family possessions are handed down, generation after generation. These include antique watches and ornate clocks, especially those with a unique history or craftsmanship. Vintage photographs, especially those of ancestors, significant events, or old family gatherings, serve as tangible memories.

High-quality or antique pieces of furniture, such as cabinets, dressers, chairs, and tables, are often coveted and handed down. So are paintings, sculptures, and other artworks acquired or created by family members.

Handcrafted textiles (e.g., quilts), especially those made by ancestors, are often cherished for their sentimental value. So are old and rare books, or books with personal inscriptions. Personal writings that offer insights into ancestors' lives, thoughts, and experiences are often preserved. Religious items such as family Bibles, prayer books, rosaries, or other religious artifacts are often part of the family heirloom. In some families, lands or homes have been owned for generations and hold immense sentimental value. Finally, family recipes, often written in longhand, can be passed down, encapsulating culinary traditions.

With all this in mind, remember that the value of an heirloom (often) lies in its emotional or sentimental significance rather than its monetary worth. The stories, memories, and family history associated with an item can make it a treasured possession, even if it's not especially old or valuable in monetary terms. The possession of heirlooms is one particular form of possession love.

To repeat, possession love, like brand love and brand commitment, occurs when you have a strong and positive emotional connection to an object. You buy some items because you have a crush on them.

The Risks and Dangers of Possession Love

Falling in love can be a complex process influenced by a multitude of factors, including biological, psychological, social, and cultural ingredients. Chemicals in the brain like oxytocin, dopamine, and serotonin play critical roles in the sensations we associate with love, like pleasure, happiness, and attachment. Love can trigger the release of these chemicals, leading to feelings of reward and bonding. As well, subconscious factors, such as scent and pheromones, may influence attraction based on genetic compatibility and diversity.

What's important to take away from this brief foray into romance is that people love in various ways. Different types of people, such as men and women, seek and value different types of love to varying degrees. Different types of love, in turn, provide different types of pleasure, satisfying different types of needs. Finally and most relevantly, people can develop feelings of love for things they own; and we are calling this possession love.

While reading this chapter, you may have discovered that you feel possession love for one or more of your consumer goods. As we have seen, possession love is a step beyond simple materialism or enchantment with the things we possess. When attachment to a possession becomes a form of love, a number of risks and dangers can emerge:

- Fragility: Objects can be lost, stolen, or decay over time. If your happiness is tied strongly to these beloved items, such events can be emotionally devastating.
- Limited emotional range: Over-attachment to material objects can stifle the emotional richness gained from human relationships, experiences, or self-growth.
- Misunderstanding and conflict: Others may not understand or appreciate your intense attachment to particular possessions, leading to misunderstandings or conflicts.
- Neglect of relationships: Time and emotional energy devoted to objects may come at the expense of personal relationships.
- Overspending: To preserve or improve your collection of beloved objects, you may overspend, leading to financial strain.
- Unwillingness to use or share: The fear of damaging a beloved item may mean it's never actually used for its intended purpose.
- Obsession: What starts as affection can become an obsession, potentially leading to hoarding or other psychological disorders.
- Anxiety: The constant worry about the safety, maintenance, or potential loss of beloved possessions can lead to increased anxiety.

- Self-worth tied to objects: If your identity becomes too intertwined with possessions, it can lead to a fragile sense of self-worth that's dependent on the condition and value of those items.
- Loss of authenticity: You may become so engrossed in your beloved possessions that you lose touch with who you are outside those objects.
- Stagnation: Emotional and financial investments in objects can divert resources from opportunities for personal growth, such as education, travel, or other enriching experiences.
- Limited experiences: By giving possessions you love the highest priority, you may miss broader life experiences and adventures.
- Clutter: An intense love for many items can lead to clutter, which may result in a chaotic living environment.
- Safety concerns: In extreme cases, such as hoarding, accumulating even beloved items can pose direct physical risks, such as fire hazards or impediments to mobility within a living space.
- Avoidance of social interactions: If you rank your possessions over social interactions, this can lead to isolation and loneliness.
- Relatability issues: Other people may find it challenging to relate to you if your primary affection is directed towards material items.
- Living in the past: Some items, especially collectibles or antiques, can make you too nostalgic, preventing you from living in the present or planning for the future.
- Consumerism: If possession love drives you to continuously buy more items, it can contribute to environmental degradation.

It's natural to appreciate and care for the things you own. But this becomes problematic when your affection for possessions surpasses or replaces the importance of human relationships, personal growth, and mental well-being. You should preserve a balanced perspective and ensure that your possessions serve as a complement to a rich, multifaceted life rather than dominate it.

The next chapter is about our need for treats and the phenomenon of *shopping addiction*, which shares characteristics with other addictions. People like Anton may shop excessively as a form of self-medication to relieve feelings of stress, anxiety, or depression. The tendency to opt for shopping as a form of addiction may depend on personal familiarity and exposure to specific addictive behaviors within one's social environment.

Shopping addiction, also known as *compulsive buying disorder* (*CBD*) or *oniomania*, may result from efforts to cope with negative emotions. However, as we will see, this addiction often leads to harmful effects such as debt, bad credit, and strains on relationships, with the underlying emotional issues remaining unaddressed.

Chapter Thirteen
The Need for Treats

All of us like to buy treats for ourselves now and then, but you might think there's a natural limit to treat buying. "People will get sick of all the kitschy stuff," you may think. "It's a waste of time and money, as anyone can see." But, in fact, some people buy treats more often—a lot more often—than others. And while many people are indifferent to shopping for treats, or even avoid it whenever possible, others love the search for treats, and indulge in it frequently.

To see which camp you fall into, respond to the following seven statements, using the same scale as before: 5 if you strongly agree, 4 if you agree, 3 if you are neutral, 2 if you disagree with the statement, and 1 if you strongly disagree. If you score 28 or more points in total, you really love shopping for treats.

1. I think about shopping all the time.
2. I often buy things to cheer myself up.
3. I shop so much it interferes with my work and other duties.
4. I have to shop more often to feel as satisfied as I used to.
5. I have wanted to shop less but haven't been able to do so.
6. I feel bad if something keeps me from going shopping.
7. I shop so much that it affects my well-being.

This set of questions, adapted from the Bergen Shopping Addiction Scale, was designed to measure the presence of what the researchers call "shopping addiction" (Andreassen et al., 2015). In fact, it taps all the agreed-on dimensions of an addiction: salience, mood change, conflict, tolerance, relapse, withdrawal, and related problems. So, if you scored 28 or more on this scale, you may have a shopping addiction.

This may raise some questions in your mind. Is shopping addiction a bad thing? If so, what should I do about it? Can I beat this addiction? Am I a bad or weak person to have such an addiction? And so on. We will have something to say about all of these things.

Excessive shopping is a social and cultural problem, and not merely a psychological problem. It says more about our society than it does about you as a particular individual. In fact, our society is organized to promote excessive shopping and even shopping addiction. (In past years, it promoted a cigarette smoking addiction, and today it promotes alcohol, drug, gambling, eating, and sex addictions.)

That said, we have already identified Anton as someone who buys stuff—treats—to cheer himself up when he is (often) feeling depressed or anxious. So that makes him a candidate for shopping addiction, as you can see from an item on the shopping scale above.

Researchers have found that some people "self-medicate" with addictive substances or activities when they feel stressed, anxious, or depressed. Of course, people vary in the substance or activity they use. So, you may be asking, why do some people use tobacco, others alcohol, painkillers, gambling, high-calorie foods, or sex for this purpose? And why, among all these alternatives, do some people opt for shopping?

The single most likely answer is they adopt the addictive substance or practice with which they are most familiar. For example, they are likely to become alcoholics if they had an alcoholic parent or spouse. Similarly, they are likely to become problem gamblers if they had a gambling addict for a parent or spouse, and so on. The same may be true of shopping addiction. People copy behaviors that others close to them have practiced, approved, and modeled for them.

Shopping addiction, also known as compulsive buying disorder (CBD) or oniomania, is a behavioral condition characterized by an obsessive need to shop and spend money, often resulting in harmful results. Some people use shopping to cope with stress, anxiety, depression, loneliness, or low self-esteem. Shopping can provide temporary feelings of happiness and accomplishment. As well, consumer culture and a societal emphasis on material possessions can encourage excessive shopping, as do social media and advertising.

Some people have to struggle with impulse control, making them more susceptible to addictive behaviors, including shopping addiction. Shopping may trigger dopamine release, providing a "high" or pleasurable feeling that can be addictive. Conditions like depression, anxiety, obsessive-compulsive disorder (OCD), or bipolar disorder may also be associated with shopping addiction.

At the same time, many experts on the topic are wrestling with the question of how to classify a behavioral addiction like gambling addiction or, in this case, shopping addiction. Some researchers have proposed that it would be worthwhile to create a new category named "other specified disorders due to addictive behaviors." Relevant data should include self-reports, clinical interviews, surveys, behavioral experiments, and, if available, biological investigations (neural, physiological, genetic). The psychological (and neurobiological) mechanisms involved in other addictive behaviors should also be present for the proposed new addiction.

By that standard, researchers have already seen plenty of evidence of problematic forms of buying and shopping. Therefore, shopping addiction may validly fit the category of other specified disorders due to addictive behaviors (Brand et al., 2020).

Shopping addiction, research already shows, is a serious problem. For example, chronic overspending can lead to significant debt, bad credit, and other financial troubles. The compulsive shopper may experience tensions with family and friends due to their addiction and financial instability. And although shopping provides temporary relief, the underlying emotional issues persist. This often leads to feelings of guilt, shame, or frustration after shopping. Performance at work or school may decline due to the preoccupation with shopping. As well, some people may amass many items they don't need, leading to clutter and disorganization.

Researchers have discovered no specific medications for shopping addiction, but doctors may prescribe medications to treat underlying disorders like depression or anxiety. Financial advisers can help people to manage debt and create a sensible budget. Practices like meditation, yoga, and other stress-reduction techniques can also help manage the emotional triggers of shopping addiction. Beyond that, people with a shopping addiction would be wise to limit their exposure to triggers. Things like unsubscribing from marketing emails and avoiding malls can help reduce the temptation to shop.

As you can see, shopping addiction is a serious and multifaceted issue, calling for a combination of therapeutic, financial, and lifestyle interventions. Some theories hold that people are most likely to fall into addictive patterns of consumption when they suffer extreme and prolonged stress. This is especially likely to happen to people who have not learned how to avoid stress or reduce it. Some people reduce their stress through religion, others through social interaction, others still through vigorous physical activity, and so on.

Another compelling theory about shopping addiction has to do with self-esteem. A large literature suggests that much of the stress people suffer is internally generated: they are stressed because they feel they are defective, deficient, faulty, or downright bad. They may feel their life is out of their control and they can't do anything about it. So, they suffer anxiety and depression much of the time.

Some of these people buy excessive treats to make themselves feel better. To compensate for feelings of inadequacy and disappointment, they spend money and buy stuff. And in many respects, buying treats is like falling in love; it momentarily takes people's minds off their troubles.

The treats people buy themselves to "feel better" can range from an ice cream cone to a Maserati. Treats can include a pricey designer gown, an unusual dessert, or a power saw with every imaginable feature. People buy treats as "extras" to add something special to their lives.

An occasional (relatively inexpensive) ice cream or a (more expensive) trip to Ireland to see relatives can both be treats. Unlike basics, treats are normally never needed. The main benefit of a treat is that it makes the buyer feel better. However, the treat carries no social meaning—it is not typically a "ticket" to a community. People do not typically buy themselves treats to improve their social standing.

Why Do We Buy Treats?

As noted earlier, people often shop when they are sad, and sadness often accompanies a sense of powerlessness or lack of control. This may be what draws sad people to shopping. Shopping provides them with choices that restore a sense of personal control over their surroundings, reducing sadness. Deciding to buy stuff, whether in your imagination or in a store, helps to make you feel better.

Similarly, sadness increases the money people are willing to spend on a product. More than a century ago, the famous psychologist William James asserted that losing material possessions has a strong influence on people. It is so powerful it causes "a shrinking of our personality, a partial conversion of ourselves to nothingness" (James, 1890).

William James (1842–1910) was an American philosopher and psychologist who is often referred to as the "father of American psychology." James made significant contributions to pragmatism, a philosophical tradition that evaluates beliefs based on their practical implications and effects. His work *Pragmatism* is a foundational text for this school of thought.

Later in his career, James developed a philosophical perspective called "radical empiricism." This stance holds that relations between things are just as real as the things themselves, and that no kind of fact is inherently more fundamental than any other. Perhaps it is in this respect that we can understand his view that the loss of a material possession is like converting part of oneself to nothingness.

Consider the emotional state of powerlessness. People who feel powerless are more likely than average to buy status symbols, to assert and display their control. People who have been manipulated into feeling powerless will pay more for status items such as cuff links, an executive pen, a briefcase, a fur coat, or a silk tie. And when people feel powerless, they want to spend more, but only on status items.

These feelings of powerlessness and helplessness were exacerbated during the COVID pandemic. In the article "Find Covid Depressing?" the *Wall Street Journal* advised, "Buy a Ferrari," citing a sharp rebound in sales of the Italian luxury car in the summer of 2020, despite the global pandemic. In fact, Ferrari outperformed orders from the previous summer.

When the author of the article noted "[i]t turns out that retail therapy extends to the super rich," he intuitively identified a key element of the topic of this chapter, treats. Louis Camilleri, the CEO of Ferrari, expressed a similar sentiment when he credited strong sales during the COVID epidemic to customers rewarding themselves "at a time of difficulty."

Shopping can easily take on the characteristics and symptoms of a behavioral addiction, such as preoccupation, mental appropriation as well as compulsiveness and loss of control. Thus, shopping addiction is becoming an increasingly important topic in research addiction.

According to many reports, the COVID-19 pandemic resulted in an increase in "sensed risk factors." There is good reason to think that a high stress level, combined with social isolation and extensive leisure time, would all push a person toward pathological shopping behavior. In response to this, many commercial brands ran campaigns supporting self-esteem and self-acceptance (Daszkiewicz, 2022).

Now, you may think that calling this a shopping addiction is going overboard. Sure, some people go crazy with their credit card now and then, and buy more stuff than they really need. But for the most part, buying too much stuff is like taking too much food off a luscious looking buffet: just a momentary indulgence that leaves you with some regret. But you'd be wrong.

Some people go overboard just about every day and plunge themselves into debt doing so. What's more, this shopping addiction of theirs can indicate other mental illnesses. For example, it is often associated with anxiety disorders, impulsive behaviors, and substance abuse. Young people are at a greater-than-average risk of developing such a shopping addiction. And though no clear gender differences have been found in the frequency of shopping, researchers have found gendered differences in terms of buying motivation (Niedermoser et al., 2021).

Like self-esteem, mood plays a large part in shaping people's buying decisions. When compulsive shoppers are in a bad mood, they are more likely to go shopping than other people. That's why compulsive or addictive shoppers are much more likely than are the general population to report feeling negative emotions before going shopping. Sadness, depression, anxiety, and boredom are among the negative emotions they report feeling before a buying spree. So, compulsive buyers are motivated to shop by negative, rather than positive, emotions.

How We Feel and How Much We'll Spend

When people feel bad about themselves—for example, when their self-esteem is under attack—they will pay a high price for a treat. Spending money when feeling sad or distressed is a common behavior for many people, and several psychological and emotional factors underlie this tendency.

One main reason people shop when they're sad is to regulate their emotions. Buying something new can provide a temporary boost in mood or serve as a distraction from negative feelings. For some, buying stuff can be a way to enhance self-esteem. Owning new or valuable items may make people feel better about themselves or compensate for sensed inadequacies. When people feel that aspects of their life are spiraling out of control, shopping can provide a sense of agency. Choosing what to buy, where to buy, and when to make a purchase can give a feeling of control in an otherwise chaotic situation. (Remember what we said at the beginning of this book about the importance of always being able to buy new socks from Amazon!)

The term "retail therapy" reflects the therapeutic effect that shopping can have at these times. It can serve as a form of escapism, allowing people to momentarily forget their problems. But negative emotions like sadness can cloud a person's judgment, leading to less rational decision-making. When sad, people may be less attentive to prices or the effects of their spending. And just as some people turn to comfort food when they're upset, others turn to comfort purchases—items that evoke warmth, nostalgia, or security.

Buying certain items, especially those that are trendy or popular, may be a way for people to feel connected to others. If shopping has been a consistent way to cope with sadness in the past, it may become a habitual response. Over time, the brain learns to associate shopping with relief from distress, reinforcing the behavior.

Shopping may provide short-term relief from sadness, but it's not a long-term solution to emotional distress. Consistently using shopping as a primary coping mechanism can lead to financial strain and doesn't address the root causes of the sadness. It's far better to seek professional help if sadness or emotional distress becomes overwhelming or persistent. That is, far better than paying a visit to Saks Fifth Avenue.

We know a lot about the effects of sadness on buying from controlled experiments that researchers have done. In one study, the researchers discovered when students learned they were in the bottom 10 percent on an assigned task, they were willing to pay a high price for an allegedly valuable item—a photograph. However, when the same photograph was described as mass-produced and of little value, students, regardless of their alleged performance, were unwilling to pay a high price for it. The researchers concluded that "an increased desire to acquire it … is better accounted for by the desire to restore one's self-worth than by the desire to signal one's wealth to others."

To repeat, people in an induced state of sadness will pay more for a consumer good than people in an emotionally neutral state. People who are depressed, for example, will pay more for a "sporty insulated water bottle" than people who are not. The result—buying an unnecessary water bottle—fits in nicely with our definition of a treat. People rarely need a water bottle, and a water bottle lacks the status to be considered a ticket or a trophy.

Consider, now, the inverse of this self-esteem and compensatory consumption issue. Will people with high self-esteem buy things that will make them feel even better? According to research, people with high levels of self-acceptance are willing to pay a premium for items that will improve their lives. They may, for example, buy a self-help book on power and influence or a subscription to a brain fitness program. People with lower self-acceptance, on the other hand, are more likely to pay a premium for items that will distract them from their sensed shortfall. Such items may include a travel magazine or a limited-edition fountain pen.

Treat Buying as a Compensatory Process

Buying oneself treats or engaging in "self-gifting" or "retail therapy" is a common behavior for various psychological, emotional, and social reasons. Some people buy themselves treats as rewards for achievements, hard work, or reaching personal milestones. This self-reward system can provide motivation and reinforce positive behaviors. Others buy treats to lift their spirits. Buying treats for oneself may bring joy, comfort, and temporary relief from stress, anxiety, or sadness. Buying treats can be seen as a form of self-care, where people indulge in products or experiences that provide relaxation, pampering, or pleasure. Buying new items, especially those seen as valuable or desirable, can boost self-esteem and confidence.

Beyond this, as we have said, some use shopping as a strategy to cope with negative emotions, personal challenges, or emotional distress. It can provide a sense of control and agency during times of doubt or instability.

People who feel insecure about their status or worth will treat themselves frequently to raise their spirits. And people who feel unpopular, overlooked, or unsuccessful may also buy themselves frequent treats to make themselves feel better.

The simplest explanations for these behaviors are psychological. The immediate pleasure gained from buying and enjoying treats often outweighs long-term financial considerations. Impulsive tendencies can lead people to buy treats without planning or consideration of the results. Buying treats can also help reduce the discomfort experienced when a gap arises between one's beliefs and behaviors. For example, rewarding oneself after a stressful period can restore a sense of balance and self-worth.

Learning theory proposes that people learn to treat or self-gift themselves the same way they learn to do everything else. They see someone else enjoying the pleasure of a gift they have given themselves, then copy this to gain the same or a similar reward.

Compensation theory, on the other hand, proposes that treat buying is motivated by needs and wishes that cannot be met immediately or directly. According to this theory, people spend money on treats to relieve negative emotions they are experiencing. Compensatory consumption is a reaction to threats to one's self-esteem. These threats are caused by a lack of personal agency (not feeling in control of one's life) or by intense emotions (feeling sad, guilty, or insecure, for example).

They may even stem from social anxieties, such as feeling excluded or inadequate in comparison to the standards of one's own group.

Both social learning theory and compensation theory should explain why some people buy things they don't need. Each, however, makes a different prediction. If social learning theory is valid, teens whose parents and peers treat themselves will be more likely than other teens to also treat themselves. If compensation theory is valid, teenagers with hostile or unsupportive parents are more likely than other teenagers to treat themselves, regardless of the behavior modeled by their parents and peers.

Without carrying out an experiment, we can't tell which theory is better at predicting self-gifting. Fortunately, a similar experiment examined the effects of learning and compensation on materialism. We will use this to get some insight into how the proposed experiment on self-gifting may go.

In an actual study, two researchers asked fifty boys and fifty girls aged 12 to 18 whether they agreed or disagreed with the following statements:

- "I feel good about myself" and "I like how I look." The answers to these questions were used to assess participants' self-esteem.
- "My mother makes me feel special" and "My mother devotes time and energy to helping me." The answers to these questions assessed parental support.
- "My friends like me for who I am," and "My friends dislike me." The answers to these questions assessed participants' peer support.
- "My mom would love to buy expensive things," and "My mom believes the more money you have, the happier you are." The answers to these questions showed how materialistic the parents of the participants were.
- "I'd love to buy expensive things" and "I think the more money you have when you grow up, the happier you'll be." The answers to these questions were used to assess the adolescents' materialism.

The study's findings supported compensation theory, not social learning theory. Adolescents who received the least support from parents and peers held the most materialistic beliefs and had the lowest self-esteem. In fact, low self-esteem was far more important in predicting materialistic views than parental or peer values. According to these findings, low self-esteem promotes materialism, and materialism is an effort to compensate for low self-esteem. It is a pattern of rewarding oneself to feel better. This finding suggests poor parenting can have negative results, such as excessive treat buying. As well, by extension this finding suggests that people who buy themselves a lot of treats are (likely) people with low self-esteem.

Love and Compensatory Spending

The idea that consumers use products to feel good about themselves is a basic principle of marketing. Yet, besides the motive to self-improve, consumers also strive to confirm their views of themselves (that is, to self-verify). Researchers also propose that low (vs. high) self-esteem consumers gravitate toward inferior products because those products confirm their pessimistic self-views.

Five studies supported this theorizing. First, they found that participants with low (as opposed to high) self-esteem preferred inferior products when—and perhaps because—those products signaled negative and pessimistic self-views, and could therefore confirmed the participants' own negative view of themselves.

Now you may be thinking to yourself, "This is pathetic. Some down-in-the-dumps mope insists on buying himself junk because he feels like junk himself. Okay, I get that. Too bad for that guy; he'll never feel right." But in fact a negative state of mind can be erased and replaced with a positive state of mind, resulting in changed behavior. According to another study, the inclination of low self-esteem consumers to choose inferior products disappears after they are induced to view themselves as worthy of superior products (Stuppy et al., 2019).

Wouldn't it be nice if all negative thinking could be erased so easily? But often it can't be, and the result is compensatory spending. With compensatory spending, people buy goods or services to address their feelings of inadequacy, discomfort, or distress and to enhance their self-image. Essentially, it's the act of shopping to compensate for sensed shortfalls in their life or self.

This behavior can be driven by various underlying emotional or psychological needs. If someone feels inadequate or insecure about a particular aspect of their identity, they may buy items they think will bolster their image. For instance, someone feeling a lack of success may buy an expensive car or branded items to portray an image of success. People may also buy things to cope with negative emotions like sadness, anxiety, or boredom. Shopping can provide a temporary emotional lift, acting as a form of retail therapy. And as we have seen, some people buy things to fit in with a specific group or social class, buying items they see as popular or status-improving within that circle.

If someone has faced financial hardship or deprivation in the past, they may overspend when they have the means, to make up for earlier times of scarcity. When people feel they lack control in certain areas of their life, they may shop as a way to exert control or agency. Shopping can also serve as a distraction from other problems or stressors, diverting attention away from unpleasant situations or feelings.

Compensatory spending provides short-term emotional relief or a boost in self-esteem. However it can lead to long-term problems if it becomes a primary coping mechanism. Over-reliance on compensatory spending can contribute to financial strain, clutter, buyer's remorse, and even compulsive buying behaviors. Recognizing the underlying motivations and triggers can help people develop healthier coping strategies and spending habits.

As mentioned earlier, people buy treats to fill an emptiness or distract themselves from feelings of anxiety, loneliness, and depression. How, you may wonder, does this relate to the most powerful expression of human need: falling in love? Is falling in love like buying a treat that one "needs" to relieve loneliness and depression? The similarity seems striking, doesn't it?

One French psychotherapist pithily described falling in love as "giving something you don't have to someone you don't know."

Constantly feeling the need to buy oneself a "treat" or reward can stem from various psychological or emotional sources. However, when this need becomes frequent or compulsive, several risks and dangers emerge. If, in reading this chapter, you have discovered you have a frequent need for treats, you should consider the following risks and dangers carefully:

- Substance abuse: For some, the idea of a treat may extend to alcohol, drugs, or other harmful substances, leading to addiction or health complications.
- Avoidance behavior: Continually seeking treats can be a way to avoid dealing with underlying emotional or psychological issues.
- Decreased resilience: Relying on external rewards for comfort can decrease the ability to cope with stress or adversity without such aids.
- Overspending: Regularly indulging in treats, especially if they're costly, can lead to financial difficulties.
- Debt accumulation: Using credit to fund these desires can lead to incurring significant debt.
- Habit formation: Over time, the brain can start associating certain actions or emotions with the need for a treat, leading to a habit that's hard to break.
- Reduced satisfaction: The more often you indulge, the less satisfying each treat becomes, leading to a need for bigger or more frequent rewards.
- External motivation: Over-reliance on treats can shift motivation from intrinsic to extrinsic, making it harder to pursue tasks without an external reward.
- Eroded discipline: Constantly giving in to the desire for treats can erode your discipline and ability to delay gratification.
- Misunderstanding or conflict: Others may not understand your constant need for treats, leading to potential conflicts, especially if shared finances are involved.
- Isolation: If the need for treats interferes with social activities or commitments, it can lead to social isolation.
- Missed opportunities: Resources (time, money, energy) spent on frequent treats may divert you from other growth opportunities or long-term goals.
- Lack of contentment: A constant need for treats can stem from or lead to a perpetual feeling of discontent with your current state.

- Overconsumption: Regularly buying material goods as treats can increase the environmental costs associated with production and disposal of such goods.
- Tolerance build-up: Over time, you may need larger or more frequent treats to achieve the same feeling of pleasure or satisfaction, like how tolerance builds with substance use.
- Decreased value: When treats are constant, the joy gained from special occasions or achievements may be diminished because the baseline for pleasure is constantly elevated.

Recognizing and addressing the root causes behind a constant need for treats is critical. This doesn't mean denying yourself all pleasures. Rather, it means understanding the motivations and ensuring that indulgences are balanced and healthy within the broader context of one's life.

As we have seen, compulsive buying is a personal and social problem. It results from an irresistible need to buy something, almost anything. And it can run people into debt. In the next chapter, we will explore the idea of *remedial treat-buying* or *retail therapy*, also known as *compulsive* or *addictive shopping*.

There, we will also discover that compensatory buying, meant to provide relief from negative emotions, offers no long-term relief from feelings like depression, loneliness, and low self-esteem. Despite people continuing to rely on shopping as a source of happiness, research suggests that material possessions don't significantly contribute to happiness.

Chapter Fourteen
Compensatory Buying, Compulsion, and Debt

As we saw in the last chapter, remedial treat-buying—retail therapy—is compulsive or addictive shopping. It is predicted by many of the same variables that predict other addictive behaviors such as substance abuse (drugs and alcohol), gambling addiction, and sex addiction.

Addictions are complex conditions characterized by compulsive, habitual behaviors that continue despite harmful results. These behaviors often provide a reward or pleasure, which reinforces the activity, creating a cycle that is hard to break. Addictions can be classified into two main categories: substance addictions and behavioral addictions.

Substance addictions include a dependency on illegal drugs (such as cocaine, heroin, or methamphetamine) or misuse of prescription medications (like opioids). They also include alcohol addiction. Also known as alcoholism, this involves the compulsive consumption of alcoholic drinks. A third kind of substance addiction is dependency on tobacco products, mainly cigarettes.

Behavioral addictions include gambling addiction, sex addiction, gaming addiction, food addiction, and shopping addiction. Gambling addiction leads to compulsive gambling despite negative financial effects. Sex addiction means compulsively engaging in sexual activities without regard to the negative effects. Internet and gaming addiction refer to excessive use of the Internet, social media, or video games in a way that interferes with daily life. Food addiction means engaging compulsively in specific eating behaviors, often linked with other disorders like bulimia or binge eating.

Finally, shopping addiction, also known as compulsive buying disorder, involves impulsive and uncontrollable buying behaviors.

All these addictions have underlying causes that range from genetic to cultural. Genetic tendencies, changes in brain function, and neurochemical imbalances are often implicated in addiction. Mental health disorders, emotional trauma, and childhood distress may increase a person's susceptibility to addiction. And family environment, social pressure, and access to addictive substances can play a significant role.

All addictions have a few common characteristics. These include compulsion—feeling an irresistible urge or compulsion to engage in the addictive behavior. Loss of control, another common characteristic of addiction, is the inability to limit or stop the addictive behavior despite attempts to do so. Addicted people tend to continue the addictive behavior despite being aware of and experiencing negative effects. They also deny, or fail to admit and recognize, the harmful effects of the addictive behavior. Finally, cravings—experiencing intense needs or cravings for the addictive substance or activity—are common among addicts.

With these symptoms in mind, researchers have identified seven major predictors of shopping addiction. These are low self-esteem, low self-regulation, negative emotional state, search for enjoyment, female gender, preference for social anonymity, and exposure to cognitive overload (Rose and Dhandayudham, 2014).

The relationship between mindfulness and compensatory buying is a growing area of research. Mindfulness is awareness and focused attention to one's actions, as well as their surroundings. Lack of mindful (attentional) awareness is significantly related to impulsive compensatory buying. An increase in mindful attention to the present moment may influence people to make more thoughtful decisions rather than acting impulsively. Impulsivity may be associated with compensatory buying because impulsive people may not pay much attention to internal (e.g., mood) or external (e.g., debt) stimuli. They pay much more attention to the potential short-term rewards associated with compensatory buying (Brunelle and Grossman, 2022).

Research repeatedly finds women are more likely to be compulsive and addictive shoppers than men. Perhaps this is because in Western countries women are expected to do most of the family's shopping. They fulfill a recognized and rewarded social role when they shop. As well, shopping has traditionally been a social activity, providing women with social interaction (with other shoppers or retail employees). By contrast, men tend to dislike and avoid shopping.

For people who crave anonymity and an absence of interaction, the anonymity of online shopping is a key benefit, promoting frequent and extended shopping activities. For many people, therefore, the online retail environment may increase buying. Anonymity also lets the buyer keep their buying habits hidden from others, including members of their family.

Now you may think that people who shop online are likely to buy less stuff than usual, because they do not see other people around them modelling the pleasures of shopping. But you would be wrong. People who shop online tend to buy *more* than other consumers.

That's because shopping online allows the consumer to feel less restricted. When people are online and cannot be seen by others, they feel less inhibited in their shopping behavior. Thus, disinhibition is a distinguishing feature of Internet behavior, and one that promotes many kinds of inappropriate or impulsive behavior. The anonymity of the online environment encourages inappropriately excessive shopping because controls are lacking. This includes the absence of environmental cues, such as other people's response behaviors.

However, both in-person and online shopping provide arousal, a factor that encourages compulsive buying. Graphic displays and "pop ups" displaying product information or announcements of special deals are two kinds of exciting stimuli that tempt repeated buying.

Faced with such stimuli, many people experience cognitive overload. Increases in a person's cognitive load tend to overpower self-control, resulting in a loss of willpower. This depletion of resources increases the power of temptation and leads to impulsive buying.

Retailers and marketers use many strategies to overcome consumers' resistance to buying, aiming to encourage purchases. For example, limited-time offers, flash sales, and countdown timers encourage quick decision-making. Phrases like "while supplies last" or "limited stock" can spur faster action. Highlighting popular or trending products creates a fear of missing out on something desirable or valuable. Sales, discounts, and promotions make consumers feel they are getting a deal, which can justify the purchase.

Beyond that, retailers are likely to use eye-catching displays that draw attention to specific products. Placing impulse buys near the checkout areas can encourage last-minute additions to the shopping cart. And pleasant music, appealing scents, and comfortable lighting create an enjoyable shopping atmosphere, positively influencing customers' mood and openness to buying.

Does Compensatory Spending Work?

No, it doesn't. Compensatory spending—spending money to provide relief from anxiety or depression—is a false cure. This is the case whether you are an adolescent seeking approval from peers or a lonely older person looking for a bit of social interaction. Spending does not provide long-term relief from feelings of depression, loneliness, or low self-esteem. It is only a temporary solution.

This finding is consistent with a large and growing body of research on happiness, contentment, and life satisfaction. Once people have the necessities of life, additional income (and the things money can buy) has only a limited influence on happiness. Extra money (and the things it can buy) contributes little to happiness among people who live above the subsistence level. In terms of happiness and life satisfaction, money is unimportant to middle- and upper-income people, when compared with good health, good family relationships, and a fulfilling job.

Overall, happiness research shows material possessions are unimportant in the face of low self-esteem. Despite this, many people continue to turn to shopping to make themselves feel better.

Debt and Compensatory Spending

People need money to buy themselves treats, and many people buy on credit if they don't have the cash. Credit is so easily available today that it's easy to assume this has always been the case; but widespread consumer borrowing is relatively new, dating back only about eighty years.

People (rightly) expected a higher standard of living after all the sacrifices required by World War II. That higher standard of living was achieved through two channels: public spending and private investments. In Canada, the federal government provided financial help to everyone who had served in the war. In the U.S., the Department of Veterans Affairs provided loans to veterans' families, allowing them to buy new homes with a small down payment and a large mortgage.

Equally important, new shopping malls and department stores sprang up all over the country, and stores began encouraging consumers to make large purchases "on credit." This credit buying allowed them to acquire household appliances and luxuries such as television sets with small consumer loans from individual stores. Some consumers were earning enough money to buy expensive refrigerators, cars, and houses on credit, confident they could repay their loans eventually.

Banks also contributed to the new postwar debt culture. They expanded financial services by offering people credit cards and lines of credit. Gradually, debtors became more and more fully bound to the institutions that lent them money. Debt enabled people to buy more, but it also bound them to particular jobs and lifestyles.

Credit cards became widely available during the 1970s. Credit card companies promoted and normalized debt in North American culture, rather than encouraging prudent borrowing. Can't afford it? No worries. Just use your credit card to borrow money from the bank. Baby Boomers, the children of postwar borrowers, grew up in this new culture of indebted living. It gave them an expectation of comfort and pleasure, through credit buying.

Consumers who paid off their credit card debt every month did not accrue interest charges and thus were not profitable for lenders. Banks preferred to loan money to people who could not pay their bills on time each month. Most of them would eventually pay off their debts, but their unpaid balances would accrue interest charges. Increasingly, banks expanded their offerings so people could even use credit cards to pay for household bills and insurance.

Financial services marketing further encouraged compensatory spending habits. To this day, the North American middle-class lifestyle is "artificial," only possible through credit financing. According to data from Statistics Canada, the median indebtedness of Canadians as of 2019 varies significantly by age. The average debts are as follows:

Under 35:	$19,000
35 to 44:	$35,200
45 to 54:	$55,000
55 to 64:	$30,000
65 and older:	$10,000

From 2021 to 2022, consumer debt increased significantly, and this was especially true for credit card debt. The average monthly spending per credit card increased by 17.5 per cent in the first quarter of 2022 compared to the previous year, according to a report by Equifax Canada. In the report, Rebecca Oakes of Equifax Canada stated that "Gen Z and Millennials are driving up higher consumer spending the most. With gas and food prices increasing at a higher rate than overall inflation, it's very important for consumers to revisit their budget allocations."

In short, we now live in a debt-based culture. People are more likely to engage in compensatory spending now that debt is normalized. Yet 39 percent of Canadians say they are overwhelmed by debt. Mortgage debt accounts for 26 percent of this total, followed by credit card debt (18 percent), car financing (17 percent), and line of credit balances (17 percent). But people continue to incur debt by spending more than they earn. Every month, half of all Canadians spend their entire paycheck or more. Some part of this indebtedness is due to treat buying.

Deviant Spending

Excessive treat buying is especially common among impulsive consumers—people who spend money on a whim, without forethought. But impulsive buying is normal in some situations.

Innovations, such as self-service kiosks, product exchange offers, credit cards and monthly instalment schemes, have significantly simplified shopping for consumers. Consequently, impulsive and frivolous buying has become effortless, and a topic of great interest to academics.

Researchers define *impulse buying* as an unplanned and unintended purchase made rapidly, on the spot, without much reflection, preceded by exposure to a stimulus and a sudden and powerful buying urge. While practical considerations influence planned and habitual buying, high-arousal emotions and hedonic (pleasure-seeking) motives are more likely to influence impulse buying.

Marketers and retailers traditionally use in-store promotions and advertising to trigger impulse shopping. From consumers' perspective, a moderate level of impulse buying is relatively harmless and considered a socially acceptable recreational activity. Excessive levels, however, can be harmful to shoppers and lead to financial and psychological hardship.

Today, impulse buying accounts for a large proportion of sales within the modern retail industry. In the United States alone, impulse purchases generate $17.78 billion in annual profit for retailers, with consumers spending an average of $5400 per year on unplanned purchases. In 2020–22, the COVID-19 crisis led to a surge in impulse shopping. Surveys show that American consumers' average monthly spending on impulse purchases increased by 18 percent from the beginning of the pandemic (Redine et al., 2022).

In Las Vegas, sudden and impulsive shopping is part of the city's sex, gambling, and drinking culture. Sex, gambling, and alcohol—all parts of the Las Vegas experience—attract and encourage impulsive spending by visitors. Sudden windfalls (such as gambling wins) motivate people to spend impulsively. As well, remorse over misbehavior or gambling losses also motivates spending, as consumers seek to make themselves feel better.

This is what the slogan "What happens in Vegas stays in Vegas" means. There, actions considered deviant or improper in any other setting are seemingly excused. They are not talked about in places where they may cause shame or embarrassment.

In other words, Las Vegas has evolved into a "deviance service center"—a place where misbehavior (including impulsive buying) is acceptable and even encouraged as part of the "Vegas experience." One can indulge in heavy drinking, high-stakes gambling, sex with strangers, and big-ticket impulse buys without feeling guilty! It's all part of a brief "fantasy life" that says nothing about who you are, only where you are.

The airport—any airport—is another example. Like casinos, airports separate people from their normal activities. In both locations, people buy impulsively as a treat for themselves, or to bring home a souvenir of the trip for a spouse or children. Some airports report that non-aviation sources (such as shopping) account for up to 53 percent of total airport revenues. People are also more likely to buy on impulse at airports because they are under time constraints and feel they must decide quickly.

As we've said repeatedly, treats, ranging from food to luxury items, are often bought during moments of sadness or low self-esteem. When people experience sadness or a sense of powerlessness, shopping offers them choices, restoring a sense of personal control and reducing sadness. Emotions, especially negative ones like sadness, anxiety, and boredom, drive compulsive shoppers to engage in retail therapy. When people are feeling down, they are willing to spend more on items they see as valuable or those that may raise their mood or status. And they do this even if these items aren't objectively valuable or necessary.

Compensatory or compulsive buying involves buying stuff as a way to cope with stress and negative emotions, or to achieve a temporary feeling of happiness. So buying can offer a short-lived boost in mood. However over-reliance on such behavior can result in various risks and dangers. Perhaps, while reading this chapter, you have realized you rely too much on compensatory spending and retail therapy. If so, here are some risks and dangers to consider:

- Debt: One of the most immediate risks is accumulating substantial debt, especially if purchases are made using credit.
- Financial insecurity: Spending beyond your means can jeopardize your ability to pay for essential expenses or save for future needs.
- Temporary relief: Shopping can provide momentary relief from negative emotions but does not address their root causes, leading to a cycle of buying and regret.
- Increased stress: The initial euphoria from buying can be replaced by stress or anxiety, especially when you consider the financial effects.
- Addictive behavior: Compulsive buying can become an addiction,

like substance abuse, where increasing amounts of shopping are required to achieve the same "high."
- Strain on relationships: Disagreements over finances or the implications of compulsive buying can cause tension in your personal relationships.
- Secrecy: You may try to hide your buying habits from loved ones due to guilt or fear of judgment, leading to mistrust.
- Accumulation of unnecessary items: Frequent purchases, especially of items not truly needed, can lead to cluttered living spaces, which can be mentally overwhelming and create additional stress.
- Post-purchase regret: The realization that you have spent beyond your means, or bought unnecessary items, can lead to feelings of regret.
- Guilt: This can emerge from recognizing the impulsive nature of the purchase or the financial implications it may hold.
- External validation: Reliance on retail therapy can shift the basis of your self-worth from internal qualities to external possessions.
- Identity crisis: Continuous buying can lead to confusion about your identity, especially if you buy stuff to fit into certain trends or societal molds.
- Overconsumption: Compulsive buying contributes to overconsumption, which has environmental implications due to increased production, transportation, and waste.
- Fast fashion consequences: Retail therapy that is focused on constantly changing fashion trends may support industries known for unsustainable practices and poor working conditions.
- Neglecting underlying issues: Using shopping as a coping mechanism can prevent you from seeking healthier ways to deal with stress or negative emotions, such as therapy, exercise, or meditation.
- Opportunity cost: Money spent on impulsive purchases could have been used for more fulfilling experiences or personal growth opportunities.
- Economic vulnerability: Over-reliance on credit to fund retail therapy can expose you to economic vulnerabilities, like increased interest rates or inability to pay back loans.
- Time consumption: Excessive shopping, especially when it's a form of

procrastination, can waste a lot of time that you could have used more productively or enjoyably.

Understanding the reasons behind your compensatory or compulsive buying and finding healthier coping mechanisms is essential for long-term well-being. If you find yourself repeatedly turning to retail therapy, it may be sensible to seek professional help or counseling to address the underlying issues.

In the next chapter, we focus on the role of comfort food as a treat, and the results of relying on comfort food for emotional relief.

Chapter Fifteen
Comfort Food and Other Treats

You may think that people eat when they're hungry and don't eat when they're not hungry: end of story. And people who eat more than they "need" are just responding politely to other people's invitations to "eat a little more." But you'd be wrong.

Buying and consuming food is one popular, cheap, and effective way of improving your mood. That's why we have a category called "comfort food." *Comfort food* refers to foods that are typically high in calories, carbohydrates, fats, and/or sugar, and are often linked with a nostalgic or sentimental feeling. These foods are sought after because they provide a sense of well-being and can help soothe negative feelings.

By why do comfort foods provide comfort? Partly, the desire for comfort foods is innate. Consider the taste infants have for sweets. Infants as young as 7 months of age show food patterns that can also be observed in older children and adults. Between the ages of 7 and 24 months, from 18 percent to 33 percent of infants and toddlers refuse to eat vegetables, and 23 percent to 33 percent don't eat fruit. French fries are one of the three most common "vegetables" consumed by infants 9 to 11 months of age.

By 15 to 18 months, French fries are the "vegetable" toddlers most often agree to eat. Almost half (46 percent) of 7- to 8-month-olds consume some type of dessert, sweet, or sweetened beverage, and this percentage increases as age increases. By 19 to 24 months, 62 percent of toddlers will consume a baked dessert, 20 percent consume candy, and 44 percent consume a sweetened beverage (Fox et al., 2004).

People like eating sweets for various reasons, including biological, psychological, and cultural factors. Humans evolved to seek out high-calorie foods as a survival mechanism in times when food was scarce. Eating sweets also stimulates the release of dopamine, a neurotransmitter associated with pleasure and reward, which creates a feeling of happiness or satisfaction.

Thus, humans are born with a preference for sweet tastes. Babies' preference for sweet flavors is thought to be related to the sweetness of mother's milk. From birth, sweets are associated with comfort and reward. Sweet treats are often also associated with positive memories, celebrations, and holidays, contributing to a sense of nostalgia and a desire to recreate those happy moments.

The widespread availability of sweet foods in our society also makes them accessible and appealing to people. In the United States and elsewhere, government agricultural policy and technical breakthroughs have led to an immense increase in production of high-fructose corn syrup, which has become a near-ubiquitous additive in processed foods—even ones that normally are not thought of as being sweet.

Sweets are a central part of many cultural traditions and celebrations, further reinforcing their desirability. Beyond that, the combination of sweetness, fat, and salt found in many sweet treats creates a pleasurable sensory experience. There is a vast variety of sweet foods available, and new products are constantly being developed, keeping the category exciting and appealing.

In summary, the desire for sweets is rooted in a complex interplay of biological drives, emotional needs, cultural influences, and sensory pleasures. Enjoying sweets in moderation is a normal part of a balanced diet.

Innate tastes aside, sweet comfort foods often have strong emotional associations. They may remind people of happier times, childhood memories, and special occasions. Eating these foods can evoke these memories and bring a sense of nostalgia and warmth. As well, foods high in carbohydrates can increase the level of serotonin, a neurotransmitter associated with feelings of calm and happiness. The brain can link the relief from distress to these foods, leading to a craving for them during times of stress or sadness.

Researchers have found that the desire to eat comfort food and expect a hedonic reward (i.e., a feeling of pleasure) depends to some degree on the interaction with music and location. More specifically, both eating at home and hearing relaxing music significantly increases a person's desire to eat comfort food and expect a hedonic reward. Further, a desire to eat comfort food leads people to pick foods with a high calorie content (Mathiesen et al., 2022). People who want comfort foods want high-calorie eating.

Many comfort foods are traditionally shared dishes, associated with family gatherings, celebrations, or communal meals. So the act of eating them can evoke feelings of belonging and love.

High-fat, high-sugar foods can also provide a feeling of fullness and satiety. This physical sensation can be reassuring for some people, especially during moments of emotional turmoil. For them, eating can serve as a distraction from emotional pain, stress, or anxiety. Consuming comfort foods becomes for them a way to temporarily escape or alleviate negative feelings.

The definition of comfort food varies across cultures and regions. In cold climates, for example, hearty and warm dishes may be favored for the physical warmth they provide. Comfort food can provide short-term relief from negative emotions. However, consistently using food as a coping mechanism can lead to unhealthy eating habits, weight gain, and other health-related issues. It's best to enjoy comfort foods in moderation and balance them with other coping strategies for dealing with stress and emotions. In other words, if you're feeling down, either eat a cream puff or ask a friend to compliment you. Both will make you feel better, but the latter is less fattening.

Overeating is a common behavior influenced by various factors, ranging from biological and psychological to environmental and social. Some of the factors that cause people to overeat are hormonal.

Hormones play a critical role in regulating hunger and satiety. Imbalances in hormones like ghrelin (which increases appetite) and leptin (which signals fullness) can lead to increased hunger and a tendency to overeat. Some people may be genetically predisposed to have a higher appetite and a tendency to overeat. These factors aside, foods high in fat, sugar, and salt can trigger the release of neurotransmitters like dopamine, creating a sense of pleasure and reward, which can encourage overeating.

As we noted earlier, people often eat in response to emotions like stress, anxiety, sadness, or boredom, rather than physical hunger. Distractions during meals (like watching television or scrolling through social media on your phone) can also lead to a lack of awareness of the quantity of food consumed, leading to overeating. Some people may develop an addictive-like relationship with certain types of food, particularly those high in sugar, fat, and salt.

However, many other social and cultural factors also play a part in overeating, and especially the overeating of high-calorie foods. For example, larger portion sizes can lead to overeating, as (not surprisingly) people tend to eat more when more food is placed in front of them. Easy access to high-calorie, palatable food can contribute to overeating. People often eat more when they are in social settings, influenced by the amount others are eating. Indeed, in some cultures, there is a social expectation to eat large quantities of food or to always finish the food on one's plate. Food advertising, especially for high-calorie, palatable foods, can increase cravings and encourage overconsumption.

Eating out of habit, rather than responding to physical hunger cues, can lead to overeating. Using food as a reward or as a way to celebrate can also establish patterns of overeating. A lack of understanding about portion sizes, calorie content, and the importance of a balanced diet can contribute to overeating. Finally, failing to practice mindful eating, which involves paying full attention to the experience of eating and drinking, can lead to overconsumption.

Understanding the factors that contribute to overeating is critical for developing strategies to prevent it and promote healthier eating habits.

Now, you may think that some people occasionally eat more than they need to make themselves feel better, but that doing so is nothing like alcohol or drug addiction. But that's not true. In fact, it's almost exactly like alcohol and drug addiction.

Throughout the world, more and more researchers are studying eating disorders such as food addiction, binge eating, anorexia, and rising obesity rates. And according to one theory, people become addicted to food in the same way people become addicted to drugs. Food addiction can then lead to overeating, which can lead to weight gain or obesity. Some have provided clinical accounts of self-identified food addicts who use food to escape a bad mood.

Some experts have also applied the substance abuse criteria in the *Diagnostic and Statistical Manual of Mental Disorders*, Fifth Edition (DSM-V) to human food addiction. And, with the increased use of brain imaging, clinical studies have revealed food craving activates the same brain regions as those signaled by drug craving.

Binge eating is an obvious symptom of food addiction. Some have suggested binge eating is like traditional drug addiction. Binge eating, also known as bingeing, alternates rapid consumption with abstinence or deprivation. And because binge eaters often consume sugary or fatty foods, many have developed a concurrent sugar addiction. When the abused substance is no longer available or is chemically blocked, withdrawal symptoms emerge.

Researchers have discovered evidence of addiction in sugar-bingeing rats. However, the addiction-like behavioral and neurochemical changes associated with binge-eating fat-rich foods have yet to be fully documented in humans. Indeed, work remains to be done on food-bingeing behaviors and their causes in general. The body of research on bulimia— binge eating followed by purging—is also growing, but gaps remain.

Evidence on eating disorders such as bulimia and anorexia shows that sociocultural factors play a part. These include media and peer influences, family stresses, depression, low self-esteem, and body dissatisfaction. These are all proposed causes of eating disorder, none of which are enough on their own. However, as a first guess, eating disorders may be one way for people to cope with issues of identity and personal control. In short, people seek out food treats when they are unhappy with themselves.

Self-Esteem and Eating Disorders

Self-esteem, which refers to a person's overall sense of self-worth or personal value, has a complex relationship with eating disorders. Numerous studies have shown that low self-esteem can be both a contributor to and result of eating disorders.

People with low self-esteem often have a negative perception of their body. Societal pressures, which emphasize certain body ideals, may exacerbate feelings of inadequacy or unattractiveness. These feelings may lead people to engage in disordered eating behaviors in attempts to achieve their ideal body shape and size. Some people with low self-esteem strive for perfection in various areas of their lives, including their appearance. This may lead to restrictive eating or over-exercising in the pursuit of a "perfect" body. For those who feel a lack of control in their lives, regulating food intake may be a way to regain a sense of mastery or control. Low self-esteem may make these people more susceptible to using food as a coping mechanism.

As eating disorders progress, they often further erode an individual's self-worth. Despite efforts to control food and body size, many people with eating disorders continue to feel that they are not "good enough," perpetuating a vicious cycle. Many people with eating disorders experience feelings of shame about their behavior and go to great lengths to hide their disorder, further isolating themselves and decreasing their self-esteem.

Positive feedback on weight loss or appearance can serve as validation for people with low self-esteem, reinforcing the behaviors associated with the eating disorder. If people can't achieve their strict and often unrealistic standards, their self-esteem may further decrease, leading them to intensify their disordered eating behaviors.

Both low self-esteem and eating disorders are often associated with other psychological disorders, especially depression and anxiety. Under this circumstance, people with eating disorders often withdraw from social situations, especially those involving food. This can lead to feelings of loneliness and further decrease self-esteem. Finally, the secretive and isolating nature of eating disorders can strain relationships with friends and family, leading to further decreases in self-worth.

In summary, self-esteem and eating disorders are deeply interconnected. Low self-esteem can contribute to the onset and perpetuation of eating disorders, and the disorders themselves often further degrade self-worth. Addressing both the physical and psychological aspects of eating disorders, including self-esteem issues, is critical in the recovery process. Recovery from eating disorders is not just about restoring physical health but also about building up self-esteem. Without addressing underlying self-worth issues, relapse is likely.

Now, we may ask, what is the connection between eating disorders and compulsive buying, addictive buying, and retail therapy? Eating disorders and compulsive buying (or addictive buying) are distinct conditions, but they share some overlapping features, especially in the underlying psychological mechanisms and emotional triggers.

Both eating disorders and compulsive buying serve as maladaptive strategies for managing negative emotions, stress, or trauma. For some, restrictive eating or binging and purging provide a temporary sense of control or relief from distress. Similarly, compulsive buying can offer a short-lived euphoria or distraction from unpleasant feelings. Both disorders are characterized by challenges with impulse control. For instance, binge eating and compulsive shopping both arise from an inability to resist immediate gratification, even in the face of negative long-term consequences.

People with either condition are seeking external validation. In the context of eating disorders, this could manifest as a desire to fit societal standards of beauty or thinness. With compulsive buying, acquiring new and often unnecessary items may be seen as a way to gain admiration, fit in, or bolster self-esteem. Low self-esteem is a common thread in many psychological disorders, including both eating disorders and compulsive buying. The perceived "failures" (for example, a binge episode or impulsive shopping spree) can further decrease self-worth, creating a reinforcing cycle.

Eating disorders and compulsive buying coexist with other psychological conditions like depression, anxiety, and personality disorders. These comorbid conditions influence and exacerbate the primary disorder. Of note is the new concept of "poly-dependencies" that involve common behaviors and trap sufferers in a vicious circle. One recent study found a direct effect of anxiety on eating disorders and on compulsive buying behavior. However, self-esteem mediated the effect of anxiety in slightly different ways. Specifically, the effect of anxiety varied depending on whether a person with an eating disorder was a compulsive or a non-compulsive buyer (De Pasquale et al., 2021).

Many people with eating disorders or compulsive buying behaviors engage in secretive behaviors due to feelings of shame or fear of judgment. This can lead to isolation and strained relationships, further exacerbating mental and emotional distress. Also, some people may switch between these maladaptive behaviors over time. For instance, someone may turn to compulsive buying during periods of recovery from an eating disorder, essentially replacing one coping mechanism with another.

Research has suggested that there may be similar neurobiological mechanisms at play in both conditions, particularly in areas of the brain related to reward and impulse control. As well, both disorders can be influenced by societal pressures and cultural ideals. The modern consumerist culture often equates possessions with success and happiness, just as it frequently emphasizes thinness as an ideal.

Recognizing the interconnectedness of these conditions is critical for clinicians and therapists, as it can influence treatment approaches. A holistic understanding of a patient's behaviors and triggers can aid in the development of more effective intervention strategies.

Compulsive food-buying, sometimes likened to forms of compulsive or impulsive shopping, often involves buying excessive amounts of food, often beyond what is needed or can reasonably be consumed. In reading this chapter, you may have realized you have a problem with buying and eating too much food. If so, you should consider some of the dangers and risks associated with this.

- Overeating: Having excess food readily available can lead to overconsumption, especially if there's a compulsion to eat what has been bought to prevent waste.
- Unbalanced diet: Compulsive buying may focus on specific types of foods, potentially leading to an unbalanced diet. For instance, if someone compulsively buys snack foods or sweets, it may result in excessive intake of sugars, fats, and salts.

- Health risks: Regular overconsumption of high-calorie foods can lead to weight gain, obesity, and associated health risks like heart disease, diabetes, and joint problems.
- Guilt and shame: Similar to other forms of compulsive behavior, people may feel guilt or shame after realizing they've purchased excessive food or allowed it to go to waste.
- Stress: The realization of overspending, wasting resources, or gaining weight can lead to increased stress.
- Avoidance and denial: People may avoid confronting their compulsive behavior, leading to further isolation and perpetuation of the issue.
- Increased waste: Excess food that is *not* consumed usually ends up as waste, contributing to environmental problems.
- Carbon footprint: The production, transportation, and disposal of excess food contributes to carbon emissions and other environmental impacts.
- Strain on relationships: The financial implications of compulsive food buying, coupled with the potential health risks, can strain personal relationships.
- Isolation: People may withdraw from social events or gatherings out of embarrassment or to hide their compulsive behavior.
- Clutter: Buying excessive amounts of food requires ample storage space, leading to cluttered living spaces, which can increase feelings of overwhelm and stress.
- Pest attraction: Stored food, especially if not properly sealed or if left to expire, can attract pests.
- Skewed priorities: Spending too much money on food can mean neglecting other essential expenses, such as bills, health needs, or other important personal or family requirements.
- Increased tolerance: Over time, the amount of food consumed may need to increase to achieve the same "relief," akin to how tolerance builds in addictive behaviors.

Understanding the reasons behind a food addiction is critical for addressing the issue. People with a food addiction should seek counseling or therapy to explore underlying emotional triggers and develop healthier coping mechanisms. Additionally, practical measures, such as creating shopping lists, setting budgets, or shopping with a trusted friend or family member, can help curb compulsive buying behaviors. Similarly, counseling, planning, and social support will eventually help a person to overcome their food addiction.

Given the deep emotional connection many people make with the things they buy, it's not surprising that many people find nostalgic purchases to be especially appealing. With this in mind, let's now talk about the role of nostalgia in marketing and selling consumer goods.

Chapter Sixteen
Nostalgia Marketing

Nostalgia is the sentimental or wistful affection for the past, typically for a period or place with happy personal associations. People often think of it as a return to something we used to enjoy. It's a complex emotional state that often involves fondly reflecting on previous experiences, objects, or people that were significant in one's life.

Nostalgic advertising appeals that emphasize a bittersweet yearning for the past typically make use of four themes: self-restoration, continuity, social relationships, and culture. As well, some "moderators" (or marketing features) make nostalgic appeals in advertising more effective, including such things as the advertisement's emotional flow, the kind of consumption being portrayed in (or encouraged by) the advertisement, and other elements (Srivastava et al., 2022).

Nostalgia reawakens sentimental, warm and fond feelings about a person's past experiences. As such, it's mainly a positive emotion. However, nostalgia can also include feelings of loss or longing for the past, resulting in a bittersweet or melancholic mood. For most people, however, nostalgia serves as a comforting emotion that provides solace and reassurance during times of stress, loneliness, or doubt.

Typically, nostalgia involves reminiscing about the past, bringing up specific memories, events, people, places, or experiences. Often, people engaging in nostalgic reflection idealize or romanticize the past, focusing on positive aspects and downplaying negative ones. Nostalgia also allows people to view their life and identity from a broader perspective, connecting the past with the present and future.

People often share their nostalgic memories with others, fostering social connection and strengthening bonds with family and friends. Engaging in activities that help preserve or collect artifacts, memorabilia, or tokens from the past is a common behavior among nostalgic people.

Nostalgic sentiments can be triggered by various stimuli. Smells, sounds, tastes, or visual cues can trigger nostalgic feelings, instantly transporting people back to a specific time or place in their minds. Milestones, transitions, or significant life events often prompt people to reflect nostalgically on their past. The loss of a loved one, ending a significant relationship, or changing one's environment can also evoke nostalgia as a way to cope and find comfort.

Nostalgia serves important psychological functions. For example, it helps us ease feelings of anxiety or sadness, providing a sense of consolation and comfort. Reflecting on the past contributes to a stronger sense of identity and self-continuity. Sharing nostalgic memories also fosters a sense of belonging and strengthens social ties. Nostalgic reflection can provide life with a sense of meaning and purpose. However, excessively idealizing the past without recognizing or addressing current realities can hinder personal growth and adaptation to present circumstances.

Originally, the word nostalgia meant "homesickness" in Greek, and that may be something useful to keep in mind. Many things, both tangible and intangible, make people nostalgic and lead to the purchase of nostalgic goods. For example, nostalgic people define themselves as having grown up in a particular era, and they feel nostalgic when they recall that era.

Successful marketing campaigns often increase their effectiveness by incorporating nostalgia. Nostalgia in marketing can make people feel happier and more powerful by reminding them of times in their lives when they felt successful, happy, and sometimes even powerful. Evoking a sense of nostalgia for our own personal past is especially effective because it reminds us of a time, usually twenty or thirty years ago, that we fondly recall. Thus, it represents a "personal best" image of ourselves.

A marketer who can make someone nostalgic is more likely to persuade them to buy their product or service. An older person is more likely to be affected by nostalgia than a younger person because the older person has more history, making nostalgia more powerful. Because nostalgia is associated with strong social bonds and the warmth of self-esteem, people use it to cope with negative emotions by recalling happy memories. Nostalgia for a brand or product, which associates a product with warm feelings, is one factor that drives purchases.

Nostalgia causes people to reflect fondly on their past. One way to look at nostalgia is as a person's tendency to seek emotional comfort in a familiar past. People who are going through a lot of trouble, turmoil, or change (such as moving, divorce, or retirement) are more likely to have nostalgic feelings than others. A century ago, some doctors thought nostalgia was a mental illness that caused people to feel depressed. Others, conversely, discovered nostalgia can make you happy. Knowing this, marketers began to view nostalgia favorably.

Nostalgia and Feelings

Because nostalgia is associated with enchantment, which has a strong positive effect on people, many consumers find it appealing. However, researchers haven't done much work on why and how nostalgia marketing makes people happy.

What emotions do people experience when they recall the good old days? To find out, researchers have examined people's written descriptions of nostalgic experiences and the emotions they expressed. The stories they told showed how nostalgia can elicit various emotions. Warmth, joy, affection, and gratitude were mixed with sadness and desire, or a longing for something else. When we think about things we used to love and things we've lost, we can feel both sad and happy.

When people are nostalgic, they do not place as much value on money as they normally do. Indeed, when they reflect on their past, various emotions bubble to the surface. People may even feel as if they can communicate with people from the past. People who are excessively nostalgic seem to enter an emotional, non-rational state. They become more willing to consider new products and to consider these products in a less rational way.

We can identify two kinds of nostalgia: personal and group (or collective) nostalgia. *Personal nostalgia* is the wish to return to a time in which one was a participant—for example, a family vacation when you were a child. *Collective nostalgia*, on the other hand, makes us want to return to a time experienced by an entire country, generation, or culture. Donald Trump's "Make America Great Again" slogan was successful in capturing this collective nostalgia and converting it into votes.

In many ways, nostalgia—a fanciful and distorted vision of one's personal past—is like other fanciful visions of the past. Consider the example of so-called "Orientalism." Many people from the Global North travel to the Global South because they want to experience life in a different way than they do at home. Edward Said (1935–2003) coined the term "Orientalism" to describe something like this. According to him, much of the early Western "understanding" of the East was based on projection and imagination, which served important economic and geopolitical needs. It allowed people to imagine another part of the world in ways that were safe and comfortable—also, subordinate.

Said, a Palestinian-American professor of literature at Columbia University, became best known for his work on postcolonial studies, particularly his book *Orientalism* (1978). There, Said critiques the Western representation of the East (particularly the Middle East) as a way of exerting power over it. He argued that the West has a long history of portraying Eastern societies as exotic, backward, uncivilized, and at times dangerous, a characterization that has served to justify colonial and imperial ambitions. "Orientalism" as a construct, he argued, is not a neutral or objective portrayal of the East but is deeply entwined with power dynamics.

In short, because of their ignorance and colonial ambition, Westerners are more likely to think that Easterners are less developed socially, technologically, and morally. When Westerners "orientalise" another group of people, they imagine a society that is backward but under control. And in many ways, that is what we imagine when we get nostalgic about the past: a world that was simpler than the world today—also, backward and under control.

Marketing's Use of Nostalgia

Based on what we've discussed so far in this book, one might think using nostalgia to market goods is unlikely to succeed. As a culture we are fascinated by new things, not old ones; we idealize progress and the future, and always want to "get ahead." Nonetheless, nostalgia, a sentimental longing for the past, is a powerful emotion that marketers often harness to connect with consumers and promote products or services.

Marketers use nostalgia in a wide variety of ways to sell their products. Many brands reintroduce older, beloved products from their lineup or revive discontinued ones because of consumer demand. (McDonald's, for instance, regularly brings back old menu items like the "McRib" sandwich for a limited time, and to celebrate its sixtieth anniversary, Tim Hortons brought back "vintage" donuts like the dutchie and the blueberry fritter that had been dropped from the menu over the years.) These classic products evoke memories of the past and can attract both older consumers who are familiar with them and younger ones intrigued by their "retro" appeal. Other products that use narratives harken back to "the good old days" and can also connect emotionally with consumers. Advertisements may depict scenes from previous decades that emphasize values, aesthetics, or experiences that resonate with certain age groups.

Packaging designs that mimic historical versions or use visual cues from past decades can also evoke feelings of nostalgia. Vintage fonts, colors, and graphics are especially effective. Brands with a long history can leverage their legacy by emphasizing their timelessness, tradition, and consistency over the years. Similarly, featuring celebrities from past decades or reusing older commercials with familiar faces can appeal to consumers' nostalgic feelings.

Using iconic tunes or jingles from past decades can immediately trigger memories and emotions. The right soundtrack can transport consumers back to a particular time in their lives. Incorporating TV shows, movies, toys, games, or other cultural touchpoints from the past in advertisements can also evoke nostalgia.

Even platforms like Instagram, Facebook, or TikTok can be used to engage with users over shared memories, or run campaigns that encourage users to share their nostalgic moments related to the brand. As well, brands can collaborate to release products that merge nostalgia from multiple sources. For example, a clothing brand may partner with a classic video game or cartoon to create themed merchandise.

Using nostalgia in marketing can, however, be a double-edged sword. Recalling the past is effective in evoking emotions and establishing a connection with the audience. However, over-reliance on the past can make a brand seem outdated.

Marketers sometimes use historical nostalgia to make the past seem like it occurred before the audience was born. The advertisement, like a historical romance—or *Star Wars*—is set a long time ago in a place far away. The characters are idealized and larger than life. They are also symbolic heroes, rather than people. The values are traditional and conservative, as they would be in an era when (people imagine) times were good. The fictional "golden age" removes real-world negatives (such as war, crime, and disease) while increasing virtues everyone can agree on (goodness, faith, and generosity). To make this work, marketers have to persuade consumers to think about people they don't know and to feel they share something with those people by buying a certain product.

Nostalgia marketing can also be used to remind people of a company's history while distracting them from the brand's current state. Bushells was an Australian tea company founded in 1883. However, in the late 1970s, the Bushell family sold the company to an English firm, Brooke Bond. (Brooke Bond in turn was bought out by consumer goods giant Unilever, which still owns the Bushell tea brand.) Despite foreign ownership, Bushells continued to emphasize its Australian roots when marketing to Australians, using local symbols and images and selling old Bushells items as memorabilia.

Marketers sometimes use nostalgia to link a product to a certain time. Luxury brands like Dolce and Gabbana can't get new customers by being the cheapest or the most cost-effective. Instead, they promote such qualities as authenticity, heritage, craftsmanship, and the brand's overall reputation.

For instance, in advertisements Dolce and Gabbana highlights its Italian heritage by using symbols like the Italian flag. In one ad, we see a picture of a boy with a white bow tie. This picture is meant to show the long-standing Catholic tradition of First Communion. These and other images work together to make the consumer feel nostalgic about the Italian way of life.

Playful nostalgia can turn history into a show, but that does not mean the show is a faithful picture of reality. Marketers can use nostalgia to play with historical facts in many ways, like showing George Washington crossing the Delaware River in a modern yacht or Benjamin Franklin getting hair implants. Such nostalgia doesn't look at the bad parts of history, but instead rewrites the past. And because real life is almost always a mix of sadness and happiness, nostalgia makes history into a myth. It blurs the complicated parts of real life. This way of showing the past invariably avoids any references to unpleasant facts (for example, the role of slavery in American history).

Personal nostalgia, unlike historical nostalgia, is about a time in one's own past. A literary precedent for this is the sentimental novel, which hides everything but the nicest parts of the story from the reader. The characters in both personal and historical nostalgia are idealized. The values on display in these depictions are old-fashioned, and make us think of the love and care that our parents gave us when we were young. Personal nostalgia connects a person with his or her past. For example, it may lead you to recall the day you came home from sledding in the park and ate a hot bowl of Campbell's soup for the first time.

As at Disney World, re-imaginings of history can turn things that were ordinary, primitive, and ugly into symbols of humor and coolness. In art or fiction, this re-imagining of history helps people see specialness in things that were once common and far from special.

Some people don't like this, of course. When they start to think about how history has been rewritten, and how consumer culture has turned the past into brand stories, they feel dislocated and alienated.

Nostalgia and Older People

People aren't all affected the same way by references to the past. It's more likely an older person will be nostalgic because they have more history to remember. But older people may remember negative features about a particular time or place, and the marketer needs to figure out how to provide a more positive, present-day image of the past using nostalgia. Take just one example of this: Japanese tourism marketers had to figure out how to get tourists to visit small rural cities. They decided to focus on the culture and spirituality of these smaller places, and targeted older people.

To do this, marketers used nostalgia marketing. They said that rural areas in Japan would give tourists a sense of what life was like in Japan a long time ago.

The same nostalgic materials can make different people feel different things. People, for example, react differently to material from their youth that makes them think of the past. However, older women don't get as nostalgic about their youth as men do. That's because when they look back, men think about their experiences, and women think about how their looks have changed, presumably, they think, for the worse.

In marketing, nostalgia helps customers feel powerful when they think about past events in their lives or the history of a country or culture. Consumers' nostalgic feelings can be influenced by how they've thought about brands in the past (especially, in-home childhood brand exposure and past emotional attachment). Marketing grounded in nostalgia has a bigger effect on people who once had a personal connection with a brand than on people with no connection at all.

Buying goods and services for nostalgic reasons means buying stuff that evokes memories of the past or elicits sentimental feelings. In reading this chapter, you may have realized that you have a weakness for nostalgia and nostalgic goods and services. Nostalgia can be a powerful and usually positive emotion that connects people to their personal histories. However, there are risks and concerns associated with making purchases based solely or primarily on nostalgic motives:

- Overspending: Driven by the emotional pull of nostalgia, you may make impulsive purchases without considering their practical value.
- Prioritizing wants over needs: Nostalgia-driven purchases can overshadow essential expenses, leading to potential financial imbalances.
- Idealization of the past: Nostalgia can sometimes lead people to remember the past in an overly positive light, which may result in disappointment when the purchased item or service doesn't fully capture the desired feeling.
- Avoidance of present challenges: Over-reliance on nostalgic pur-

chases can be a way of avoiding current life challenges or emotional distress. This avoidance can delay necessary growth or problem-solving.
- Accumulation: Buying multiple items for nostalgic reasons can lead to clutter, especially if the items are not often used or are only meant for display.
- Storage problems: Storing nostalgic items, especially larger ones, may necessitate additional storage space, incurring more cost.
- Misunderstood motives: Friends or family may not understand the sentimental value of certain purchases, leading to potential misunderstandings or judgments.
- Generational gaps: Nostalgia often differs across generations. What is nostalgic for one generation may seem outdated or irrelevant to another, leading to generational divides.
- Commercialization: Recognizing the powerful pull of nostalgia, marketers and companies may exploit these sentiments by re-releasing, rebranding, or remarketing products at a premium price.
- Impulse purchases: Companies often bank on the impulsive nature of nostalgia-driven purchases, which can result in consumers buying items without thorough consideration.
- Reproductions vs. originals: In the pursuit of nostalgia, you may end up buying reproductions or simulations of original items. These may lack the authenticity of the original, leading to potential disappointment.
- Chasing feelings: The initial emotional satisfaction of a nostalgia-driven purchase may diminish with time, leading you to make more purchases in an attempt to recapture the feeling, resulting in a cycle of purchases and disappointments.
- Over-reliance on the past: Excessively focusing on the past can hinder personal growth and the development of a multifaceted identity grounded in the present.
- Unexpected responses: Engaging with nostalgic items may evoke unexpected emotions, including sadness, regret, or longing, especially if associated with challenging memories.

Engaging with nostalgia can be a beautiful and enriching experience, offering comfort, connection, and a sense of identity. However, you should remember the potential pitfalls associated with making purchases driven by nostalgia. Balancing sentimental values with practical considerations can lead to wiser and more varied consumer choices.

In the next chapter, we will discuss something entirely different. Up to this point, we have focused on the positive inducements marketers use to get consumers to buy their products. But now we will consider how some marketers also capitalize on negative inducements like shame, guilt, and embarrassment to sell their product.

Chapter Seventeen
Embarrassment, Shame, and Guilt

After reading the title of this chapter, you may think, "Advertisers would never try to use embarrassment, shame, and guilt to get people to buy stuff. People would be turned off by that approach, not turned on." But in fact, marketers use a wide range of emotional triggers to influence consumer behavior, including negative emotions like shame and guilt. While these tactics can be effective, they can also be controversial because of their manipulative nature. So marketers have to overcome and avoid controversy by taking a hidden or indirect approach.

For example, advertisements may present an idealized version of beauty, success, or lifestyle, subtly implying that the consumer is lacking in some way. By creating a gap between the portrayed ideal and consumer's current state, marketers can make people feel that buying a particular product or service will help bridge that gap. They leave the consumer to make their own comparison and draw their own conclusion.

Many other campaigns emphasize the environmental impact or ethical implications of consumer choices. For instance, advertisements may highlight the consequences of not recycling, or the benefits of buying ethically-sourced products, thereby leveraging guilt to guide people's buying decisions.

Marketers may play on the fears and anxieties of parents by implying that they aren't doing enough for their children's health, education, or future unless they buy a particular product. And as mentioned, the health and beauty industries often use advertisements that suggest people aren't fit, slim, or youthful enough. This can induce feelings of shame, leading consumers to buy products they think will help them fit the ideal standard.

Marketers sometimes enlist the bandwagon effect to shame and guilt consumers. By suggesting that everyone else is part of a trend, marketers can make buyers feel left out or less than their peers. In turn, this can push them to buy out of a sense of embarrassment or guilt. Some advertisements emphasize the suffering of others and suggest that by not buying a certain product (where a portion goes to charity), the consumer is neglecting their moral duty. Advertisements may also imply that not using a specific product or service will result in social exclusion or judgment from peers.

By stressing the superiority of one product over another (for example, sugar-free, organic, natural), marketers can make consumers feel guilty about their previous or typical choices. Or by playing on personal responsibility, a marketer can highlight the consumer's role in larger problems, suggesting that not buying a certain product contributes to the issue. An example may be highlighting the role of individual consumers in global plastic waste.

These tactics may be effective, but they must be used judiciously. Overt, blatant manipulation can backfire, leading to consumer backlash and damage to the brand's reputation.

In our society, many people are ashamed of their low income and seeming lack of success. They go into debt buying consumer goods to prove they did not fail. However, people often have other reasons to feel shame, embarrassment, or guilt, and therefore many reasons to buy things to make themselves feel better.

With this in mind, let's see how many of these emotions influence your buying decisions. To do so, please respond to the eight items listed below. As before, assign a score from 1 to 5, showing whether you strongly agree (= 5) or strongly disagree (= 1) with the item. Remember, there are no correct or wrong answers.

1. Most people I know have much better stuff than I do.
2. I don't have especially good taste, compared with other people.
3. I don't have enough money to buy good stuff.
4. My friends have much better stuff than I do.
5. I don't have enough time to shop carefully.
6. Most of my stuff is useless and has no practical value.

7. People would laugh at me behind my back if they saw my stuff.
8. Having my stuff doesn't make me feel any happier at all.

Now, tally up your total score. If it is 32 or higher, you are easily embarrassed or shamed.

It's hard but necessary to distinguish between guilt, shame, and embarrassment. "Embarrassment is that unpleasant state of mortification, awkwardness, and chagrin that can occur when unwelcome events in public threaten one's social identity," writes psychologist Rowland Miller. In other words, *embarrassment* is a distressing state of psychological and physiological arousal that causes people to feel exposed and ashamed. Then, people avoid doing anything that may make them look bad and try to fix things quickly when they do. Today, embarrassment, including empathic and sympathetic embarrassment, continues to have an impact on our behavior, with some people feeling it more keenly than others.

When a person feels *guilty*, they may do (or not do) something over which they think they have control, then use coping skills to deal with the outcome (Pounders et al., 2017: 38). So if an advertisement makes people feel bad in order to make a sale, it must also let the customer think they can solve the problem with the product being offered.

Shame, on the other hand, is a sense of failure beyond the person's control. For that reason, shamed people cannot quickly or easily rid themselves of their shame. People who are shamed avoid further shame with "avoidance coping."

Advertisements are effective in shaming people, but it is hard for marketers to use shame as an advertising tool. That's because a consumer cannot repair their shame by buying something. Only guilt can be remedied by buying something. A shame appeal with a "preventative message," on the other hand, merely encourages people to avoid bad things by focusing on how to avoid them.

So, to change people's buying behavior, an advertising message must combine guilt and focused messaging. This must emphasize action and its corresponding benefits. For example, marketers often use advertisements with thin models to encourage people to improve their own bodies. Yet many of these appeals harm and offend the women who see them. Promotional messages work better when they make people feel bad about something that has not happened to them and may not happen if they take the appropriate steps. Loss-framed (or prevention-framed) messages are effective when they make people want to avoid bad outcomes. For example, by buying life insurance, the consumer protects their family if they die.

People often use elaborate methods to avoid feeling embarrassment and guilt. For example, they may feel embarrassed about buying condoms and prefer self-service checkouts to avoid dealing with a cashier. Or they'll buy other items, such as magazines, to "hide" the condoms from public view. They may even buy a mound of unnecessary items to hide their embarrassment and end up spending more money than they had intended.

People who feel embarrassed often want to avoid other people, so they hide their faces under big sunglasses, a wide-brimmed hat, or restorative cosmetics. However, research shows these two coping strategies produce different outcomes. When people use cosmetics to hide their faces until they feel comfortable again, they reduce their feelings of embarrassment. Hiding their with sunglasses or a large hat is apparently much less effective.

Though some consumers buy extra goods to hide embarrassing ones, such as condoms, others do not buy the embarrassing goods at all. So marketers look for ways to reduce the embarrassment that comes with buying such products. One method they use is to change the packaging of a product. For example, they can alter the colour and design of the packaging to make the product appear sophisticated, rather than strange or silly. As well, they can sell their products online, through the mail, or through vending machines to make the products less visible to others. Other marketers try to change the social norms and stereotypes associated with sensitive products, but this is a much slower, more costly process.

Some people feel guilty or embarrassed about shopping for luxury items, especially in swanky stores. So, pop-up stores can be a solution. "Pop-up" refers to a temporary, mobile store that is only open for a brief time. Most customers do not think these stores are as swanky as traditional luxury stores, because of their improvised appearance. As a result, buying luxuries there causes less embarrassment and attracts more customers.

Neutralizing Feelings of Guilt

Some people who break the rules, or otherwise fall short of public expectations, avoid feeling bad by employing "neutralization" techniques (Sykes and Matza, 1957). Techniques of neutralization are justifications or rationalizations that people use to dismiss their guilt or responsibility for deviant behavior. These techniques allow people to engage in deviant or morally questionable activities while still maintaining a positive self-image. The five original techniques of neutralization are:

1. Denial of responsibility: The person believes that their actions were the result of circumstances beyond their control, so they cannot be held accountable.
2. Denial of injury: The person insists that their actions did not cause any harm or damage, and thus should not be considered wrong.
3. Denial of the victim: The person convinces themselves that the victim deserved the treatment they received, justifying the behavior.
4. Condemnation of the condemners: The person shifts focus from their own deviant behavior to the hypocrisy or misconduct of those who disapprove of their actions.
5. Appeal to higher loyalties: The person argues that their behavior was for the greater good, with loyalty to a specific group being prioritized over societal norms or laws.

Since the introduction of these first five techniques, researchers have proposed additional neutralization strategies, such as:

- Claim of normalcy: The person asserts their behavior is normal or typical, suggesting that most people would have acted in the same way in similar circumstances.
- Claim of necessity: The person argues that their actions were necessary under the circumstances, perhaps as a means of survival or to protect others.

- Claim of entitlement: The person believes they had a right to engage in the behavior, perhaps because of their status, position, or previous experiences.
- Defense of necessity: The person claims they had no other choice but to engage in the behavior.

These techniques of neutralization can be applied to a wide range of deviant behaviors, from juvenile delinquency to white-collar crime. Accordingly, researchers have tried to figure out how these techniques work, and have come up with interesting results, some of which marketers use to sell their products.

Some of these marketing strategies prompt consumers to make a purchase, donate to a charitable cause, or otherwise change their behavior. But guilt is a personal experience. People with weak moral principles are less likely to feel bad or to look for ways to feel better. So guilt-based appeals may sometimes fail. As an example, consider ads that aim to encourage environmental sustainability. These might depict the negative impacts of pollution, deforestation, or climate change, and then urge consumers to buy "green" or eco-friendly products. Similarly, some ads promote products that are made under fair labor conditions or from ethically sourced materials, and are intended to make consumers feel guilty for not choosing these options. Highlighting the health risks associated with certain lifestyles or product choices prompts consumers to buy healthier alternatives. Ads targeting parents with messages about providing the healthiest options for their children are intended to make them feel guilty for not choosing a particular product.

Or marketers may appeal to pity. Showing images or telling stories of people in need creates a sense of guilt and responsibility to donate. Depicting abused or abandoned animals encourages donations to shelters or animal welfare organizations. Using influencers or popular figures to endorse a product make consumers feel morally obligated to follow suit. Suggesting that not purchasing a product or service is a form of self-neglect may prompt guilt about not taking proper care of oneself.

Finally, advertising low-calorie or "guilt-free" versions of indulgent foods may make consumers feel guilty about choosing the regular versions. And offering something for free may create a sense of obligation to reciprocate by making a purchase or signing up for a service. To get people to buy things using guilt, marketing must rely on "ego-depletion"—wearing down the consumer's resistance to the marketing appeal.

One strategy of ego-depletion marketers employ is strategic message framing, which reduces the customer's power to resist. A guilt-laden message, to be effective, must give people the opportunity to lessen their guilt by acting. That's why some people are more likely to respond to messages that are guilt-laden rather than shame-laden. Shame fades only with time, but guilt can be quickly removed with action.

With this in mind, marketers employ various strategies to wear down consumer resistance to guilt-laden marketing messages, aiming to influence purchasing decisions and build brand loyalty. For example, repeating the same guilt-laden message across various advertising platforms ensures that consumers are continuously exposed to it. Sending regular reminders via email, social media, or other channels keeps the message at the forefront of consumers' minds. Creating compelling stories or testimonials that evoke strong emotions makes the guilt-inducing message more relatable and impactful.

Using powerful imagery and music may also enhance emotional appeal and create a stronger connection with the audience. Leveraging popular figures or influencers to endorse guilt-laden messages may tap into their followers' trust and admiration. Showcasing positive experiences and testimonials from other consumers will provide social proof and reduce resistance. Presenting guilt-laden messages as time-sensitive may urge consumers to take immediate action before they miss out. Similarly, highlighting the limited availability of a product or service will create a sense of urgency and prompt a quicker response.

Other tactics may include offering helpful content, advice, or incentives alongside guilt-laden messages to reduce resistance. Presenting the guilt-laden message alongside positive outcomes or benefits will shift the focus from guilt to the positive impact of taking action. Starting with an extreme request or statement will make the subsequent guilt-laden message seem more reasonable and acceptable. Highlighting that the desired behavior is a common or standard practice will make consumers feel out of step if they resist. And finally, creating a sense of belonging or community around the desired behavior will encourage people to conform.

It's important for marketers to be mindful of the ethical implications of using guilt-laden messages. Over-reliance on guilt can lead to negative consumer experiences, damage brand reputation, and contribute to unhealthy societal norms. Responsible marketing practices that prioritize transparency, honesty, and consumer well-being are essential for building long-term trust and loyalty.

In reading this chapter, you have perhaps realized that you sometimes—or often—buy things to avoid feelings of guilt, shame, or embarrassment. If so, you should consider some of the risks and dangers of doing this. Buying items to avoid or alleviate feelings of guilt, shame, or embarrassment can be seen as a form of emotional or compensatory spending. Here are some risks and dangers associated with this behavior:

- Debt accumulation: Consistently buying items to cope with negative emotions can lead to accumulating debt, especially when using credit cards without promptly paying them off.
- Temporary relief: Buying may provide a brief respite from negative emotions. However, it doesn't address the root causes, which means feelings of guilt, shame, or embarrassment may return.
- Increased guilt or shame: Ironically, the act of emotional spending may amplify the initial feelings if you realize you've acted impulsively or irresponsibly.
- Dependence: Over time, you may become increasingly reliant on buying as a primary coping mechanism, limiting your ability to develop healthier emotional regulation strategies.
- Disappointment: Items bought impulsively may not meet your actual needs or expectations, leading to buyer's remorse.
- Strained relationships: Emotional spending can put a strain on your relationships, especially if it impacts shared financial resources or if partners don't understand the underlying emotional triggers.
- Isolation: You may hide your spending habits out of shame, leading

to secretive behaviors and potential isolation from friends and family.
- Skewed priorities: Emotional purchases can divert your funds and attention away from genuine needs or long-term goals.
- Physical health neglect: In extreme cases, the financial implications of frequent emotional spending may impact your ability to afford basic necessities or health care.
- Avoidance: Buying to escape negative feelings reinforces an avoidance pattern, preventing people from confronting and resolving their emotional challenges.
- Cycle of guilt: The act of buying to alleviate guilt may, in turn, induce more guilt, creating a vicious cycle.

To counteract the risks of buying things to avoid negative feelings, you should recognize the behavior, understand its triggers, and develop healthier coping mechanisms. This may involve seeking therapy, financial counseling, or engaging in activities that offer genuine emotional relief without financial costs.

In the next chapter, we will discuss a topic that would interest frugal Angelyn, who only buys basics. If you are like Angelyn, it should interest you too. The chapter is about the expansion of basics that is constantly taking place, and always threatening to overwhelm the most cautious, budget-conscious consumer.

Chapter Eighteen
The Expansion of Basics

Many buyers today want to be frugal like Angelyn but end up spending more than they intended. They want to save their money for future needs and spend it only on necessities.

However, our views of what we need are constantly shifting. Life's "must-haves" change with social pressures and cultural values. This is due, in part, to planned obsolescence, but it is also a result of rising expectations and marketers' efforts to raise people's expectations. Regardless of the reason, new "basics" are constantly added to our list of needs. These can be both real and imagined.

Over the past few decades, we have experienced rapid technological advancement, societal shifts, and global economic changes. These have introduced a range of new products and services that consumers today consider essential, but which were rare or didn't exist a generation ago. They include smartphones and apps. A generation ago, mobile phones were just emerging and were primarily used for voice calls. Today's smartphones are multifunctional devices essential for communication, entertainment, work, and more. Additionally, a plethora of apps, from social media to mobile banking, have become everyday necessities for many. Streaming service platforms like Netflix, Disney+, Spotify, and others have largely replaced traditional cable TV and physical media for many consumers.

Products like Amazon Echo (with Alexa), Google Home, smart thermostats, and smart lighting systems have become common household items. Services like Uber, Lyft, Door Dash, and Grubhub have transformed transportation and food delivery. Services like iCloud, Google

Drive, and Dropbox offer digital storage solutions that didn't exist a generation ago. Devices like the Amazon Kindle have changed the way many people read. Fitness trackers like Fitbit, smartwatches like the Apple Watch, and even smart glasses are now commonly used.

Monthly or quarterly subscription services can provide everything from beauty products to snacks to clothing. Websites and platforms like Coursera, Udemy, and Khan Academy have emerged as significant sources of education and skill development. While still emerging, augmented reality games represent a new frontier in entertainment. As environmental consciousness has grown, products like reusable straws, biodegradable goods, and electric vehicles have become more prevalent.

Finally, companies like 23andMe or AncestryDNA offer personal genomic testing, again something not directly available to the general public a generation ago. (It was only in 2003 that the Human Genome Project was declared complete, having mapped 92 percent of the human genome. The rest has been filled in since.) Doorbell cameras, home surveillance systems, and smart locks have become common security additions to many homes. And services like Apple Pay, Google Wallet, and contactless credit cards have changed the way transactions are conducted.

This long list is by no means exhaustive, and the "newness" of some items may vary based on region and specific local developments. Not every consumer feels the need to buy all these new goods and services. However most consumers at least consider buying many of them, especially if they have children in their household.

Now, you may be saying that this list of "new" basics goes far beyond the things you would ever consider basics. What's more, that list is exhaustive and it would be impossible to think of any more "new basics." But you would be wrong. Two new basics that no one can ignore today are higher education and Internet access, so let's take a few minutes to discuss each of these in greater detail.

A New Basic: Higher Education

Education has long been regarded as a basic need of modern life. However, in the last generation or two, the definition of "basic education" in Canada has broadened. Most who read this book will have completed secondary education and, likely, have earned a postsecondary diploma or degree as well (or be in the process of earning one).

Postsecondary education has become increasingly important, even for low-wage jobs and careers. If you want to compete effectively in the job market today, you must have a postsecondary degree or diploma. Many careers and jobs require significantly higher qualifications than they did a generation ago. This is largely due to credentialism and credential inflation.

The belief in or reliance on formal qualifications (especially academic degrees) as the best measure of a person's ability, intelligence, status, and so on is referred to as *credentialism*. However, credentialism has created a new problem to solve: *credential inflation*. Credential inflation is the tendency to require ever-increasing, often unnecessary, levels of education or qualifications—for example, certificates, degrees, and diplomas—for a specific job. Because of this, a position that might have required a high school degree thirty years ago now may require a bachelor's degree.

At the same time, postsecondary education itself has changed, becoming more market-oriented. In Canada, even domains that aren't mainly about making money adopt money-making, business-oriented thinking. When it comes to education, dominant political thinking—known as neoliberalism—favors making students pay for their own education, since only they will (supposedly) benefit from it. In effect, then, credentialism has created a market need which postsecondary institutions gladly fill.

The problem with this increased demand (along with reduced government funding), however, is that it raises tuition and forces low-income students into debt while they finish their studies. Statistics Canada found that tuition's contribution to overall Canadian university revenues increased by more than a third just between 2011 and 2021, from 21.5 percent in 2010–11 to 28.8 percent in 2020–21. And according to the Ontario Student Assistance Program, new graduates with student loans need about nine years to repay their debt.

Yet, even if they have to borrow the money, people continue to invest in higher education. In our society, having a postsecondary credential—a community college diploma, if not a university degree—is desirable. Sociologist Ivar Berg (1970) was among the first to coin the phrase "the great training robbery" to describe this new extension of often unnecessary (or ill-suited) education.

Employers—even those who think they need well-educated workers— are unwilling to invest in training and skill development. They put young job seekers in charge of their own training. Employers want students—the future workers—to pay for their own education and training because it lowers the employers' costs and increases their profits.

Tuition is expensive, even before you factor in living expenses and wages lost while studying. A university degree benefits workers financially, though the situation is less clear-cut for those who complete an apprenticeship or get a community college diploma. According to Canadian census data, workers (both men and women) with a bachelor's degree earn more than those with a high school diploma, apprenticeship certificate, or college diploma.

But note the nuances. Women with an apprenticeship certificate initially earn less than women with only a high school diploma. The difference amounts to an average of $5,000 per year. On the other hand, having an apprenticeship certificate nets a man an immediate gain of $17,000 annually compared to those who only finished high school. In fact, in the 25-to-29 age bracket, holders of apprenticeship accreditations had higher earnings than high school, college, or university graduates, according to the 2016 Canadian census. It is only in their thirties that university graduates begin to outearn apprenticeship graduates, and only in their forties that holders of college degrees pull ahead of those with apprentice training. By their late fifties, however, university graduates earned 82 percent more than those with apprenticeship credentials, and 72 percent more than college graduates. Looked at cumulatively over an entire working lifetime, all types of postsecondary education will provide higher incomes than holding only a high school diploma, but how quickly those gains will come, and how much they will add up to in total, depends heavily on the type of accreditation, the type of apprenticeship, diploma, or degree program, where one lives, and, of course, gender.

With a dollars-and-cents mindset dominating education today, colleges and (especially research) universities now run like private-sector corporate entities. They all want to make a profit, even if it means sacrificing educational quality by wedging students into gigantic classes and classrooms.

Today, more than half of all Canadians aged 25 to 64 have a college diploma or university degree. In fact, Canada now has the OECD's highest percentage of college and university graduates. With so many Canadians entering the labor force with postsecondary credentials, students with only a secondary education are at a disadvantage. This effectively forces people to aim for postsecondary education, even if they do not want to.

An educated citizenry is useful to society. However, when the costs of education are high, people will continue to disagree about who should pay the cost. So far, consumers of higher education are footing most of the bill themselves, though society as a whole benefits.

A New Basic: High Speed Internet

The ability to get information from a server located tens or even thousands of kilometres away is critical today for education, work, commerce, and entertainment. And that means that, in our technologically advanced world, Internet access has become a necessary expense.

Reliable, affordable Internet access has become a critical part of daily life for people, communities, and businesses around the world. The Internet provides access to a vast array of educational resources, including online textbooks, articles, videos, and courses. Especially important during crises like the COVID-19 pandemic, the Internet enables students to continue their education remotely when in-person attendance is not possible. Many job opportunities are now primarily or exclusively listed online, and the application process often requires Internet access.

The ability to work from home or from remote locations has become increasingly common, requiring reliable Internet access. The Internet also allows for virtual doctor's appointments and consultations, making healthcare more accessible. There is a wealth of health and wellness information available online, helping people make informed decisions about their health. The Internet enables people to stay in touch with family and friends through email, social media, and video calls. Online communities can provide valuable support and connection, especially for people in isolated or marginalized groups.

Many government services are now available online, making them more accessible to the public. The Internet enables easier participation in civic activities, such as voting information, community organizing, and advocacy. The Internet also provides tools and resources for entrepreneurs to start and grow their businesses. Online platforms enable businesses to reach global markets, essential for growth and competitiveness.

Finally, the Internet provides access to movies, music, games, and other forms of entertainment. There are online communities and resources for nearly every hobby and interest, helping people connect and learn. The Internet is a powerful tool for research and self-directed learning on an infinite variety of topics. Access to diverse sources of news and media helps people stay informed about the world around them. As the world becomes increasingly digital, having Internet access is critical for developing digital literacy skills.

The Internet can also prepare you for the future. Many of the jobs and industries of the future will require proficiency with digital tools and the Internet. The Internet plays a vital role in disseminating information and coordinating responses during disasters. Access to information and resources via the Internet can help people and communities prepare for and recover from emergencies.

Affordable Internet access helps ensure that these benefits are available to all, reducing inequalities and fostering a more inclusive society. In short, the Internet is an essential utility, much like water or electricity, and plays a critical role in individual empowerment and societal progress.

Yet the Internet bill is a major source of stress for low-income families in Canada. According to one Canadian survey, 59 percent of households cut other budgets to pay for Internet access: "71 percent went without food, 64 percent cut back on recreation, and 13 percent delayed paying their rent." In our new-media universe, this cost sometimes creates a divide between "information-rich" and "information-poor" people.

People living in large urban centers may think that by now everyone who needs high-speed Internet access has it, or has easy access to it at the public library or the nearest Starbucks. But that's not so.

High-speed Internet service is expensive everywhere and relatively inaccessible in many places. For example, people living in remote or rural areas with limited Internet access may be unable to access such services, or may only be able to do so using costly satellite providers like Elon Musk's Starlink. According to the CRTC, all Canadians should have access to broadband speeds of at least 50 Mbps download and 10 Mbps upload. However, in rural communities, less than half of the population (45.6 percent) can meet this standard, and the situation is even worse on First Nations reserves, where access is only 34.8 percent.

Internet access became increasingly important during the COVID-19 pandemic. Without good access, many low-income families were unable to provide their children with the necessary education.

Basics Added and Upgraded

One marketing strategy is to persuade people that a product (or service) is something they need rather than something they merely want. If you merely want something, you have a better chance of convincing yourself not to spend the money. A need, on the other hand, is less susceptible to such arguments. If you need something, you must find a way to get it.

Realizing this, marketers strive to give the most mundane or insignificant items new meaning. People buy products not because they meet immediate needs, but because they relieve anxiety and promise to fulfill previously unconsidered desires. Consider, as an example, marketing by Volvo. With the title "For Everyone's Safety," a 30-second Volvo advertisement tries to manipulate our fears about our children in the following way.

The advertisement shows a young couple in their Volvo with their twins, surviving what could have been a fatal accident. They avoid being t-boned as they back out of their driveway thanks to a safety feature of the vehicle that tells them when another car is approaching from behind. In this way, the Volvo secures the family and helps these twins reach adulthood. Volvo, in this way, becomes more than just a necessary mode of transport. It becomes a uniquely valuable possession.

So, advertising makes us want things we didn't know we needed. We weren't aware of this need, and we didn't know a car could successfully meet it, either.

As another example, consider the advertisement for a vacation to a Jamaican resort. It plays on our need for rest, sun, pampering, and sexual pleasure. Before seeing the advertisement, we may not have realized just how ready we were for this—how played out we were. And we had no idea that a Jamaican resort could meet all our needs at the same time. Now that we are aware of our need for rest, sunshine, pampering, and sex, we begin to think that such an expensive vacation, would pay for itself many times over. It would energize and enthuse us for work. This would result in promotions and pay raises. And a happier and less stressful family life at home would also be great! Just like that, marketing has installed a new need in our minds.

But marketing also makes people less happy with their daily lives, so they look for ways to improve their lives. For example, advertising encourages us to associate happiness with clean kitchens, shiny cars, people in wide-open natural spaces, and elegant, perfectly prepared food. We begin to think that if we only had the same kitchen, car, vacation, and classy-looking food, we, too, could be happy.

Advertising imbues mere objects with meaning in this and other ways. We come to associate a sit-down roast beef dinner with family life, a can of beer with popularity, and a sports car with virility. A car with new safety features communicates to the world that you are an exceptional parent who is always thinking about his family. A card with a high credit limit and airline points communicates you are a sophisticated traveler.

In short, the intended role of advertising in the marketplace is to sell goods. Whether they're selling you real or fictitious basics, it's the advertiser's job to convince you, the consumer, that you need a particular product. Advertising does this by transforming and creating new meanings for consumer goods, drawing on a cultural treasure trove of symbols and ideas. In the end, marketing influences every other aspect of society: our culture, politics, economy, and of course, social lives.

To repeat, our views of what we need—the essentials—are constantly shifting. With the aid of marketers, we are constantly updating our list of "needs." Consider the following two examples from this chapter—higher education and high-speed Internet access. They were previously unavailable to a large portion of the Canadian population and continue to be so for much of the rest of the world. But today, to "make it" in our knowledge economy, you absolutely need these things.

In reading this chapter, some of you may have discovered you are excessively frugal—so frugal you are reluctant to invest even in higher education or high-speed Internet. If so, you may want to consider the risks of such a decision. Both higher education and access to high-speed Internet can have significant impacts on an individual's opportunities and quality of life.

Failing to get a higher education may result in lower earning potential. On average, people with postsecondary qualifications earn more over their lifetimes than those without. Many professions require specific degrees as a minimum qualification. Colleges and universities often provide opportunities to network, which can be vital for career advancement. Future income aside, college can be a time for broadening horizons, meeting people from diverse backgrounds, and being exposed to new ideas and experiences.

Studies suggest that people with higher education are often more engaged in civic activities, like voting. On a societal level, lack of access to higher education can exacerbate economic disparities. Unfortunately, people without higher education may face biases or stereotypes in certain social or professional circles.

Similarly, a failure to pay the price of high-speed Internet may reduce your opportunities. Many jobs, especially post-pandemic, offer remote working opportunities that require reliable high-speed Internet. Small businesses may struggle to operate efficiently without high-speed Internet. Without reliable Internet, students may struggle with online classes or accessing educational resources. The Internet, as we have seen, is a vast repository of information. Lacking high-speed access can limit one's ability to research and learn.

As well, social interactions, especially in the digital age, often happen online. Without high-speed Internet, people may feel isolated or out of the loop. Many essential services, like banking, government services, or medical consultations, have online components. Streaming platforms, online gaming, and other forms of digital entertainment require high-speed Internet. The Internet is a primary source of news for many, especially breaking news or international events. Finally, lacking high-speed Internet can exacerbate the "digital divide," where certain groups lack digital resources and hence face disadvantages.

Both higher education and high-speed Internet access provide people with opportunities and resources. However, just as with more traditional basics like food, shelter, and transportation, with the "new" basics alternatives exist at varying price points, and a careful consumer will weigh both the benefits and the costs of those alternatives. It should also be remembered that, for economic reasons, many people lack adequate access to these new basics (and, for that matter, to many of the old basics as well). Addressing these disparities requires collective societal effort.

In the next chapter, we look at the problem of planned obsolescence. This is another problem frugal Angelyn must face. Though she may have no desire to replace her phone, her toaster, her stove, or any of the other household devices and appliances she owns, she may find it impossible to avoid buying replacements.

Chapter Nineteen
Planned Obsolescence

You may think that we live in a society that is very progress-minded. Scientists and engineers are constantly making new discoveries and helping to create new products that make our lives endlessly better. But there's another way of looking at things. A manufacturing strategy known as *planned obsolescence* does not make our lives better and drives even people like Angelyn to buy things that aren't necessities. Planned obsolescence is the corporate decision to make consumer goods go out of style or become unusable after a limited period of time.

Planned obsolescence makes more money for manufacturers by making their products less durable. And even if companies try to hide the environmentally damaging aspects of obsolescence with greenwashing, as an educated consumer, you can see beyond that marketing charade. Planned obsolescence leads to vast waste and a throwaway culture.

Consider one popular example: Apple releases a new iPhone in the fall, and last year's model, which was once the newest and coolest thing, no longer signals that its owner is on the cutting edge. Because most people like "new and improved" things, one reason for planned obsolescence is that people prefer to buy the latest version of a product. It gives the appearance of progress and modernity.

To understand planned obsolescence, consider why we buy things in the first place. People don't buy things just to satisfy their needs. They also buy things to signal others. Most of the items we buy are items we use every day: ink for the printer, paper towels for the kitchen, gas for the car. When we buy such things, we don't give them much thought. But even in our basics buying, we are sending messages to others.

Angelyn doesn't necessarily want to signal others that she is poor or a cheapskate. So, planned obsolescence disguises itself as a necessary part of consumer buying. That broken toaster? You'll need a new toaster, won't you? No sense trying to fix it. Buying a new one will cost only a little bit more, even though the new one may not last as long as the older one did.

The March toward Planned Obsolescence

When things are no longer as valuable or appealing as they once were, obsolescence drives people to seek out "the new." People buy current fashions, for example, because fashion critics change their minds about what to like. What we bought last year is no longer cool, so we go shopping for new stuff. Even the arts change from one year to another, and gradually these changes translate into new products with new styles. For example, during the 1920s and early 1930s, a new artistic style emerged that expressed modernist ideals. Critics considered it a significant improvement over how objects had appeared in the past. Quickly, this new style came to signify speed and progress.

With this in mind, manufacturers started producing new products—radios and refrigerators, among others—to look more aerodynamic. Newly streamlined, they came to look like cars and planes, which are designed with the need to reduce wind resistance in mind. So, modernism helped us think about these new products in a new way. We came to think that products that appear modern are likely to be innovative and superior to older products.

Many new products are better than the ones they replaced—few people want to return to using typewriters and manually correcting errors with Liquid Paper!—so the cost of progress (not to mention economic growth) may indeed be obsolescence.

Ironically, however, sometimes obsolescence isn't all it's cracked up to be. Take the computer programming language COBOL, for instance. Our modern banking infrastructure was coded in the COBOL language, which has since been superseded to the point where most universities have stopped teaching it. Updating financial systems by coding in more recently developed languages would cost an immense amount of money and would run the risk of new bugs in the system. As a result, banks have been relying on retirees with expertise in COBOL to keep their systems working. That would mean that a young programmer who learned COBOL would be in great demand. (And, in fact, numerous online courses in COBOL are now available, offered by IBM and others.)

The lesson here? Not every new product or service is an improvement on the one it replaced. Here's a prime example for classic music buffs and other antiquarians: no one has yet figured out how to make a violin as well as Stradivarius made violins. Antonio Stradivari, commonly known as Stradivarius, was an Italian luthier (a maker of stringed instruments) who is widely considered one of the greatest craftsmen in his field. He was born in 1644 and lived in Cremona, Italy, until December 1737.

Stradivari is celebrated for his exceptional skill in crafting stringed instruments, including violins, cellos, guitars, and harps. He continuously experimented with and refined his designs, contributing to the development of the modern forms of these instruments. His instruments are known for their meticulous craftsmanship, superior quality woods, and varnish. Stradivari developed a distinct style, with innovations in the shape and proportions of his instruments, contributing to their exceptional sound quality.

Stradivari produced an estimated 1,100 instruments during his lifetime, and around 650 of these survive today. His instruments are sought after and have been played by many of the world's most renowned musicians. Stradivarius instruments are among the most valuable in the world, with violins selling for millions of dollars at auctions. Their rarity and the mystique surrounding Stradivari's craftsmanship contribute to their high value.

The exceptional sound quality of Stradivari's instruments has been the subject of much study and debate. Some attribute the sound to his craftsmanship, choice of materials, or the varnish he used. Others believe the wood he used benefited from the unique climate conditions during the Little Ice Age. Stradivari's instruments are not only considered to be works of art but also remain unparalleled in their acoustic qualities, setting a standard for excellence in instrument making that endures to this day.

So, the "Stradivarius" name remains synonymous today with excellence in craftsmanship and the pinnacle of sound quality in stringed instruments. Yet, we don't know how to reproduce (or improve on) its quality. Planned obsolescence in the seventeenth-century Italian violin-making industry would not, then, have improved the performance (or composition) of music.

Similarly, people have increasingly come to appreciate Indigenous people's knowledge of medicines and other plant-based chemicals. Pre-industrial societies had extensive knowledge of plant-based drugs and medicines, much of which was accumulated over generations of observation, experimentation, and oral tradition.

Some of this knowledge remains integral to contemporary herbal medicine and has even informed the development of pharmaceutical drugs. However, certain aspects of this traditional knowledge may have been lost, overlooked, or undervalued in the transition to modern medicine.

Pre-industrial societies had in-depth knowledge of the local flora and understood the seasonal variations in plant potency. They knew when to harvest specific parts of plants to maximize their medicinal effectiveness. They approached healing holistically, considering the mental, emotional, and spiritual aspects of health alongside the physical.

Remedies were often part of broader healing rituals and practices. Traditional medicine practitioners had intricate methods for preparing remedies, involving specific combinations, timings, and techniques. They understood the importance of the method of preparation on the final product's efficacy. They were adept at combining different plants to create synergistic effects, enhancing the efficacy of the remedy. The knowledge of which plants worked well together was a critical aspect of their pharmacopeia.

Their knowledge was empirical, based on direct observation and experience rather than controlled scientific studies. This experiential knowledge allowed for a nuanced understanding of how remedies worked in different contexts and for different people. They were able to adapt their practices and remedies based on changing conditions, new observations, and individual patient needs. This adaptability allowed for a personalized approach to medicine.

Many pre-industrial societies also practiced sustainable harvesting methods to ensure the continued availability of medicinal plants. They understood the importance of preserving plant populations and ecosystems. Plants used in medicine often held cultural or spiritual significance, intertwining medical practices with broader cultural and spiritual beliefs. Knowledge was passed down orally or through apprenticeship, creating a direct lineage of knowledge transmission. This method ensured that nuanced, contextual information was preserved and communicated.

Practitioners developed highly tuned sensory and intuitive skills to assess the quality of medicinal plants and the needs of their patients. These skills, developed over a lifetime of practice, were a vital part of their medicinal toolkit.

Modern medicine has brought about incredible advances in healthcare. However, there is a growing recognition of the value of traditional plant-based knowledge. Integrating this traditional wisdom with contemporary scientific approaches can provide a more holistic and nuanced understanding of plant-based medicine, potentially leading to new discoveries and therapeutic applications. The challenge remains in accurately documenting and validating this traditional knowledge before it is lost with the passing of elder practitioners and the erosion of traditional practices.

Large Corporations Want Consistent Profits

Everywhere, competition forces businesses to reduce production costs, lower prices, and seek new markets. Planned obsolescence makes companies more money by making products less durable, so people buy more over time.

Researchers have identified three types of planned obsolescence. The first is purposefully making products obsolescent. Parts are deliberately designed to wear out. This would include flimsy knobs or levers that break off prematurely. Your appliance service provider will tell you that, increasingly, household appliances (stoves, refrigerators, and the like) are being designed to last no longer than three to five years, no matter what they cost. And if you'd rather hold on to your old appliances, you'll find that it's almost impossible to get parts for them.

A second type is "stylistic obsolescence," which occurs when manufacturers create consumer goods that go out of style quickly, so that people think they aren't as cool as they once were, even if they still work just fine. Sneakers are a great example. Models like Nike's Air Max are constantly updated using new colours and materials, but the basic design remains the same. And because form is now more a choice than a necessity, new styles can come and go quickly. Products are designed to satisfy an aesthetic desire rather than a practical need.

We see the third form of planned obsolescence in products that are designed to be hard to repair. For instance, some electronics are hard to fix, because doing so requires special tools you don't have, or because their cases are sealed, leaving the working parts inaccessible.

Or consider another example of this that is creating problems for schools and the environment: Chromebook laptops. Alphabet, the maker of this computer, admits that Chromebooks have planned expiration date, after which they'll no longer load software and security updates. That means the computer's performance will degrade and it may become impossible to run certain apps. This fact has created a crisis for many school systems in the United States that purchased Chromebooks during the pandemic to allow for remote learning. Just doubling the lifespan of a Chromebook could save these schools an estimated $1.8 billion.

The Environmental Issue

One obvious problem with planned obsolescence is that it increases societal waste. Waste is a huge and growing problem around the world.

Almost a century ago, Stuart Chase's *The Tragedy of Waste* (1925) considered the harm caused by a society obsessed with producing and consuming "adulterated" goods. Chase's book explored the vast inefficiencies and wasteful practices present in the American economic system of the time. Chase, an economist and social theorist, delved deep into the various sectors of the American economy to reveal inherent wastefulness, emphasizing its moral, economic, and social implications.

Chase expanded the concept of waste beyond the traditional sense of useless expenditure or material excess. He considered waste in various forms—from physical waste in production processes to wasteful advertising practices and even the waste of human potential. He highlighted how waste in one sector of the economy could have ripple effects throughout the system. He demonstrated that wasteful practices were not isolated incidents but interconnected symptoms of larger systemic issues. Chase also critiqued the inefficiencies inherent in the capitalist economic system, especially during the boom years of the 1920s. He pointed out that a system that produced excessive and often needless goods, while leaving some in poverty, was inherently flawed.

Beyond economic inefficiencies, Chase discussed the social implications of waste, especially in terms of lost human potential. He argued that by not utilizing human resources effectively, society was missing out on potential contributions from vast swathes of its population. Chase approached waste not just as an economic or social issue, but also as a moral one. He contended that the unchecked consumption and production-driven mindset were eroding societal values. One of the significant contributions of the book was its critique of the advertising industry. Chase thought that advertising often promoted unnecessary consumption, leading to increased waste and inefficiencies.

Chase's examination of waste culminated in a call for systemic change. He thought that the issues he highlighted were not just minor aberrations but core flaws in the system that required fundamental rethinking and restructuring. Thus, *The Tragedy of Waste* resonated with many progressive thinkers of the time and influenced discussions on economic reforms and the role of government in regulating industries to reduce inefficiencies and waste.

Environmentalism as we know it today was not the primary focus of the book. However, Chase's ideas on waste reduction and efficiency have gained renewed importance in present-day discussions on sustainability and environmental conservation.

By "adulterated goods," Chase meant goods that are intended to be obsolete at a specific point in time. These goods come in various shapes and sizes. Some are poorly made, some have parts that don't work, and some are luxuries disguised as needs. Adulterated goods quickly degrade and run out, as the manufacturer intended. And then they're thrown out.

Today greater efforts are being made to reuse and recycle things that are no longer useful. For example, recycled plastic can be used to make a patio chair or an eco-friendly shopping bag. In this way, used items can be essentially turned into raw materials again. Yet waste keeps filling up landfills. Why? We still teach people to not value their purchases, to toss them away without regret, and to want the next shiny thing. This is the most important difference between a sustainability approach and a profit-driven approach. Environmentally responsible designers re-use materials without sacrificing the quality of their products.

To lessen waste, it's important for us to think more deeply about the life cycle of raw materials. Different types of raw materials have shorter or longer lives. "Life-cycle assessments" evaluate how raw materials are used, re-used, and thrown away. Some of your favorite online clothing stores may make T-shirts out of recycled cotton, but the recycled cotton came from a recycling plant in a different country. The negative environmental effect of getting your shirt from China to Canada may offset the benefit of re-using the raw material. So, you need to be strategic when doing a life-cycle analysis.

The best way to fight planned obsolescence is to get more out of our products. The more useful a product is and the longer it lasts, the less often we need to replace it. And some progress is being made. In 2023, the average U.S. passenger vehicle had been on the road for 12½ years, up more than four years compared to the 1990s. It's often cheaper to repair a product than discard it. But the fact many products today (including cars) can only be repaired with specialized equipment the average person doesn't have (and wouldn't know how to use even if they did) presents a challenge.

Another choice is to reduce the emphasis on style in the things people buy. If we value products more for their utility than for their looks, then style obsolescence can end. No one will make you buy that "shiny new thing." For example, most trash cans look the same and are made to be useful. Few people replace them every few years to keep up with the latest style trends. Reducing the emphasis on style isn't a perfect solution because it cuts down on giving people choices and being creative. Still, we may be better off if we change our focus from looks to usefulness.

As well, we need to change the way we think about what matters in life in general. Conspicuous consumption encourages a life of excess. People get rid of things because their wants and needs change. Many people would rather buy something new than look at what they already own.

Sustainable design considers the value of materials not only for the market but also for the health of the environment. To keep the environment safe, manufacturers should be environmentally friendly at every step of a product's life cycle. Planned obsolescence means people aren't taking care of their environmental responsibilities. No matter how well a product is made, we can still use our things more efficiently.

As we have seen, planned obsolescence is a huge problem for people like Angelyn, who is prudent, careful, and sensible about the things she buys. What can someone like Angelyn do to avoid or deal with the problem of planned obsolescence? Here are strategies consumers can use to counteract or mitigate the effects of planned obsolescence:

- Research before buying: Look for products known for their durability and longevity. Reading online reviews, consulting resources like *Consumer Reports* or the *New York Times*' "Wirecutter" feature, and seeking out products with favorable warranties can help.
- Understand the product life cycle: Be aware of product release cycles, especially for tech products, to avoid buying something shortly before a new version is released.
- Regular maintenance: Proper care and maintenance can extend the life of many products. This may include cleaning, software updates, and other routine activities.
- Learn basic repairs: For products that are prone to minor damage, learning to do basic repairs can significantly extend their life.
- Support repairable products: Choose products that are designed to be repairable rather than those sealed or constructed to discourage user repairs.
- Buy quality over quantity: Investing in higher-quality items that may have a higher upfront cost but last longer can save money and reduce waste in the long run.
- Support ethical companies: Patronize companies that have sustainable practices and avoid those known for intentionally designing products with a short lifespan.
- Custom software: In some cases, third-party or custom firmware can breathe new life into devices that manufacturers no longer support.

For instance, some users of desktops and laptops have switched to alternative operating systems when those machines are too old to use current versions of Windows.
- Avoid unnecessary upgrades: Just because a new model is out doesn't mean the old one is obsolete. If it still serves its purpose, continue using it.
- Buy secondhand: Buying used items can sometimes counteract the cycle of planned obsolescence.
- Recycle or upcycle: If a product can no longer serve its original purpose, consider repurposing it. If that's not feasible, ensure that it's recycled properly.
- Support right-to-repair legislation: This type of legislation requires manufacturers to provide consumers and repair shops with the tools, parts, and information to repair their products.
- Raise awareness: Discussing and raising awareness about planned obsolescence can drive more conscious consumer choices and push companies to change their practices.
- Support product-as-a-service models: Some companies are moving away from selling products to leasing them, which may mean they take responsibility for maintenance and longevity.
- Participate in circular economies: This economic model focuses on reusing, sharing, repairing, refurbishing, and recycling to create a closed-loop system, minimizing the use of resource inputs and the creation of waste.
- Join or support repair cafés: These are community-driven workshops where people can repair household electrical and mechanical devices, reducing the need to buy new ones.
- Share knowledge: Share knowledge about products that have served you well over the years and listen to others' recommendations.

By making informed choices and advocating for more sustainable production practices, consumers can counter the impacts of planned obsolescence and promote a more sustainable and ethical consumer culture. In the next and final chapter, we will discuss the environmental impact of all the buying we have discussed in this book.

Chapter Twenty
Final Words

By now, you may realize that consumer behavior is a uniquely social practice that, largely, takes place in the company of others. You feel a sense of solidarity and group support when you buy things. You express your own preferences, usually with the encouragement and approval of the group.

You buy stuff because it is a part of your social life. Your actions are motivated by the social activity of buying rather than the consumer item itself. This explains why you do so much of your shopping in groups or discuss it online.

And if shopping is about sociability—whether real or imagined—you may never be able to give up consumerism. Doing so would force you to replace your ritual enjoyment with new (non-consumer) items.

Throughout this book, we've seen that consumerism is a social activity, but people disagree on the nature of this activity. On the one hand, consumerism is a pleasurable dance of desire. People who buy items sit on one side of the dance floor. People who sell things are on the other side. They want people to buy their products so they can profit. Both are willing—even eager—to take part in these mutual acts of seduction. Consumers—people like you—are doing what they enjoy in this dance of desire. Nobody has a gun to your head.

But you rarely buy things without being persuaded or even duped. Many social forces are at work in marketing, as we have seen, and they have a significant impact on what you buy and how you buy it. We've seen how marketers use the media to persuade you to buy one thing over another. That being said, you have agency and awareness. You are not forced by media messages to think, feel, or act in a certain way. You have control over what you buy and when you buy it.

Some people think advertising is like brainwashing. And yes, some consumers do act like robots, buying things without thinking. However, you are not a passive victim, and you don't have to be. You usually buy things for good reasons. You think that buying is part of "the good life," and that is what you desire.

But think about this: consumer buying—especially, the vast volume of consumer buying in our society—speaks to the sense of powerlessness, isolation, anonymity, and meaninglessness that so many people feel. It is a way you use to feel you have control over your life, in the face of heavy evidence that you do not. In other words, consumerism is a response to what some sociologists have called alienation. You buy stuff because you are alienated from your life and from yourself.

This is important, because in the end, you can choose what you buy and even what you desire. We have created the consumer society we live in, and we keep it going with our spending. And we are all responsible for the environmental impact of our shopping.

Keep in mind the four buyers we discussed in the first few pages of this book. Tamara enjoys buying tickets that show she is, or wishes to be, a member of a particular group. She does not think this will have an impact on global climate change. And most people don't think about the climate crisis when they're looking for a new car or other desirable possessions. Nonetheless, as the middle class expands everywhere, hundreds of millions more Tamaras join the ticket-buying class each year. That means that every year, more people want (and can afford) cars, household goods, and other middle-class items to "keep up with the Joneses."

Timothy may have the most direct influence on climate change. His desire for global trophies at any cost promotes the extinction of animal species and the destruction of natural habitats. It also ignores the reckless extraction of natural resources in previously protected areas. People who are trophy hunters like Timothy enjoy wasting time and money because it displays their wealth. But waste, or the systematic and competitive production of garbage, is bad for the environment.

Anton, for his part, is a big fan of treats, and he always buys more than he needs. In this sense, Anton deserves our sympathy. At the same time, we must ask ourselves how and why we have created a society with so many Antons, each of whom is desperate for treats. It begs the question of whether our society provides any sort of human or spiritual meaning for many people.

Even Angelyn is a problem. Sure, she carefully budgets and plans her shopping; and she never buys more than her family needs. However, because of global population growth, each year sees a larger number of Angelyns than the previous year. The issue is the inescapable rise in the world's population. Population growth is expected to continue until around 2100, when the world's population will be around 11 billion people (an increase of 3 billion over its current level).

Each of our four consumer types contributes to environmental destruction. This problem will worsen in the coming years unless we act now.

True, everyone who buys something does so for somewhat different reasons. Whatever their motivation, the more people who buy things like treats, tickets, and trophies, the worse the environmental problem becomes. In response to this environmental climate crisis, some people have turned vegetarian or vegan. According to Statista, 2.3 million Canadians are vegetarians, and among them, roughly 850,000 are vegans, while there are roughly 13 million vegans in the United States. This is one sign of people's growing desire to make more ethical buying decisions when they shop. And because many of these people are under the age of 35, the future will see more vegans—and more ethical shoppers in general—because present-day people will raise children with similar values.

Similarly, we have seen the rise of the so-called "share economy" over the last twenty years. Many people hail the share economy as progressive and innovative. But to say it is "new" ignores a long history of sharing among the working class and people of colour. The key innovation of the current sharing economy is that it promotes "stranger sharing." Previously, sharing was limited to family, friends, and neighbours. Now new technology enables people to share with other people they don't know.

For instance, the new technology brings together strangers to share the use of a home or a car. Risk is reduced by requiring prospective sharers to provide information about themselves and be "reviewed" by others. Uber drivers, for example, rate their passengers to tell other drivers about passengers who may be rowdy or otherwise difficult, while passengers in turn can rate the quality of their ride. Similarly, Airbnb allows guests to leave reviews so others who want to go on vacation can see what they're getting into.

Some people think the sharing economy can help people consume goods and services in ethical and community-based ways. It may also help employees to become financially independent. If so, the share economy has the potential to make the economy as a whole more human. However, platforms in the sharing economy do not always adhere to their stated ethical objectives. Some players in the share economy, such as Uber and Airbnb, are beginning to resemble traditional businesses.

We simply don't know how these sharing platforms will evolve. For example, we don't know the degree to which governments will impose stricter rules to correct abuses; or the extent to which workers will band together to demand better treatment. And we can't know whether changes to the economy will create a more humane market, where production is done on a "size appropriate" scale and workers are treated fairly.

Marketing may be becoming more sophisticated, but so are consumers. Just as the Internet has changed the way businesses advertise, it has also made it easier for buyers to find trustworthy information. Previously, comparison shoppers had to spend a lot of time reviewing various products and prices. Today, they can do this quickly and easily. They can also get word-of-mouth recommendations from strangers, and not just from their "real-life" friends and family. So, more people than ever are knowledgeable about the products, services, and brands they buy. This makes them less likely to make ill-informed decisions.

As well, because people's trust in advertisements has dwindled, they have become more cautious shoppers. People today are more likely to see advertisements from any source as obvious money grabs. People are even becoming more adept at spotting sponsored content promoting products that is disguised to look like everyday postings by friends and familyu members. Tired of being bombarded with sales pitches, more people are turning to traditional word-of-mouth for brand recommendations.

However, some aspects of our consumer society are not improving and cannot be ignored. One huge problem is that we live in an economically unfair society. Inequality, excess, and despair are all on the rise. Inequality benefits a few at the top while harming many people at the bottom. And, as previously stated, this system ranks profit over environmental protection.

Consumerism serves to mask much of this bad stuff. When people think they will have plenty of things, they are more likely to ignore the unfair and exploitative system they live in, or even like and support it. Enchanted, they ignore the tedium of their jobs for the availability of instant satisfaction. They join social groups to show they belong. They use their possessions to express themselves, stay connected to others, and think about their identities.

People in consumer societies become engrossed in the competition for status. They also enjoy rewards such as belonging and inclusion, which make them content with the way things are. We eventually lose our willingness to fight back, revolt, or rebel. Even when we protest, we often do so by buying different goods. This is what keeps us bound to a system that we should be questioning.

According to Benjamin Barber's book *Consumed* (2007), many of us have been "infantilized." These "child" consumers have few strong beliefs or political ideas. They don't have well-thought-out goals or ideas about what makes up a "good society." They cannot take part in democracy, act morally, or perform their civic duties. They are obsessed with things and think that consumerism is the best way to make a lot of money and to be liked by others. They have grown used to the way things are. As Barber put it, they've been "made to look like babies."

Is Barber talking about you or someone you know? It's critical for all of us to consider why we buy stuff and whether we've been sacrificing too many other things in life to get it.

Sources and Selected References

As we noted in the preface, the earlier book *Consumer Society* includes an extensive list of references. Many of those works informed the discussion in this book, too. We encourage you to read the earlier book if you're interested in a deeper look at consumerism.

In this book, we refer frequently to four key authors who write about consumerism from a critical perspective: David Riesman, Jean Baudrillard, Theodor Adorno, and Thorstein Veblen.

In *The Lonely Crowd* (1953), Harvard researcher David Riesman and his colleagues Nathan Glazer and Reuel Denny identified three main types of people, whom they call tradition-directed, inner-directed, and other-directed. They assert that in twentieth-century North America, people became more other-directed, more concerned with how their neighbours were living their lives. North Americans wanted to win social approval. These other-directed people lost sight of themselves as they pursued social acceptance and material well-being. This rise in other-directedness thus coincided with the rise of consumerism and materialism. Interestingly, at the same time, Canadian-born sociologist Erving Goffman was publishing his classic work, *The Presentation of Self In Everyday Life* (1956). Here, Goffman urged us to think of all social life as a theatre, with scripts, props, rehearsals, front stages, and back stages. Life in this dramaturgical world is aimed wholly at gaining, keeping, and influencing an audience of observers. Life, in Goffman's eyes, is the ultimate version of "other-directedness."

Two decades after the publication of *The Lonely Crowd*, French sociologist Jean Baudrillard wrote a classic book on consumer behavior aptly titled *The Consumer Society* (1970). This is a book about the culture of consumer societies. In the simplest terms, Baudrillard proposes that whenever you buy a car, a sweater, or a snow shovel—whatever you buy—you are buying a sign. Every consumer good is a sign that sends signals or messages to other people. They help us belong to groups we want to join, mark our distance from other groups, and show off our position in the social hierarchy.

To repeat, for Baudrillard, signs are objects, behaviours, or events that stand for something else. Signs give our world and our relationships meaning. They also help us share our thoughts and ideas—that is, to have social lives. Religion once provided this sense of shared meaning and social connection. But religion has, in general, lost its hold on mainstream secular culture throughout the West. Consumer buying has largely taken its place as a source of meaning and communication.

Theodor Adorno and other members of the so-called Frankfurt School viewed many types of consumer buying as symptomatic of cultural degeneration: a loss of human integrity and taste that accompanies the rise of a capitalist "cultural industry." Early critical theorists included Max Horkheimer, Theodor Adorno, Erich Fromm, and Herbert Marcuse. Critical theorists like Adorno offer an approach to social and cultural analysis that reflects the influence of philosophy and psychoanalysis. It focuses on social inequalities in wealth and power and criticizes the social order that preserves this inequality. The most famously relevant work by Adorno and Horkheimer is on the cultural industry and its role in promoting capitalism and consumerism (Adorno and Horkheimer, "The Culture Industry" [1944], in *Dialectic of Enlightenment* [1947]). Critical theorists recognize that no single discipline can adequately study the cultural complexity of the modern world. To address this problem, the Frankfurt School usefully combined philosophy, psychoanalysis, Marxist theory, sociology, and economics.

Finally, Thorstein Veblen was among the first to examine the idea of conspicuous consumption in his classic text, *The Theory of the Leisure Class* (1899). His book, though more than a century old, still helps us understand the connection between class, status, and consumption today. *The Theory of the Leisure Class* is about class divisions in late nineteenth-century America. It uses historical research and observation to analyze how the leisure class—what we might call the "one percent" today—promoted economic inequality during the early industrial period. It wasn't until the early days of industrialism that the leisure class as Veblen defined it began to flourish. People in the leisure class made money from land, investments, and by exploiting the lower classes. They spent their wealth conspicuously to show where they stood on the socio-economic ladder, consuming in ways that no one in the working or even middle classes could afford to emulate.

Works Cited

A number of other works are also cited in *Why You Buy*. Below you'll find a list of references, organized alphabetically.

Ahmad, S., and Khan, M.A. (2019). Tesla: Disruptor or sustaining innovator. *Journal of Case Research*, 10(1): 12–24.

Ahuvia, A., Rauschnabel, P. A., and Rindfleisch, A. (2020). Is brand love materialistic? *Journal of Product and Brand Management*, 30(3): 467–480.

Andreassen, C.S., et al. (2015). The Bergen Shopping Addiction Scale: Reliability and validity of a brief screening test. *Frontiers in Psychology*, 6: 1374.

Arceneaux, K., et al. (2021). Some people just want to watch the world burn: The prevalence, psychology and politics of the "Need for Chaos." *Philosophical Transactions of the Royal Society of London. Series B, Biological sciences*, 376(1822), 20200147.

Ashill, N., Semaan, R.W., Williams, P. (2019). Measuring brand charisma: An exploratory study of luxury brand consumers. *2018 Annual Meeting of the Decision Sciences Institute Proceedings*, 1074–1093. Available at SSRN: https://ssrn.com/abstract=3349642

Atalay, A.S., and Meloy, M.G. (2011). Retail therapy: A strategic effort to improve mood. *Psychology and Marketing*, 28: 638–659.

Atik, D., and A. F. Fırat. (2013) Fashion creation and diffusion: The institution of marketing. *Journal of Marketing Management*, 29(7–8): 836–860.

Balderas-Cejudo, A., I. Patterson, and G.W. Leeson. (2019). Senior foodies: A developing niche market in gastronomic tourism. *International Journal of Gastronomy and Food Science*, 16, Article 100152.

Banks, Jaime, and Edwards, Autumn. (2019). A common social distance scale for robots and humans. In *2019 28th IEEE International Conference on Robot and Human Interactive Communication (RO-MAN)*. IEEE Press, 1–6.

Barber, Benjamin R. *Consumed: How Markets Corrupt Children, Infantilize Adults, and Swallow Citizens Whole*. New York: Norton, 2007.

Bazaki, Eirini, and Cedrola, Elena. (2022). Becoming a fashion blogger entrepreneur: The case of Chiara Ferragni. In Eirini Bazaki and Vanissa Wanick (eds.), *Reinventing Fashion Retailing: Digitalising, Gamifying, Entrepreneuring*. Berlin: Springer Nature.

Beall, Justin M., et al. (2020). What drives ecotourism: Environmental values or symbolic conspicuous consumption? *Journal of Sustainable Tourism*, 29: 1215–1234.

Belk, R., Weijo, H., and Kozinets, R. V. (2021). Enchantment and perpetual desire: Theorizing disenchanted enchantment and technology adoption. *Marketing Theory*, 21(1): 25–52.

Berg, I. (1970). *Education for Jobs: The Great Training Robbery*. New York: Praeger.

Berger, Jonah, and Ward, Morgan. (2010). Subtle signals of inconspicuous consumption. *Journal of Consumer Research*, 37(4): 555–569.

Bradshaw, H.K., Rodeheffer, C.D., and Hill, S.E. (2020). Scarcity, sex, and spending: Recession cues increase women's desire for men owning luxury products and men's desire to buy them. *Journal of Business Research*, 120: 561–568.

Brand, M., et al. (2020, June 30). Which conditions should be considered as disorders in the International Classification of Diseases (ICD-11) designation of "other specified disorders due to addictive behaviors"? *Journal of Behavioral Addictions*, 11(2):150–59.

Brunelle, Caroline, and Grossman, Hanna. (2022). Predictors of online compulsive buying: The role of personality and mindfulness. *Personality and Individual Differences*, 185, 111237.

Campbell, Colin. (1992). The desire for the new: Its nature and social location as presented in theories of fashion and modern consumerism. In *Consuming Technologies: Media and Information in Domestic Spaces* (pp. 48–66), edited by Roger Silverstone and Eric Hirsch. London: Routledge.

Campbell, Colin. (2018). *The Romantic Ethic and the Spirit of Modern Consumerism, New Extended Edition*. London: Palgrave Macmillan.

Campbell, Margaret C., et al. (2020). In times of trouble: A framework for understanding consumers' responses to threats. *Journal of Consumer Research*, 47(3): 311–26.

Chase, Stuart. *The Tragedy of Waste*. New York: Macmillan, 1925.

Clark, Andrew V., Carol Atkinson-Palombo, and Norman W. Garrick. (2019). The rise and fall of the Segway: Lessons for the social adoption of future transportation. *Transfers: Interdisciplinary Journal of Mobility Studies*, 9(2): 27+.

Cooper, Robert G. (2019). The drivers of success in new-product development. *Industrial Marketing Management*, 76: 36–47.

Cummins, R. Glenn, Gong, Z.H., Reichert, T. (2021). The impact of visual sexual appeals on attention allocation within advertisements: An eye-tracking study. *International Journal of Advertising*, 40(5): 708–732.

Curasi, C.F., Price, L., and Arnould, E. (2004). How individuals' cherished possessions become families' inalienable wealth. *Journal of Consumer Research*, 31(3): 609–622.

Currid-Halkett, Elizabeth. *The Sum of Small Things: A Theory of the Aspirational Class*. Princeton, NJ: Princeton University Press, 2017.

Dalton, Matthew. (2019, September 6). Why luxury brands burn their own goods. *Wall Street Journal*. https://www.wsj.com/articles/burning-luxury-goods-goes-out-of-style-at-burberry-1536238351

Daszkiewicz, M. (2022). Supporting self-esteem and self-acceptance in commercial brand campaigns created during a pandemic: Social and marketing aspects. *Ekonomia: Wroclaw Economic Review* 28(3): 109–127.

De Pasquale, C., et al. (2021). Relations between mood states and eating behavior during COVID-19 pandemic in a sample of Italian college students. *Frontiers in Psychology*, 12, 684195.

Denny, Iain. (2021). The sneaker—Marketplace icon. *Consumption, Markets and Culture*, 24(5): 456–467.

Du, H., et al. (2022). Perceived income inequality increases status seeking among low social class individuals. *Asian Journal of Social Psychology*, 25(1): 52–59.

Dunn, E. W., et al. (2020). Prosocial spending and buying time: Money as a tool for increasing subjective well-being. In B. Gawronski (ed.), *Advances in Experimental Social Psychology* (pp. 67–126). Cambridge, MA: Elsevier Academic Press.

Dunn, M. J., and Searle, R. (2010). Effect of manipulated prestige-car ownership on both sex attractiveness ratings. *British Journal of Psychology*, 101(1): 69–80.

Elhefnawy, Nader. (2021, July 21). "What makes an action film an action film?": How the James Bond movies defined the genre. Available at SSRN: https://ssrn.com/abstract=3890883 or http://dx.doi.org/10.2139/ssrn.3890883

Fiske, S. T., et al. (2019). A model of (often mixed) stereotype content: Competence and warmth respectively follow from perceived status and competition: Correction to Fiske et al. (2002). *Journal of Personality and Social Psychology*. Advance online publication.

Fox, Mary Kay, et al. (2004). Feeding infants and toddlers study: What foods are infants and toddlers eating? *Journal of the American Dietetic Association*, 104: 22–30.

Gacek, J. (2020). Corporate greenwashing and Canada Goose: Exploring the legitimacy–aesthetic nexus. *International Journal for Crime, Justice and Social Democracy*, 9(4): 148–162.

Galambos, N. L., et al. (2020). The U shape of happiness across the life course: Expanding the discussion. *Perspectives on Psychological Science*, 15(4): 898–912.

Ganassali, S., and Matysiewicz, J. (2021). "What a lot of things I don't need!": Consumption satiation, self-transcendence and consumer wisdom. *Journal of Consumer Marketing*.

Gilal, Faheem Gul, et al. (2020). Corporate social responsibility and brand passion among consumers: Theory and evidence. *Corporate Social Responsibility and Environmental Management* 27(5): 2275–2285.

Hackman, D.A., et al. (2019). Neighborhood environments influence emotion and physiological reactivity. *Scientific Reports*, 9, Article 9498.

Han, Y. J., Nunes, J. C., and Drèze, X. (2010). Signaling status with luxury goods: The role of brand prominence. *Journal of Marketing*, 74(4): 15–30.

Hanke, E., Scaff, L., and Whimster, S. (eds.), *The Oxford Handbook of Max Weber*, Oxford Handbooks (2020; online edn, Oxford Academic, 11 Feb. 2019).

Hennighausen, C., et al. (2016). What if the rival drives a porsche?: Luxury car spending as a costly signal in male intrasexual competition. *Evolutionary Psychology*, 14(4), Article 1474704916678217.

Ho, F. N., Wong, J., and Brodowsky, G. (2023). Does masstige offer the prestige of luxury without the social costs? Status and warmth perceptions from masstige and luxury signals. *Journal of Business Research*, 155(Part A), Article 113382.

Howell, R. T., Pchelin, P., & Iyer, R. (2012). The preference for experiences over possessions: Measurement and construct validation of the Experiential Buying Tendency Scale. *The Journal of Positive Psychology*, 7(1): 57–71.

Iyer, G.R., et al. (2020). Impulse buying: a meta-analytic review. *Journal of the Academy of Marketing Science*, 48: 384–404.

Jamal, Tazim. (2019). *Justice and Ethics in Tourism*. Milton Park, England: Routledge.

James, William. (1890). *The Principles of Psychology, Vol. 1*. Henry Holt and Co.

Jennings, Rebecca. (2019, August 1). E-girls and e-boys, explained. *Vox*. https://www.vox.com/the-goods/2019/8/1/20748707/egirl-definition-what-is-an-eboy.

Kennedy, David. (2022). The World Cup football: A case study in commodity fetishism. *Critique*, 50(4): 727–38.

Khandizaji, A., and M. Caputi, *David Riesman and Critical Theory: Autonomy Instead of Emancipation* (London: Palgrave Macmillan, 2021).

Kim, Jung-Hwan. (2020). Luxury brands in the digital age: Perceived quality and gender difference. *International Review of Retail, Distribution and Consumer Research*, 30(1): 68–85.

Kiverstein, J., Miller, M. and Rietveld, E. (2019). The feeling of grip: Novelty, error dynamics, and the predictive brain. *Synthese*, 196: 2847–2869.

Krier, D., and Swart, W. J. (2016). Trophies of surplus enjoyment. *Critical Sociology*, 42(3): 371–392.

Letheren, Kate, Russell-Bennett, Rebekah, and Whittaker, Lucas. (2020). Black, white or grey magic? Our future with artificial intelligence. *Journal of Marketing Management*, 36(3–4): 216–232.

Lewis-Kraus, Gideon. (2013, May 7). "Yelp and the Wisdom of 'The Lonely Crowd.'" *The New Yorker*.

Lins, S., and Aquino, S. (2020). Development and initial psychometric properties of a panic buying scale during COVID-19 pandemic. *Heliyon*, 6(9): e04746. https://doi.org/10.1016/j.heliyon.2020.e04746

Lins, S., et al. (2022). From panic to revenge: Compensatory buying behaviors during the pandemic. *International Journal of Social Psychiatry*, 68(4): 921–922.

Lury, Celia. (2011). *Consumer Culture*, 2nd ed. New Brunswick, NJ: Rutgers University Press, 2011.

Mark, Margaret, and Pearson, Carol S. *The Hero and the Outlaw: Building Extraordinary Brands Through the Power of Archetypes*. New York: McGraw-Hill, 2001.

Marks, Shawna. (2019, July 26). Representations of "WAGs" and the state of play of women's Australian football. https://shawnamarks.com/2019/07/26/representations-of-wags-and-the-state-of-play-of-womens-australian-football/

Martensen, Anne, Brockenhuus-Schack, Sofia, and Zahid, Anastasia. (2018). How citizen influencers persuade their followers. *Journal of Fashion Marketing and Management*, 22(3): 335–353.

Mathiesen, S. L., et al. (2022). Leaving your comfort zone for healthier eating? Situational factors influence the desire to eat comfort food and simulated energy intake. *Food Quality and Preference*, 100, 104605.

Mears, Ashley. (2020). *Very Important People: Status and Beauty in the Global Party Circuit*. Princeton, NJ: Princeton University Press, 2020.

Medeiros, S.A. et al. (2020) A viagem que mais contribuiu para quem eu sou: Explorando as dimensões da Experiência Turística Eudaimônica. *Revista Brasileira de Pesquisa em Turismo* 14(1): 14–33.

Meißner, Martin, et al. (2020). How virtual reality affects consumer choice. *Journal of Business Research*, 117: 219–231.

Milic, A. (2019). Envy—An unwanted, yet unavoidable and necessary emotion. *Psihologijske Teme*, 28(2): 355–375.

Müller, M. (2023). Masstige and luxury consumption: The relationship between political attitude, dark triad, technology propensity, and masstige/luxury products. Master's thesis, Catholic University of Portugal. https://ciencia.ucp.pt/en/studentTheses/masstige-and-luxury-consumption

Negulescu, Andrei. (2021, June 11). *The Enchanted World of Marketing*. Retrieved from http://hdl.handle.net/2105/57145

Niedermoser, D. W., et al. (2021). Shopping addiction: A brief review. *Practice Innovations*, 6(3): 199–207.

Okulicz-Kozaryn, Adam. (2022). Review of "Wealth(s) and Subjective Well-being" by Gael Brule. *Journal of Happiness Studies*, 23(2), no. 21: 813–814.

Ongis, M., & Davidai, S. (2022). Personal relative deprivation and the belief that economic success is zero-sum. *Journal of Experimental Psychology: General*, 151(7): 1666–80.

Otterbring, T. (2021). Evolutionary psychology in marketing: Deep, debated, but fancier with fieldwork. *Psychology & Marketing*, 38: 229–238.

Otterbring, Tobias, and Sela, Yael. (2020). Sexually arousing ads induce sex-specific financial decisions in hungry individuals. *Personality and Individual Differences*, 152, Article 109576.

Redine, Artem, et al. (2022). Impulse buying: A systematic literature review and future research directions. *International Journal of Consumer Studies*, 47. 10.1111/ijcs.12862.

Richins, M. L., and Dawson, S. (1992). A consumer values orientation for materialism and its measurement: Scale development and validation. *Journal of Consumer Research*, 19(3): 303–316.

Rose, S., and Dhandayudham, A. (2014). Towards an understanding of Internet-based problem shopping behaviour: The concept of online shopping addiction and its proposed predictors. *Journal of Behavioral Addictions*, 3(2): 83–89.

Saad, G., and Vongas, J. G. (2009). The effect of conspicuous consumption on men's testosterone levels. *Organizational Behavior and Human Decision Processes*, 110(2): 80–92.

Scheidt, Stefan, et al. (2020). Old practice, but young research field: A systematic bibliographic review of personal branding. *Frontiers in Psychology*, 11, Article 1809.

Schneider, Mark A. (1993). *Culture and Enchantment*. Chicago: University of Chicago Press.

Schouten, Alexander P., Janssen, Loes, and Verspaget, Maegan. (2020). Celebrity vs. Influencer endorsements in advertising: The role of identification, credibility, and Product-Endorser fit. *International Journal of Advertising*, 39(2): 258–281.

Sedikides, C., and Hart, C. M. (2022). Narcissism and conspicuous consumption. *Current Opinion in Psychology*, 46, 101322.

Shimp, T.A., and Madden, T.J. (1988). Consumer-Object Relations: a Conceptual Framework Based Analogously on Sternberg's Triangular Theory of Love. *ACR North American Advances*.

Shrum, L.J., et al. (2013). Reconceptualizing materialism as identity goal pursuits: Functions, processes, and consequences. *Journal of Business Research*, 66(8):1179–85.

Simmel, Georg. 2004 [1900]. *The Philosophy of Money* (3rd enlarged ed.), edited by D. Frisby, translated by D. Frisby and T. Bottomore. London: Routledge.

Sokolova, Alla. (2013) Jewish memory and family heirlooms (based on materials from field studies in St. Petersburg, 2010–11). *East European Jewish Affairs*, 43(1): 3–30.

Srivastava, Ekta, et al. (2022). Nostalgia: a review, propositions, and future research agenda. *Journal of Advertising*, 52: 1–20.

Stuppy, Anika, Mead, Nicole, and van Osselaer, Stijn. (2019). I am, therefore I buy: Low self-esteem and the pursuit of self-verifying consumption. *Journal of Consumer Research*. 10.1093/jcr/ucz029/5522913.

Sykes, G.M., and Matza, D. (1957). Techniques of neutralization: A theory of delinquency. *American Sociological Review*, 22(6): 664–670.

Tiberghien, G. (2020). Neo-nomadic culture as a territorial brand for 'authentic' tourism development in Kazakhstan. *Europe-Asia Studies*, 72(10): 1728–1751.

Varghese, N., and Kumar, N. (2020). Femvertising as a media strategy to increase self-esteem of adolescents: An experiment in India. *Children and Youth Services Review*, 113, Article 104965.

Wang, W., et al. (2020). The pauper wears prada? How debt stress promotes luxury consumption. *Journal of Retailing and Consumer Services*, 56, 102144.

Xu, Ziyu. (2022). The analysis of the marketing strategy of Lululemon Athletica. *BCP Business and Management*, 34: 8–12.

Zhang, Min, et al. (2021). What type of purchase do you prefer to share on social networking sites: Experiential or material? *Journal of Retailing and Consumer Services*, 58, Article 102342.

Zhang, Y., Zhang, J. and Sakulsinlapakorn, K. (2020). Love becomes hate? Or love is blind? Moderating effects of brand love upon consumers' retaliation towards brand failure. *Journal of Product and Brand Management*, 30(3): 415–432.

Zielińska-Szczepkowska, J. (2021). What are the needs of senior tourists? Evidence from remote regions of Europe. *Economies*, 9(4): 148.

The Questionnaires

A distinctive feature of this book is its use of questionnaires to help readers identify their own shopping habits. Below, we discuss the origins and sources of those questionnaires. From the sources listed below (and others), we gathered ideas and—in some cases, questions from existing questionnaires—that we then adapted for our own use. Having chosen and (sometimes) reworded these questions, we created a large questionnaire and tested it on over 600 undergraduate students at the University of Toronto. Doing so allowed us to confirm and refine the questions we would use in the questionnaires in this book. We are grateful to doctoral student Soli Dubash for helping us run this survey, cleaning the data, and helping to interpret the results. Through this method of validation, all the questionnaires we use in this book have high (Cronbach alpha) reliability scores.

Below, we identify the published books and articles that were most useful to us, classified by key concept.

Branding

As you have gathered from chapters in this book, the creation of brand identities is a key feature of marketing and advertising strategy. Here, among other works, are research studies we examined to prepare materials for our questionnaires. The main objective in this domain is to conceptualize and operationalize the construct of consumers' brand love by drawing on the concept of love from interpersonal psychology as well as on studies carried out in the consumer-object context.

On brands and branding generally, *Consumer Brand Relationships: Meaning, Measuring, Managing*, edited by Marc Fetscherin and Tobias Hellmann (2015).

On brand loyalty, "An empirical model for brand loyalty measurement," by M. Punniyamoorthy and M. Prasanna Mohan Raj (2007); "Developing a scale to measure customer loyalty," by Claudia Bobalca, Cosmina Gatej (Bradu), and Oana Ciobanu (2012); "A model to measure the brand loyalty for fast moving consumer goods," by Ahmed I. Moolla and Christo A. Bisschoff (2012); "Confirmatory study on brand equity and brand loyalty: A special look at the impact of attitudinal and behavioural loyalty," by Hardeep Chahal and Madhu Bala, (2010); "A review of brand-loyalty measures in marketing," by Mellens, Dekimpe, and Steenkamp (1996).

On brand love, "When consumers love their brands: Exploring the concept and its dimensions," by Albert, Merunka, and Valette-Florence (2007); "Two studies of consequences and actionable antecedents of brand love," by Lars Bergkvist and Tino Bech-Larsen (2010); "Determinants and outcomes of brand hate", by Hegner, Fetscherin, and van Delzen, (2017); "Why brands should fear fearful consumers: How attachment style predicts retaliation," by Thomson, Whelan, and Johnson (2012); "Love actually? Measuring and exploring consumers' brand love," by Heinrich, Albrecht, and Bauer (2012).

Control

Authors in this domain propose that consumers compensate for a loss (or lack) of perceived control by buying products—especially, basics (e.g., household cleaning agents)—because of these products' association with problem solving, which promotes a sense of control.

"Desperately seeking certainty: Narrowing the materialism construct," by Kathleen S. Micken and Scott D. Roberts (1999); "Control deprivation motivates acquisition of utilitarian products," by Chen, Lee, and Yap (2017).

Embarrassment

Authors in this domain examine situations in which embarrassment can affect consumer behaviour. They also discuss the implications of embarrassment for consumer behavior and review the strategies that both consumers and practitioners can use to mitigate embarrassment and its negative consequences.

"A review of consumer embarrassment as a public and private emotion," by Krishna, Herd, and Aydınoglu (2018);"Provocative sexually appealing advertisements: The influence of embarrassment on attitude towards the ad.," Virginie De Barnier and Pierre Valette-Florence (2006); "Effects of consumer embarrassment on shopping basket size and value: A study of the millennial consumer," by Nichols, Raska, and Flint (2015); "Do men and women use different tactics to cope with the embarrassment of buying condoms?" by A.D. Arndt and C. Ekebas-Turedi (2017); "Coping with condom embarrassment," by Moore, Dahl, Gorn, and Weinberg (2006)

Enchantment

Authors in this domain assert that desire is at the heart of consumption's enchantments, even when the product consumed is technology. They also consider how the fulfilment of such desire is temporary, skeptical, and ironic. Still, enchantment replaces reason with wonder. The act of buying creates desirous senses of wonderment and anticipation.

"Many happy returns: Preliminary study on retrospective and prospective experiences of enchantment," by Rense Lange, James Houran, and J. Bruce Tracey (2022); "Understanding consumer enchantment via paranormal tourism: Part I—Conceptual review" by Drinkwater, Massullo, Dagnall, Laythe, Boone, and Houran (2020); "Enchantment and perpetual desire: Theorizing disenchanted enchantment and technology adoption," by Belk, Weijo, and Kozinets (2020); "Creating enchanted customer experiences," by J. Bruce Tracey and James Houran (2021); "Measuring patterns of fantasy behavior in children," by Rosenfeld, Huesmann, Eron, and Torney-Purta (1982); "Enchantment and modernity," by Patrick Curry (2012); "Retail luxury strategy: Assembling charisma through art and magic," by Delphine Dion and Eric Arnould (2011); "Narrative and persuasion in fashion advertising," by Barbara J. Phillips and Edward F. McQuarrie (2010).

Experiential Buying

Authors in this domain note that many consumers have shown a preference for experiential buying over the purchase of goods. However, some buyers show this preference more strongly than others. Some research finds that an experiential buying tendency is related to more extraversion, openness, empathic concern, and reward seeking. It is also related to non-materialistic values which increase subjective well-being. In turn, this may be a function of a person's emotional sensitivity to rewards, events, and natural beauty.

"The role of the rural tourism experience economy in place attachment and behavioral intentions, by Sandra Maria Correia Loureiro (2014); "The preference for experiences over possessions: Measurement and construct validation of the Experiential Buying Tendency Scale," by Howell, Pchelin, and Iyer (2012); "Buying life experiences for the "right" reasons: A validation of the motivations for experiential buying scale," by Zhang, Howell and Caprariello (2013); "Consumption experience: Past, present and future," by Chaney, Lunardo, and Mencarelli (2018); and "The mediators of experiential purchases: Determining the impact of psychological needs satisfaction and social comparison," by Ryan T. Howell and Graham Hill (2012).

Guilt

Many people feel guilty about things they want to buy, especially, if they are non-essential; so, marketers need to find ways to prevent or relieve these feelings. Authors in this domain find that various strategies work. For example, gift-with-purchase promotions diminish guilt when the gift is practical or necessary, if intended for use by the purchaser. They diminish guilt when the gift is self-indulgent but is intended for the enjoyment of someone else.

"Introducing the GASP scale: A new measure of guilt and shame proneness," by Cohen, Wolf, Panter, and Insko (2011); "The influence of temporal frame on guilt and shame appeals," by Pounders, Royne and Lee (2018); "A little something for me and maybe for you, too: Promotions that relieve guilt," by Sooyeon Nikki Lee-Wingate and Kim P. Corfman (2009); "Consumer guilt: Preliminary construct assessment and scale development", by Sammy Bonsu and Kelley Main (2006); "Consumer guilt: Examining the potential of a new marketing construct," by D. Lascu (1991).

Materialism

Definitions of materialism vary widely. Some scholars view materialism as a personal value, others as a personality trait, an extrinsic motivation focus, a preference for products over experiences, or even a focus on lower-order needs at the expense of higher-order needs. However, despite these variations, most commentators view materialism as a stable trait that is harmful to people's well-being.

"Living in wealthy neighborhoods increases material desires and maladaptive consumption," by Zhang, Howell, and Howell (2016); "Materialism: Trait aspects of living in the material world," by Russell W. Belk (2014); "Reconceptualizing materialism as identity goal pursuits: Functions, processes, and consequences," by L. J. Shrum et al. (2013); "Implicit and explicit assessment of materialism: Associations with happiness and depression" by Muñiz-Velázquez, Gomez-Baya, and Lopez-Casquete (2017); "A cross-cultural investigation of the materialism construct: Assessing the Richins and Dawson's materialism scale in Denmark, France and Russia," by Griffin, Babin, and Christensen (2004); "Interpersonal influences on adolescent materialism: A new look at the role of parents and peers," by Lan Nguyen Chaplin and Deborah Roedder John (2010); "Materialism pathways: The processes that create and perpetuate materialism," by Marsha L. Richins (2017); "Materialism: The good, the bad, and the ugly," by L. J. Shrum et al. (2014); "Stigmatizing materialism: On stereotypes and impressions of materialistic and experiential pursuits," by Van Boven, Campbell, and Gilovich (2010); "Coping with loneliness through materialism: Strategies matter for adolescent development of unethical behaviorsm" by Gentina, Shrum, and Lowrey (2018); "Three scales to measure constructs related to materialism: Reliability, validity, and relationships to measures of happiness," by Russell W. Belk (1984); "A consumer values orientation for materialism and its measurement: Scale development and validation," by Marsha L. Richins and Scott Dawson (1992).

Niche Marketing

Authors in this domain note that niche marketing is nothing new. What is new, however, is the increased diversity of markets, technologies that enable new marketing approaches, and the disappearance of large companies and their traditional marketing approaches. Another factor is the increased participation of more varied types of people in certain previously restricted markets—for example, international tourism. Niche marketing seems an appropriate method to use in this changing environment.

"Retailers' use of niche marketing in product development," by Erin Parrish (2009); "Niche marketing revisited: Concept, applications and some European cases," by Tevfik Dalgic and Maarten Leeuw (1994); "Effective marketing of small brands: Niche positions, attribute loyalty and direct marketing," by Wade Jarvis and Steven Goodman (2005).

Novelty

Researchers in this domain recognize the size and significance of a consumer desire for new things and new experiences. Often, they are looking for a thrill, a change from routine, the alleviation of boredom, and surprise. These qualities are available in different forms, to different degrees in different kinds of products. They are especially relevant in tourism research, but may also be relevant when marketing technology, food, and sex toys.

"The role of novelty in the pleasure travel experience," by Daniel C. Bello and Michael J. Etzel (1985); "Measuring novelty seeking in tourism," by Tae-Hee Lee and John Crompton (1992)

Possession Love

Researchers in this domain are interested in emotional ties to products that emulate human-to-human love attachments. So, for example, they find love-smitten consumers nurturing their beloved possessions by buying complementary products and services. Research suggests that this possession love is empirically tied to loneliness and social affiliation deficits. In turn, that suggests these possessions are providing their owners with compensatory well-being.

"Geeks' intimate attachments to their computers: An investigation of the relationship between geekism and material possession love," by Franziska Geesen (2013); "An integrative review of material possession attachment," by Susan Schultz Kleine and Stacey Menzel Baker (2004); "Falling in love with a product: The structure of a romantic consumer-product relationship," by Yun-Oh Whang et al. (2004); "Truly, madly, deeply: Consumers in the throes of material possession love," by John L. Lastovicka and Nancy J. Sirianni (2011).

Retail Therapy

Researchers in this domain consider the degree to which consumers engage in shopping and buying to repair their negative feelings. They do this research in several ways. Some research examines the goals and motives that consumers have for shopping. Other research explores the activities in which consumers engage during the shopping process. A third approach examines the feelings that consumers experience while shopping.

"Retail therapy: A strategic effort to improve mood," by A. Selin Atalay and Margaret G. Meloy (2011); "The emotional shopper: Assessing the effectiveness of retail therapy," by Leonard Lee (2015); "The benefits of retail therapy: Making purchase decisions reduces residual sadness," by Scott, Pereira, and Burson (2014); "Retail therapy: A qualitative investigation and scale development," by Minjeong Kang (2009); "Sadness and consumption," by Nitika Garg and Jennifer S. Lerner (2012).

Shame

Research in this domain considers the effects of shame on people's buying decisions. Avoidance of shame significantly influences how people live their daily lives when it comes to making decisions—especially, decisions perceived to have an ethical content or consequence. Consumers with high guilt-proneness vary widely in their approach to unethical behaviours, but they all approach it with a fear of shame.

"The effects of sexual social marketing appeals on cognitive processing and persuasion," by Reichert, Heckler, and Jackson (2001); "Making prudent vs. impulsive choices: The role of anticipated shame and guilt on consumer self-control," by Chun, Patrick, and MacInnis (2007); and "Investigating the impact of guilt and shame proneness on consumer ethics: A cross national study," by Arli, Leo, and Tjiptono (2016).

Shopping Addiction

Research in this domain notes that shopping addiction is a lot like addiction to a psychoactive substance. Problematic shopping behaviors are best understood from an addiction perspective. Both internal factors (e.g., distress) and external factors (e.g., environmental cues) produce a craving for the activity and an anticipation of rewards. Non-addicted people are less responsive to both such internal and external cues.

"Problematic shopping behavior: An item response theory examination of the seven-item Bergen Shopping Addiction Scale," by Daniel Zarate et al. (2022); and "The Bergen Shopping Addiction Scale: Reliability and validity of a brief screening test," by Cecilie S. Andreassen et al. (2015).

Specialization

Specialization is a developmental process that entails a progression in behavior, attitudes, and preferences. As such, it reflects an individual's history of immersion in an activity. In a particular area—whether sports, tourism, or wine tasting—specialization is the progression in behaviors, skills, and commitment over a time period. As such, it points to stages of involvement, career changes, and turning points.

"Consumer specialization and the Romantic transformation of the British Grand Tour of Europe," by Andreas Chai (2010); "Recreational specialization: A critical look at the construct," by David Scott and C. Scott Shafer (2002); "Consumer specialization and the demand for novelty: A reconsideration of the links and implications for studying fashion cycles in tourism," by Andreas Chai (2012); "Specialization and marine based environmental behaviors among SCUBA divers," by Thapa, Graefe, and Meyer (2006); "Measuring birding specialization: A confirmatory factor analysis," by Jin-Hyung Lee and David Scott (2004); "Measuring specialization among birders: Utility of a self-classification measure," by Scott, Ditton, Stoll, and Eubanks (2005); and "Degree and range of specialization across related hunting activities," by Craig A. Miller and Alan R. Graefe (2000).

Index

Absolute deprivation, 136
Acquisitive materialism, 133
Addictions, 189–90; food, 201–07; see also Shopping addiction
Adopters, early vs. late, 41–42
Adulterated goods, 245
Advertising, changes in, 32; use of sexual imagery, 153–57; use of nostalgia, 209–18
Alienation, 29–37, 250; from labour, 29
Archetypal psychology, 152
Archetypes, 150–52
Arousal theory, 46
Artificial intelligence (AI), 148
Asceticism, 111–12
Aspirational class, 126
Aspirational consumers, 97–100, 126
Aspirational materialists, 126, 132
Bandwagon effect, 121–22, 220
Barber, Benjamin, 253
Basics, expansion of, 229–38; upgrading of, 235–37
Baudrillard, Jean, 24, 83, 139
Berg, Ivar, 232
Bergen Shopping Addiction Scale, 175–66
Brand affiliations, 168–69
Brand communities, 33–34, 162, 168–69
Brand distinctiveness, 109–111
Brand love, 161–64; self-congruence and, 169
Brand passion, 168–69
Brand prominence, 84–87, 107–08
Brands and branding, 21–24, 32–34, 39, 84–87, 107–11, 161–64, 168–69; personal, 22; in tourism, 67–70
Buyers, types of, 11–17
Campbell, Colin, 111–12
Canada Goose (coats), 84–85
Capital (Marx), 138
Charismatic personality (of consumer goods), 103–04
Chase, Stuart, 244–45
Chromebooks, 244
COBOL, 240–41

Collective unconscious, 150
Comfort food, 199–208
Commodities, 79–80
Commodity fetishism, 137–38
Communication, through purchases, 25
Compensatory buying/consumption, 98, 113–14; see Shopping addiction
Competitive consumption, 119–29
Compulsive buying disorder (CBD), see Shopping addiction
Conformity, social, 27–28
Conspicuous compassion, 34
Conspicuous consumption, 47, 78–84, 87, 112–13, 122–24, 246; and narcissism, 82; and eco-tourism, 82
Conspicuous waste, 87
Consumed (Barber), 253
Consumer Culture (Lury), 23
Consumer Society, The (Baudrillard), 24
Cosmetics, 94–95
Credential inflation, 231
Credentialism, 231
Credit, 91
Cultural capital, 124–25
Cultural meaning, 23–24
Currid-Halkett, Elizabeth, 126–27
Customized consumer goods, 44
Debt, 91, 180–81, 192–94; emergence of credit cards, 193
Denney, Reuel, 20
Deprivation, absolute, 136; relative, 136–37
Deviant spending, 194–96
Disenchanted Enchantment Model, 146
Disenchantment, 145–48
Durkheim, Émile, 20
Eating disorders, 201–03; and self-esteem, 203–05
Eco-tourism, 82
Ego-depletion, 225
Embarrassment, as used in marketing, 219–27; of consumers in buying certain goods, 222–23

Emotional labor, 100–01
Enchantment, 140–41, 143–55; advertising and, 149–53; and nostalgia, 211; see also Disenchantment, Re-enchantment
Environmentally friendly products, 224
Envy premium, 120–21
Envy, 120–24
Evolutionary psychology, 115–16
Ewan, Stewart, 33
Experiences, search for, 51–61; happiness and, 52–59; consumption through, 54
Experiential Buying Tendency Scale (EBTS), 54
Experiential retail, 51, 54–59, 124–26
"Experientials", 58
Ferragni, Chiara, 26
Fetishism, 137–39
Gambling, 73
Glazer, Nathan, 20
Goffman, Erving, 22
Groupthink, 27
Guilt, as used in marketing, 219–27; neutralization of, 223–24; ethical implications, 226
Happiness, 134; models of, 35–36; and experiences, 52–59
Hedonism, 111
Heirlooms, 170–71
Hero and the Outlaw (Mark and Pearson), 152–53
Hidden Persuaders, The (Packard), 149
Hierarchy of needs, 59
Higher education, as basic, 230–33; effect on income, 232; benefits, 237
High-speed Internet, as basic, 233–35; benefits, 237
Hummer, 85–86
Impulse buying, 54, 195; in Las Vegas, 195; in airports, 196
Inconspicuous luxury consumption, 110
Incrementally New Products (INPs), 42–44
Influencers, 26–27, 108–09
Inglehart, Ron, 58
Innovation, see Novelty
James, William, 179
Jung, Carl, 150–52
Las Vegas, 195
Lego, 34
Lewis-Kraus, Gideon, 21
Life, control of, 11–12
Logos, 21–22; prominence of in luxury goods, 109–10
Loneliness, 36–37
Lonely Crowd, The (Riesman et al.), 20–21, 30, 31

Love, of robots, 163–64; nature of, 164–73; dimensions of, 166; types of, 166–67; and compensatory spending, 185–86; of possessions, see Possession love; of brands, see Brand love
Lululemon, 33, 168
Lury, Celia, 24
Luxuries, 89, 91–117; as communication tools, 93; ways of distinguishing luxury brands, 95, 103–04; and social inequality, 95–97; and emotional labor, 100–01; gender differences in, 101–03, 170; total spending in U.S., 102; parenting styles and, 112–14; gender and, 114–16; automobiles as example of, 114–15, 143–44, 170
Luxury brands, use of nostalgia in marketing, 214–15
Mark, Margaret, 152
Marketing, in modern capitalism, 143; use of emotions in, 145; use of nostalgia in, 209–18
Marx, Karl, 29, 138, 146
Maslow, Abraham, 59
Masstige goods, 93–95
Materialism, 29, 129, 131–41; in city life, 133–34; types of, 133; as social and cultural problem, 135–37; and fetishism, 137–39; as a signal, 139; relationships to brands and, 161
Mears, Ashley, 83–84
Mega-spectacles, 123–24
Men, luxury buying and, 101–03
Myers-Briggs Type Indicator (MBTI), 150
Narrative transport, 152, 157–58
Neophilia, 45
Niche buying, 63–76
Niche marketing, 61, 64–70
Nostalgia, 209–18; psychological function, 210; enchantment and, 211; personal, 211–12, 215; collective, 212; vintage products, 213; use of to emphasize national roots, 214; use of by luxury brands, 214–15; older people and, 215–16
Novelty, 37, 39–50; reasons for attraction to, 40–41; advertising and, 48
Off-price retailers, 100
Old money vs. new money, 81–82, 93–94
Oniomania, see Shopping disorder
Optimal stimulation level (OSL), 46
Orientalism, 212
Overeating, 201–03, 206
Packaging of products, 22
Packard, Vance, 149
Pearson, Carol S., 152–53

Pecuniary strength, 112
Philosophy of Money, The (Simmel), 79
Pity, in marketing, 224
Place-making and place-seeking, 67–70
Planned obsolescence, 239–48; modernism and, 240; profits and, 243; style and, 243–44; repairability and, 244
Plant-based medicines, Indigenous knowledge of, 242–43
Population growth, 251
Positional goods, 96
Possession love, 160–74; risks of, 171–73
Products, anthropomorphizing of, 169–70
Protestant ethic, 131
Radical empiricism, 179
Raw materials, life cycle of, 246
Really New Products (RNPs), 42–44
Re-enchantment, 148
Reference groups, 25–26
Relative deprivation, 129, 136–37
Retail therapy, 134, 181–82, 189
Riesman, David, 20–21, 30, 31
Robots, 163–64
Romanticism, in luxury consumerism, 111–12
Said, Edward, 212
Segway, 43
Sephora, 34
Sexual imagery, in advertising, 153–57
Shame, as used in marketing, 219–27
Share economy, 251–52
Shopping addiction, 173–98; as social problem, 176; treatment for, 177–78; self-esteem and, 178–85; sadness and, 181–82; predictors of, 190; mindfulness and, 190; gender differences, 190–91; online shopping and, 191; retailers' strategies to encourage, 191–92; effectiveness in addressing people's emotional problems, 192

Shopping, and social relations, 170–71; as social practice, 249–50; as response to alienation, 250; inequality and, 253
Simmel, Georg, 79
Snob effect, 122–24
Social character, 30–31
Social distance scale, 163–64
Social hierarchy, position in, 119–20
Social inequality, 95–97
Social media, effects of, 34–35
Social relations, and consumerism, 170–71
Storytelling, and brand love, 162
Stradivari, Antonio, 241–42
Stradivarius violins, 241–42
Sum of Small Things, The (Currid-Halkett), 125–26
Sweets, human taste for, 199–200
Theory of the Leisure Class, The (Veblen), 80
Tickets, 15, 19–28, 37, 250
Tim Hortons, 33–34
Totems, 20, 32, 92
Tourism, 57–58, 66–74; culinary, 67, 70; brands in, 67–70; strategies, 69; ethical, 70–71; seniors and, 72–74; rural, 73–74
Tragedy of Waste, The (Chase), 244–45
Treats, 16, 175–88, 199–208, 251; buying as compensatory process, 182–86
Trees as luxury goods, 110–11
Trophies, 15–16, 76, 77–89, 199–29, 250; of *jouissance*, 124
Trophy husbands, 87
Trophy treadmill, 199–29
Trophy wives, 86–87
Veblen, Thorstein, 47–48, 78–81, 87, 95
Virtual reality (VR), 46–47
WAG (Wife and Girlfriend), 86
Weber, Max, 131, 145, 147
Women, luxury buying and, 101–03

www.ingramcontent.com/pod-product-compliance
Lightning Source LLC
Chambersburg PA
CBHW052134070526
44585CB00017B/1825